ROLE PLAY

DISTANCE LEARNING AND THE TEACHING OF WRITING

NEW DIMENSIONS IN COMPUTERS AND COMPOSITION

Gail E. Hawisher and Cynthia L. Selfe, editors

Digital Youth: Emerging Literacies on the World Wide Web
Jonathan Alexander

Role Play: Distance Learning and the Teaching of Writing
Jonathan Alexander and Marcia Dickson (eds.)

Datacloud: Toward a New Theory of Online Work
Johndan Johnson-Eilola

At Play in the Fields of Writing: A Serio-Ludic Rhetoric
Albert Rouzie

Integrating Hypertextual Subjects: Computers, Composition, Critical
Literacy and Academic Labor
Robert Samuels

Sustainable Computer Environments: Cultures of Support in English
Studies and Language Arts
Richard Selfe

Doing Literacy Online: Teaching, Learning, and Playing
in an Electronic World
Ilana Snyder and Catherine Beavis (eds.)

forthcoming

Webbing Cyberfeminine Practice: Communities, Pedagogy
and Social Action
Kristine Blair, Radhika Gajjala, and *Christine Tully* (eds.)

Lingua Franca: Towards a Rhetoric of New Media
Colin Brooke

Aging Literacies: Training and Development Challenges for Faculty
Angela Crow

Labor, Writing Technologies and the Shaping of Composition
in the Academy
Pamela Takayoshi and Patricia Sullivan (eds.)

ROLE PLAY

DISTANCE LEARNING AND THE TEACHING OF WRITING

edited by

Jonathan Alexander
University of Cincinnati

Marcia Dickson
The Ohio State University—Marion

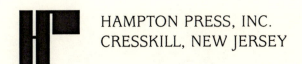

HAMPTON PRESS, INC.
CRESSKILL, NEW JERSEY

Copyright © 2006 by Hampton Press, Inc.

All rights reserved. No part of this publication may be reproduced, stored in a retrieval system, or transmitted in any form or by any means, electronic, mechanical, photocopying, microfilming, recording, or otherwise, without permission of the publisher.

Printed in the United States of America

Library of Congress Cataloging-in-Publication Data

Role play : distance learning and the teaching of writing / edited by Jonathan
   Alexander, Marcia Dickson
      p. cm. -- (New dimensions in computers and composition)
   Includes bibliographical references and index.
   ISBN 1-57273-658-5 -- ISBN 1-57273-659-3
     1. English language--Rhetoric--Computer-assisted instruction. 2. Composition
(Language arts)--Computer-assisted instruction. 3. Distance education--
Computer-assisted instruction. 4. Report writing--Computer-assisted
instruction. I. Alexander, Jonathan. II. Dickson, Marcia. III. Series.

PE1404.R634 2005
808'.042'0285--dc22

                                                         2005051582

Hampton Press, Inc.
23 Broadway
Cresskill, NJ 07626

CONTENTS

Introduction   1
    Jonathan Alexander and *Marcia Dickson*

I   PERFORMANCES

1   Pedagogical Performances in the Online Writing Class   21
   Christy Desmet, Robert Cummings, Alexis Hart,
   and *William Finlay*

2   And Now, a Word From Our Sponsor   47
   John G. Bryan

II   PROCESSES

3   A Language All Its Own: Writing in the Distance-Learning   63
   Classroom
   Ellen H. Hendrix

4   Trying to Connect: A Distance-Learning Basic Writing Course   79
   for Nontraditional Students
   Stuart Blersch and *Carolyn Stoll*

5   Anyone? Anyone? Anyone? Leading Discussions in Cyberspace: 97
   E-Journals and Interactivity in Asynchronous Environments
   Debbie Danowski

v

vi Contents

III COMMUNITIES

6 Rhetorical Violence and the Problematics of Power: 111
A Notion of Community for the Digital Age Classroom
Lori E. Amy

7 Critical and Multicultural: Pedagogy Goes Online   133
Lesliee Antonette

8 Feminist Civic Engagement and the Role of the   147
Bureaucrat: Graduate Education, Distance Learning, and
Community Action
Melody Bowden

IV FUTURES

9 Online Distance Education and the "Buffy Paradigm":   163
Welcome to the Hell Mouth"
Cynthia L. Jenéy

10 Learning at Light Speed in Neal Stephenson's   189
The Diamond Age
Veronica Pantoja

11 Distant, Present, and Hybrid   201
Peter Sands

About the Editors   217

About the Contributors   219

Author Index   223

Subject Index   xx

INTRODUCTION

DISTANCE LEARNING, TEACHING WRITING, AND LEARNING TO PLAY NEW ROLES

Jonathan Alexander
Marcia Dickson

Teachers generally come to practice distance-learning pedagogy for one of two reasons:

- their love of and faith in technology, or
- desperation.

The first group of distance-learning advocates derives its pedagogy from love of and faith in technology. Such instructors tend to share certain advantages, however, because they are usually either full time, tenure-track faculty who have the time and support to develop distance-learning classes or graduate students whose pedagogy is the focus of their research.

The desperate tend to be a more diverse population that is distressed for more than one reason. Adjunct faculty instructors need jobs, and distance-learning courses may be the only courses available. Full-time instructors or lecturers as well as assistant professors often find themselves suddenly assigned to distance-learning classes courtesy of administrators who decide that the college or university needs to provide (at best) more access to students or (at worst) to bring in more money. The only positive element for the desperate—besides a paycheck—may be that the distance-learning course may be more flexible than traditional classes.

In addition to being members of both categories, the editors of this book came to distance learning for an additional reason: a desire to create sound writing pedagogies for distance-learning courses. Having both constructed and participated in distance-learning curricula and instruction, we have had the opportunity to experience first-hand teaching English—particularly teaching *writing*—in virtual classrooms. Jonathan Alexander worked collaboratively with Michelle Gibson, a colleague at the University of Cincinnati, to develop a video writing course in which they became the star performers. Marcia Dickson and Susan Delagrange, from the Marion and Mansfield campuses of The Ohio State University, took turns serving as teachers and facilitators as they developed video-conferencing courses in literature, composition, and business writing.

Jonathan and Michelle initially fell into the category of teachers who are desperate. Their introduction to distance learning came about as part of a federally mandated curriculum change. In 1998, President Clinton signed into law PL 105-285. This act stipulated that by "September 2003, at least 50% of all Head Start teachers nationwide in center-based programs have an AA, BA, or advanced degree in early childhood education or development, a degree in a related field and experience in teaching preschool children." The fiscally minded University of Cincinnati administrators believed that the large number of Head Start teachers who live in areas where there is no easy access to on-campus programs in early childhood education would be a perfect (read "captive") audience for a distance-learning program. Such a program, designed specifically for Head Start teachers, had the potential to fill the university's coffers while expanding its reputation for meeting pressing social needs.

A number of different entities—including the university's Early Childhood Education Program and RISE (which makes educational videos for HS teachers)—secured a grant to form the Early Childhood Learning Community (ECLC). The ECLC courses would offer a portion of every course on video; the remaining instruction would occur online. This was an agreement made without consulting writing faculty or apparently any other faculty. When Jonathan and Michelle found themselves involved, they were "righteously indignant" about the use of video, claiming that if the university insisted on developing an online curriculum it should be a purely interactive, online pedagogy. They did not feel that a video presentation would best serve the needs of students who were working in isolation. Administrators told them to "think outside the box"—an ironic directive because Michelle and Jonathan felt trapped inside an electronic box.

Marcia and Susan's experiences fell under the first category of distance learning—they chose to teach distance-learning classes because they were challenged by the idea of a new forum for instruction. They saw themselves as intrepid adventurers in the unexplored territory of the virtual classroom. The deans of The Ohio State University regional campuses had begun to extol the virtues of distance learning. Although plenty of the conversation was devoted to how *soon* the university could begin distance-learning classes, little was said about the pedagogies that would be involved in this new teaching arena.

Because they had been heavily involved in computer-enhanced instruction, Susan and Marcia felt comfortable enough with technology to propose an upper-division English course, "Theories and History of Writing." They looked at distance learning as a challenge and an intellectual enterprise, and they hoped that their development of distance-learning pedagogies would be used to train future distance-learning instructors. For this particular course, Marcia served as instructor and Susan as facilitator. "Theories and History of Writing" brought together students from three campuses. The class would meet twice a week in 2-hour blocks—once via video conferencing and once by means of computer technologies: e-mail, listserv, and discussion webs. In this first attempt at distance learning, the students met in computer classrooms on each campus so they could form a face-to-face community while dealing with this unusual classroom situation. In subsequent classes—"Introduction to Shakespeare," "Intermediate Essay Writing," and "Business and Professional Writing"—the formula remained the same: one teacher, one facilitator, once-a-week video conferences, and computer labs.

Just describing our various distance-learning courses makes us conscious that the term *distance learning* has no fixed meaning. At various times, the expression "distance learning" has covered courses taught solely on the Web, courses where students watch videos and then work with facilitators to complete assignments, and courses where teachers meet with students in real time over Internet connections. The students have been as diverse as the rural students served by our courses and the urban students who have to fit learning into an already busy workweek. We decided that this collection would be concerned with distance-learning venues that make *much* use of *virtual instruction*, which editors Carine M. Feyten and Joyce W. Nutta (1999) suggested, in *Virtual Instruction: Issues and Insights from an International Perspective*, is "characterized by computer-mediated communication such as e-mail, Web-based instruction, Internet relay chat, CUseeMe, two-way videoconferencing, or any combination of these tools" (p.xvi). We decided to limit our scope for the most part to courses where students do not have much direct access to the instructor and where the classroom essentially disappears, to be replaced by TV monitors, computer screens, or some mixture of these and other electronic media.

PEDAGOGICAL PERFORMANCES, OR HOW ONE REALLY ROLE-PLAYS

The term *role*, whether used in the singular or plural, shifts in meaning as frequently as *distance learning* does. Writing teachers are not altogether in agreement about their roles in today's academic environment; teachers vary in classroom identities and in the parts they play with their students when out of class. Teachers can see themselves as mentors, coaches, friends, guides into the world of intellectual endeavor, or gatekeepers for that world. They can play rescuers of the ignorant, bringers of knowledge, or catalysts for student development. Traditionally, these roles involve or even depend on face-to-face interactions. Suspicious—not to mention cynical—teachers fear that distance-learning environments will be destructive to learning; it might be said that they fear to find themselves performers playing a role without an audience.

For us, role-play has always been a crucial component of our pedagogical practices. We want our students to approach each learning opportunity with both curiosity and creativity—essential ingredients of play *and* learning, particularly about writing. Christine Pearson Casanave's (2002) book, *Writing Games*, reconfigures writing instruction in terms of meaningful play, suggesting that "the practice of academic writing is shaped but not dictated by rules and conventions, [and] that writing games consist of the practice of playing, not of the rules themselves . . . writers have choices about whether and how to play" (p. xiv). Part of that play involves imagining oneself in different situations and different contexts. Just as they used to play make believe as children, adult learners (and writers) make believe with a variety of texts, concepts, ideas, and issues—imagining connections, possibilities of interpretation, and new ways of thinking about and approaching important topics. Approaching each role we play in the classroom with creative playfulness enhances the possibility that we will make valuable connections between ideas and insights, craft text in engaging ways, and just plain have fun in the process.

Introduction 5

The relevance of roles and play takes on new dimensions in distance-learning experiences—for both students and instructors. Students often find themselves having to renegotiate their approach to education, to their own learning. Frequently, distance-learning courses require active participation via chatrooms or discussion boards, and students must generally participate more proactively (rather than passively sitting in a classroom) if they are to benefit from the learning experience. Indeed no small amount of creativity—and even playfulness—is needed to communicate successfully and productively in such electronically mediated venues. Without the old standby of the lectern and chalkboard, faculty must utilize a new array of instructional platforms, many of which require instructors to become facilitators more than authorities. In this role, instructors coach, cajole, and encourage more than they "hold forth" knowingly, and a playful approach to such a role generally helps all participants enjoy and benefit from the experience.

When we accepted the roles of distance writing instructors, the four of us had little idea how the performance would turn out. After receiving her administrator's directive, Michelle—an avid TV-watcher convinced that watching TV is not, as some have argued, necessarily a passive activity—began to think about ways to re-create for ECLC students the kinds of opportunities for intellectual involvement that can grow out of watching TV programs related to personal interests and identities. She created a writing course curriculum based on two important ideas: (a) that well-researched documentary TV can function as a powerful text in a writing course, and (b) that instructors could quite productively focus on the intellectual exploration of text, identity, and politics in video discussions. One of the central objectives would be to transform two personable instructors into video commentators rather than simply talking heads.

The transformation occurred, but the results were often shaped in unexpected ways. When Jonathan was working with Michelle on the ECLC videotapes, he began to realize that being videotaped on a sound stage was having an effect on his teacherly performance in some curious and potentially productive ways. To his surprise, he began thinking more about the clothing he wanted to wear to the tapings, and he talked more seriously with the make-up artist about how and why she did what she did. He felt himself becoming, if not a "star," then at least the caricature of a TV personality.

That was oddly fortuitous—not just for Jonathan's vanity, but for his pedagogy. In the process of paying attention to what most teachers would consider superficial details, Jonathan felt himself acting more and more the "role" of the TV talk-show host. Part of this was aided by Michelle's deci-

6   *Alexander and Dickson*

sion to use videotexts—episodes of PBS' *Frontline* documentary series—as the primary course texts. Made up, mic'ed, and positioned on the set, Jonathan and Michelle became their own strange, academic versions of Regis and Kathie Lee. They discussed the tapes, joked, told stories, and had on-the-spot insights—all with increasing frequency and ease. Even the crew on the set, as well as the director and producer, began to quip that they should have their own show.

Jonathan and Michelle characterized their transformation from instructors into stars as learning how to think inside the box—to accept enough of the illusion in which they were participating so that some real discussion, perhaps even real learning, could take place. Instead of just being two "talking heads," they succeeded in performing roles that their viewers—excuse us, students—would recognize, be comfortable with, and perhaps even interact with. After all, many students (and their teachers) report "talking to" the TV when watching their favorite talk shows or news shows, critically questioning and responding to them. By becoming talk-show hosts, or by performing that role, Jonathan and Michelle sought to capture some of that interactive energy and even model other ways of thinking critically about video and other visual texts.

Susan and Marcia felt less like talk-show hosts and more like TV's favorite make-believe instructors. Indeed finding themselves performers on live TV was disconcerting for everyone involved. Teacher and student alike were uncomfortable with the camera, and we all felt frustrated when we tried to establish eye contact with whoever happened to be on the screen at the moment. No one seemed able to establish a comfortable presence with the character who appeared on screen. Even people in the room with an on-monitor speaker were more likely to watch and respond to his or her image on the screen than to look directly at a living person. This dislocation of attention created an altered perception of just who the audience happened to be, not to mention a heightened sense of self as a major character in the scene. Students who spoke became characters in the "play" taking place before the camera. Both Susan and Marcia felt an increased need to assume a personality and presence that combined the patience of Mr. Rogers, the rigor of the crusty professor from *Paper Chase*, and the flash of the PBS art instructor who could produce a picture in 10 minutes. Needless to say, none of these roles resembled ones Susan and Marcia assumed when going before one of our regular classes. Like Michelle and Jonathan, however, we had no other models to imitate or emulate as we played at being new kinds of teachers.

Interestingly enough, all of us came to feel that we were quick to privilege our regular classrooms as authentic, believing that they offered us an

Introduction   7

embodied teaching that seemed more real in the process. We forgot how teaching is always the performance of a role or, as Jane Gallop (1995) suggested in the title of her collection, *Pedagogy: The Question of Impersonation*, how much of teaching is impersonation, or the taking on of different roles to model and guide thinking, to act out different views and ideas, and even to offer pleasure as part of the process.

The adoption of such roles, however, has not always been a pleasurable experience for all faculty involved, and many have worried over the contorted shapes their instructional—and institutional—personas adopt in the implementation of distance-learning pedagogies. For instance, in an editorial published in the *American Journal of Distance-Education*, "Technology-Driven Change: Where Does It Leave Faculty?", Michael G. Moore (2000) posed tough questions about the structural and institutional impact on faculty when colleges and universities begin offering online courses. For instance, he wonders on whose shoulders responsibilities for such courses will fall. Will institutions have to hire new instructors? Will they be hired from a distance? Will such courses and distanced instructors change the role of faculty at their home institutions? Such questions can lead to substantial skepticism on the part of faculty—both in terms of pedagogy and institutional motivation for engaging in such ventures—and such skepticism often derails distance-learning projects before thoughtful pedagogies can be developed.

Some composition researchers worry over the potential *disappearance* of the instructor in online, distance-education spaces. In "Fault Lines in the Terrain of Distance-Education," Laura Brady (2001) noted that "student perceptions of teaching change with a distance-education approach. Without face-to-face interaction, the teacher disappears or becomes not applicable" (pp. 350-351). When viewed through a larger, political lens, this disappearance can be understood as a co-optation of academics by economics. In "The Debate about Online Learning: Key Issues for Writing Teachers," Patricia Webb Peterson (2001) suggested that, "Some teachers who fear distance-learning courses . . . assert that distance-learning technologies change the role of the professor into a deliverer of corporate values and goals, instead of a deliverer of traditional, liberal humanist goals" (p. 360).

Not all views of distance-learning teaching are negative, however, even as they acknowledge that instructors *must* take on new roles in their online and distanced teaching. Sara Guri-Rosenblit (1999), in *Distance and Campus Universities: Tensions and Interactions*, pointed out that "most scholars and practitioners believe that teachers have a firm and central role in distance-education" (p. 76). Teachers, she argued, will become more facilitators and mediators between knowledge bases and students than the main vehicle and transmitter of bodies of knowledge (pp. 247-248). Such facilitation often extends beyond the *content* of the course. As others note, the use of technology has *cultural* impacts as well. In a recent article in *Computers and Composition*, "Power, Language, and Identity: Voices from an Online Course," L. E. Sujo de Montes, Sally M. Oran, and Elizabeth M. Willis (2002), drawing on their extensive experience with majority and minority students in online courses, contended that "Web-based courses offer learning and teaching environments full of promises and challenges. The first of these challenges is to recognize and act upon the knowledge that computers are not culturally neutral but amplify the cultural characteristics that are taken for granted by those who develop them, promote them, and use them" (p. 268). We may be tempted to think of computer-mediated distanced instruction as potentially "stripping down" our participation in a course to the basic content, but this is not the case; cultural assumptions (as well as biases and prejudices) are carried into such spaces in complex ways, such as the assumption by many majority students of default "whiteness" or even heterosexuality in other participants who can not be seen. Thus, another new role for the distance-learning instructor is multicultural mediator who help students interrogate cultural assumptions and multicultural absences in online, distance-education spaces.

HOW THIS BOOK CONTRIBUTES TO THE CONVERSATION

Patricia Webb Peterson (2001) reminded us that, in "[o]nline teaching . . . technology alone cannot cause changes; it is the teacher's use of technology and the designers' construction of the technology that shapes its impact" (p. 362). Peterson's comment harkens back to what Nancy Kaplan (1991) suggested some years ago in her article, "Ideology, Technology, and the Future of Writing Instruction"—that "reading ourselves, as teachers of English in a technological world, awakens us to our roles, and our complicity, in the world" (p. 38). Although Kaplan was not writing exclusively about distance-learning environments but about teaching writing with technology in general, her point is nonetheless well taken: We need to find space to reflect on our roles in teaching environments increasingly reliant on technological mediation or interfaces—perhaps even more so because writing instruction is taking place in many venues exclusively mediated by technology.

Introduction 9

Given the diversity and complexity of our own experiences with distance learning and the teaching of English in general and writing in particular, we set out to create such a reflective space—hence, this book.

As we began assembling chapters for this collection, we were impressed with the variety of instructional and pedagogical experiments that faculty were undertaking—experiments that have since prompted us to reconsider some of our own teaching practices. Yet more than this, we were surprised by contributions to the collection that moved our thinking beyond the shifting role of the instructor. Specifically, many working with DL have turned their attention to the changing role of the writing process, to shifts in how we form and understand collaboration in writing projects, and to new expectations—and challenges—for the future of writing instruction.

At the heart of many of our contributors' discussions is both a reconsideration of the instructor's role as facilitator *and* an interrogation of changing notions of process in distance-learning writing instruction, particularly because staples of writing instruction—brainstorming, peer reviewing, drafting, revising, and editing—must be negotiated at a distance, usually electronically, and without the immediate presence of others responding to texts and offering (usually immediate) feedback. Moreover, and in a related vein, the distance-learning practitioners who have contributed to this volume also critically consider how remote environments require us to reconceive the notion of writing community in online spaces. For instance, group work assumes a different dimension in distance-learning courses because group members have to negotiate their input and feedback without the benefit of face-to-face cues and responses. Although this poses challenges for some, it also opens up new possibilities for collaboration and group writing projects as students generate text—usually a *lot* of text— through discussion boards, chatrooms, and e-mail—text that can be mined for more formal writing projects in ways that *verbal* discussions cannot. Finally, some practitioners of distance-learning writing instruction have been speculating on the future possibilities of English education and writing instruction in virtual environments. These writers see new potential roles for both delivering writing instruction and reconceptualizing what literacy means in the increasingly computer-networked academy. Given these new roles and possibilities, we have divided the chapters in this book into four sections: *Performances, Processes, Communities,* and *Futures.*

In Section I, *Performance*, authors examine the changes in teachers and students who suddenly find themselves as performers in a new medium, which often requires a reconsideration of the traditional roles of student and teacher. Given such changes, contributors to Section I reexamine and reconsider the role of distance-learning instructor as *facilitator*, particularly in terms of writing instruction. First, Christy Desmet, Robert Cummings, Alexis Hart, and William Finlay (chap.1, this volume) share some of their thought-provoking research about the difficulty of adjusting to new roles in "Pedagogical Performances in the Online Writing Class." They examine two great fears: that moving courses from brick-and-mortar to virtual classrooms will turn college education into what Clifford Stoll called a "cubicle-directed electronic experience" and that online learning will separate students from their teachers. Instead of accepting these fears, however, their chapter questions the inevitability of such negative experiences and views for both teachers and students. First, the authors report on a survey of classroom climate in traditional and online writing classrooms. Then they analyze features of a number of online classes in their study, relating the elements that may have helped students to perceive teacher–student interactions and classroom performance in a positive light.

John Bryan's "And Now, a Word from Our Sponsor" (chap. 2, this volume) examines the adoption of pedagogical roles from the perspective of a college administrator, in this case a dean, who both spearheaded and oversaw the development of a distance-learning program. Drawing on his expertise and experience as both a professional writing instructor and as an administrator, Bryan provocatively argues that the ability of distance learning to "threaten faculty comfort" is only "one of its virtues." Specifically, Bryan suggests that "Technology will push faculty toward the roles envisioned by the creators of the technology. But technology does not trump all, not even in DL." Nurturing the ability of faculty to imagine new pedagogical uses and roles for technology is thus crucial. Further, in his consideration of dealing with resistant faculty, we are reminded that, in distance-learning settings, perhaps more consciously and more acutely than in any other pedagogical site, our roles exist in the complex intersection between pedagogical *and* administrative needs. Thus, Bryan's perspective, as an administrator, is crucial in offering a fuller understanding of the DL writing instructor's role.

Section II, *Processes* examines the specific ways in which our understanding as well as our teaching of writing as a *process* shifts in distanced learning environments. Chapters in this section consider the changes in pedagogy that the electronic classroom often requires for effective instruction to take place, suggesting that anyone who attempts to transfer existing pedagogies to the cyberclass, for instance, is destined to find distance learning unsatisfactory. On the contrary, the authors suggest that those who revision practice often find themselves enthusiastic about activities

Introduction 11

they would never consider using in a face-to-face environment. In "A Language All Its Own: Writing in the Distance Learning Classroom," Ellen H. Hendrix (chap. 3, this volume) argues that, for students who are ready to embark on the journey toward learning to write, view themselves as writers, and become writers, the distance-learning class can help them in ways that the traditional classroom cannot. Specifically, if online interaction allows group members to use writing in a variety of ways and to understand writing as language used for a purpose, then the members of the class will begin to value writing in the same way that they value speech. Although not all writers will develop at the same pace or to the same level, writing group members will develop greater confidence in themselves as writers. The distance-learning experience will provide the opportunity for using language, more specifically writing, to create meaningful discourse, experiment with communications technologies, and participate actively in their learning environments.

Stuart Blersch and Carolyn Stoll's chapter, "Trying to Connect: A Distance-Learning Basic Writing Course for Nontraditional Students" (chap. 4, this volume), describes a particular approach taken by two faculty teaching in the same program in which Michelle and Jonathan taught. Specifically, Blersch and Stoll examine online communication as the means to create classes for the growing number of people for whom college has not traditionally been an option—basic writers whose locations or time constraints often make attending courses on a college campus difficult, if not impossible. As these basic writers pursue coursework and degrees in higher education, the question of whether we *should* teach basic writing online becomes mute; the question now becomes *how* can we teach such courses effectively? The authors of this chapter explore creative approaches to teaching basic writing in distance-education environments, with a specific focus on the teacher's role in facilitating the student–teacher relationship by building a community of learners—a strategy crucial in basic writing instruction.

This section of the book ends with Debbie Danowski's "Anyone? Anyone? Anyone? Leading Discussions in Cyberspace: E-Journals and Interactivity in Asynchronous Environments" (chap. 5 , this volume), which offers new insights about building active student participation. Although necessary in a face-to-face classroom, in a distance-education environment, the very survival of the course can depend on interactivity, yet the tendency for decreased sharing can be even greater. Danowski discusses the use of student e-journals as a means to promote interactivity in asynchronous environments, making important distinctions between the traditional expressive student journals currently used in many composition courses and newer methods of interactive e-journals.

In Section III, *Communities*, contributors focus on the art of community building—on ways to bring together anonymous students with each other and with their teachers. Recognizing the benefits that accrue when our face-to-face classroom experiences seem to "gel," with students and instructor excitedly working with and learning from one another as a *group* of learners, some distance-learning practitioners have sought ways to replicate such experiences in distance-learning environments, and chapters in this section explore and discuss such community-building ventures. Lori E. Amy's "Rhetorical Violence and the Problematics of Power: A Notion of Community for the Digital Age Classroom" (chap. 6, this volume) discusses previous studies of the classroom as a contact zone and suggests that we need to expand that discussion to include the "electronic contact zones" created when reading, writing, and teaching online. In addition, while recognizing the limitations of early, utopian visions of the Internet and online communication as spaces of radical equality, she describes how the electronic communication spaces of our online classrooms can be restructured as places in which we explore language as power and as an activity with civic responsibilities and consequences.

The second chapter in this section, "Critical and Multicultural: Pedagogy Goes Online" by Lesliee Antonette (chap. 7, this volume), challenges online teachers to rethink current traditional models of student–teacher interaction. Through multiple examples, she argues that a critical multicultural pedagogy that utilizes problem posing and collaborative work can allow for the production of a distance-learning space that is innovative and effective in addressing the increasingly diverse populations that inhabit U.S. college classrooms.

Antonette's chapter is followed by Melody Bowden's "Feminist Civic Engagement and the Role of the Bureaucrat: Graduate Education, Distance Learning, and Community Action" (chap. 8, this volume), which argues that when we move our courses from traditional classrooms to the Internet, we disrupt our students' and our own senses of time, space, and identity. In other words, all of us can be anyone, anywhere, at any time. The author explores ways in which teachers can capitalize on this disruption to improve our students' and our own learning experiences and begin to alter the social geography of our communities. To ground her theories, Bowden demonstrates how a combination of service-learning and Web-based learning in one graduate program helped students build a virtual community that could understand and value the power of rhetoric for social change.

In Section IV, *Futures*, the contributors devote themselves to visions of the future of cyber or distanced classes. As such these authors maintain that the future plays a role in how we conceive and understand our peda-

Introduction   *13*

gogical, programmatic, and institutional commitments and priorities. Specifically, they ask what future possibilities of instruction might be heralded by increased use of and experimentation with distance-learning venues. They also consider the limitations of such instruction and potential losses in quality of instruction as institutional pressures mount to switch to seemingly cheaper or more efficient distance-learning venues.

In "Online Distance-education and the 'Buffy Paradigm': Welcome to the Hell Mouth," Cynthia L. Jenéy (chap. 9, this volume) suggests that one of the most responsible approaches educators and administrators can take with regard to distance-education is to acknowledge that we face an uncertain mix of existing and future conditions. The unique pedagogical and practical dimensions of teaching English composition and literature in computer-mediated environments, and the task for most educators assigned to online distance courses, are often daunting—particularly considering budget constraints, poor computer programming, and a variety of seemingly inevitable technological mishaps and crashes. Jenéy argues that, by taking a more activist stance, we *can* become better designers, better online teachers, and better Internet *personae* that students can rely on and trust.

Veronica Pantoja's "Learning at Light Speed in Neal Stephenson's *The Diamond Age*" (chap. 10, this volume) creatively suggests that Stephenson's award-winning science fiction novel, *The Diamond Age or, A Young Lady's Illustrated Primer*, provides new perspectives for educators interested in constructing a critical pedagogy that integrates technology to establish effective interactive teaching and learning environments. The novel tells the story of a young girl, her technologically advanced computerized primer, and how it impacts her education. Pantoja sees Stephenson's book as an illustration of the possibilities of highly interactive technology, offering connections drawn from actual distance-learning practice to suggest future implications for a distance learning and teaching that uses interaction as its primary instructional mode.

To close the section and the book, Peter Sands argues in "Distant, Present, and Hybrid" (chap. 11, this volume) that a hybrid or blended course, combining both face-to-face and distance-education platforms, might ultimately provide both instructors and students with a richer ground for role-playing and learning. Instructors, academic staff, and administrators keen to experiment with such spaces will appreciate the theoretical savvy and practical experience Sands brings to his analysis of hybridity and distance learning.

14 Alexander and Dickson

* * *

We are quite happy with this collection of chapters on distance learning. All the authors are concerned with both philosophical and theoretical aspects of distance-education. However, they not only reflect critically on changing roles and situations, but discuss the practical implications of a variety of distance-learning strategies and approaches in writing instruction. We invite you to consider your own experiences, fears, and hopes in light of the shifting roles described in this book. It is our hope that *Role Play*, which was not designed as a "how-to" text, will allow and even encourage instructors to make their own decisions about the way their individual practice can be incorporated into distance-learning situations, provide administrators with a better sense of the problems inherent in distance-learning education, and allow those who have been resisting distance learning to see the merits as well as the challenges of virtual classrooms.

REFERENCES

Brady, Laura. (2001). Fault lines in the terrain of distance-education. *Computers & Composition, 18,* 347-358.

Feyten, Carine M., & Nutta, Joyce W. (Eds.). (1999). *Virtual instruction: Issues and insights from an international perspective.* Englewood, CO: Libraries Unlimited.

Casanave, Christine Pearson. (2002). *Writing games: Multicultural case studies of academic literacy practices in higher education.* Mahwah, NJ: Lawrence Erlbaum Associates.

Gallop, Jane. (1995). *Pedagogy: The question of impersonation.* Bloomington: Indiana University Press.

Guri-Rosenblit, Sara. (1999). *Distance and campus universities: Tensions and interactions.* Oxford: IAU Press, Pergamon.

Kaplan, Nancy. (1991). Ideology, technology, and the future of writing instruction. In Gail E. Hawisher & Cynthia L. Selfe (Eds.), *Evolving perspectives on computers and composition studies* (pp. 11-42). Urbana, IL: NCTE.

Moore, Michael G. (2000). Technology-driven change: Where does it leave faculty? *The American Journal of Distance-education, 14,* 1-6.

Peterson, Patricia W. (2001). The debate about online learning: Key issues for writing teachers. *Computers & Composition, 18,* 359-370.

Sujo de Montes, L. E., Oran, Sally M., & Willis, Elizabeth M. (2002). Power, language, and identity: Voices from an online course. *Computers & Composition, 19,* 251-271.

Introduction   *15*

FOR FURTHER READING

Atieh, Sam. (1998). *How to get a college degree via the Internet: The complete guide to getting your undergraduate or graduate degree from the comfort of your home.* Rocklin, CA: Prima Publishing.

Bates, A.W. Tony. (1995). *Technology, open learning and distance-education.* New York: Routledge.

Belanger, France, & Jordan, Dianne H. (2000). *Evaluation and implementation of distance learning: Technologies, tools, and techniques.* Hershey, PA: Idea Group Publishing.

Berge, Zane L. (Ed.). (2001). *Sustaining distance training.* San Francisco: Jossey-Bass.

Birnbaum, Barry W. (2001). *Foundations and practices in the use of distance-education.* Lewiston: The Edwin Mellen Press.

Blythe, Stuart. (2001). Designing online courses: User-centered practices. *Computers & Composition, 18,* 329-346.

Carchidi, Daniel M. (2002). *The virtual delivery and virtual organization of postsecondary education.* New York: Routledge Falmer.

Chute, Alan G., Thompson, Melody, & Hancock, Burton. (1998). *The McGraw-Hill handbook of distance learning: A "how to get started guide" for trainers and human resources professionals.* New York: McGraw-Hill.

Collis, Betty, & Moonen, Jef. (2001). *Flexible learning in a digital world: Experiences and expectations.* London: Kogan Page Ltd.

Cooper, Linda. (2001). Online courses: Strategies for success. In Richard Discenza, Caroline Howard, & Karen Schenk (Eds.), *The design & management of effective distance learning programs.* Hershey, PA: Idea Group Publishing.

Dillon, Connie L., & Cintrón, Rosa. (Eds.). (1997). *Building a working policy for distance-education.* San Francisco: Jossey-Bass.

Discenza, Richard, Howard, Caroline, & Schenk, Karen. (Eds.). (2001). *The design & management of effective distance learning programs.* Hershey, PA: Idea Group Publishing.

Dooley, Kim E., & Magill, Jane. (2001). Faculty perceptions and participation in distance-education: Pick fruit from the low-hanging branches. In Richard Discenza, Caroline Howard, & Karen Schenk (Eds.), *The design & management of effective distance learning programs.* Hershey, PA: Idea Group Publishing.

Garrison, Randy R., & Anderson, Terry. (2003). *E-learning in the 21st century: A framework for research and practice.* London: Routledge.

Gilbert, Sara Dulaney. (2001). *How to be a successful online student.* New York: McGraw-Hill.

Hailey, Jr., Dave E., Grant-Davie, Keith, & Hult, Christine A. (2001). Online education. Horror stories worthy of Halloween: A short list of problems and solutions in online instruction. *Computers & Composition, 18,* 387-397.

Hairston, Maxine, & Ruszkiewicz, John J. (1996). *Teaching online: Internet research, conversation and composition.* Austin: HarperCollins.

Harasim, Linda, Hiltz, Starr Roxanne, Teles, Lucio, & Turoff, Murray. (1995). *Learning networks: A field guide to teaching and learning.* Cambridge, MA: MIT Press.

Harrington, Susanmarie, Day, Michael, & Rickly, Rebecca. (Eds.). (2000). *The online writing classroom.* Cresskill, NJ: Hampton Press.

Harry, Keith. (Ed.). (1999). *Higher education through open and distance learning.* New York: Routledge.

Hawisher, Gail E., & Selfe, Cynthia L. (Eds.). (1991). *Evolving perspectives on computers and composition studies.* Urbana: NCTE.

Hiltz, Starr Roxanne. (1994). *The virtual classroom: Learning without limits via computer networks.* Norwood, NJ: Ablex.

Lau, Linda K. (Ed.). (2000). *Distance learning technologies: Issues, trends, and opportunities.* Hershey, PA: Idea Group Publishing.

Lockwood, Fred, & Gooley, Anne. (Eds.). (2001). *Innovation in open & distance learning: Successful development of online and web-based learning.* London: Kogan Page Ltd.

Mantyla, Karen, & Gividen, J. Richard. (1997). *Distance learning: A step-by-step guide for trainers.* Alexandria, VA: American Society for Training & Development.

McVay, Marguerita. (2000). *How to be a successful distance learning student: Learning on the Internet.* Needham Heights, MA: Pearson Custom Publishing.

Miller, Susan. (2001). How near and yet how far? Theorizing distance teaching. *Computers & Composition, 18,* 321-328.

Miller, Susan Kay. (2001). A review of research on distance-education in *Computers and Composition. Computers & Composition, 18,* 423-430.

Moore, Michael G., & Kearsley, Greg. (1996). *Distance-education: A systems view.* Belmont, CA: Wadsworth Publishing.

Palloff, Rena M., & Pratt, Keith. (1999). *Building learning communities in cyberspace.* San Francisco: Jossey-Bass Publishers.

Peterson, Patricia Webb, & Savenye, Wilhelmina C. (2001). Letter from the guest editors: Distance-education: Promises and perils of teaching and learning online. *Computers & Composition, 18,* 319-320.

Picciano, Anthony G. (2001). *Distance learning: Making connections across virtual space and time.* Upper Saddle River, NJ: Merrill Prentice Hall.

Porter, Lynnette R. (1997). *Creating the virtual classroom: Distance learning with the Internet.* New York: John Wiley & Sons.

Ragan, Tillman J., & White, Patricia R. (2001). What we have here is a failure to communicate: The criticality of writing in online instruction. *Computers & Composition, 18,* 399-409.

Rudestam, Kjell Erik, & Schoenholtz-Read, Judith. (Eds.). (2002). *Handbook of online learning: Innovations in higher education and corporate training.* Thousand Oaks, CA: Sage.

Salmon, Gilly. (2000). *E-moderating: The key to teaching and learning online.* London: Kogan Page Ltd.

Savenye, Wilhelmina C., Olina, Zen, & Niemczyk, Mary. (2001). So you are going to be an online writing instructor: Issues in designing, developing, and delivering an online course. *Computers & Composition, 18,* 371-385.

Schreiber, Deborah A., & Berge, Zane L. (Eds.). (1998). *Distance training: How innovative organizations are using technology to maximize learning and meet business objectives.* San Francisco: Jossey-Bass Publishers.

Shoemaker, Cynthia C. Jones. (1998). *Leadership in continuing and distance-education in higher education.* New York: Allyn & Bacon.

Tait, Alan, & Mills, Roger. (Eds.). (1999). *The convergence of distance and conventional education: Patterns of flexibility for the individual learner.* New York: Routledge.

Tschang, F. T., & Senta, T. Della. (Eds.). (2001). *Access to knowledge: New information technologies and the emergence of the virtual university.* Amsterdam: Pergamon.

Verdejo, M. Felisa, & Cerri, Stefano A. (Eds.). (1994). *Collaborative dialogue technologies in distance learning.* Berlin and New York: Springer-Verlag.

Willis, Barry. (1993). *Distance-education: A practical guide.* Englewood Cliffs, NJ: Educational Technology Publications.

Willis, Barry. (Ed.). (1994). *Distance-education: Strategies and tools.* Englewood Cliffs, NJ: Educational Technology Publications.

Wolcott, Linda L. (1993). Faculty planning for distance teaching. *The American Journal of Distance-Education, 7,* 26-36.

I PERFORMANCES

Pedagogical Performances in the Online Writing Class

Christy Desmet, Robert Cummings,
Alexis Hart, and William Finlay

And Now, a Word From Our Sponsor

John G. Bryan

1

PEDAGOGICAL PERFORMANCES IN THE ONLINE WRITING CLASS

Christy Desmet, Robert Cummings, Alexis Hart, and William Finlay

VIRTUAL PROBLEMS: ISOLATED STUDENTS AND INVISIBLE TEACHERS

Many educators fear that moving their courses from brick-and-mortar to virtual classrooms will turn college education into what Clifford Stoll, in *Silicon Snake Oil: Second Thoughts on the Information Highway*, called a "cubicle-directed electronic experience." In this world of virtual cubicles, students are isolated, "psychodynamically separated from one another even while inhabiting the same campus or dorm building" (cited in Anson, 1999, p. 269). Critics of virtual classrooms also fear that online learning separates students from their teachers. David Noble (2001), an outspoken opponent of mass-produced distance-education, wrote that, "[e]ducation is a process that necessarily entails an interpersonal (not merely interactive) relationship between people—student and teacher (and student and student)" (p. 2).

Laura Brady's (2001) study of distance-education courses at West Virginia University seems to confirm the fear that computers isolate students from their teachers. When studying the responses on student evaluations of online courses over several semesters, Brady found that 35% of students rated the instructor's teaching as "not applicable," and a staggering 56% rated the instructor's advance preparation and organization as "not applicable." According to Brady, without face-to-face interaction, "the teacher disappears or becomes not applicable" (p. 351). David Hailey, Keith Grant-Davie, and Christine Hult (2001) reached a similar conclusion, cautioning that although "online classes require more of the teacher's time than face-to-face classes," the instructor's "time investment is not necessarily noticed and appreciated by online students *unless the teacher works to create the appearance of being present at all times*" (p. 394; italics added).

In online education, the teacher's time and effort can be invisible and therefore irrelevant to the students' perception of classroom climate. As the studies cited earlier suggest, the problem manifests itself quite literally as a matter of perception. The teacher and her labor become *invisible*; she must work extra hard to create and maintain a *presence* in the virtual classroom; only by creating an illusion of perpetual presence, therefore, can the teacher meet her students' expectations. This chapter, however, questions the inevitability of such negative experiences for both teachers and students—first by reporting on a survey study of classroom climate in traditional and online writing classrooms, and second by analyzing features of some online classes that participated in the study that may have helped students perceive teacher–student interaction and classroom performance in a positive light.

POSITIVE PERCEPTIONS: ONE STUDY OF CLASSROOM CLIMATE IN ONLINE COMPOSITION

This chapter takes as its starting point data that were gathered in a larger research project—a comparative study of e-learning in different departments across the University of Georgia (UGA) campus. As part of the project, members of the Deans' Forum, a collaborative group of faculty from

Pedagogical Performances in the Online Writing Class 23

the Colleges of Arts and Sciences and Education, studied the online writing classes in Christy Desmet's first-year composition program.[1]

In Fall 2001, on behalf of the Deans' Forum Technology group, William Finlay of the University of Georgia Department of Sociology conducted random focus groups of students in online first-year composition classes and interviewed their teachers. In Spring 2002, the group followed up with a survey study of the online composition classes and traditional classes that met at the same days and times, using an instrument based on the fall findings and constructed by Dr. Finlay. Responses to individual questions in the survey were grouped into themes or measures as follows:

- Instructor is helpful (four items)
- Easy to participate in discussion (three items)
- Don't enjoy class (three items)
- Better critical thinking skills (two items)
- Know what is needed to succeed (three items)
- Would take this type of class again (one item)
- Satisfied with decision to take class (one item)

Surprisingly, students in the online classes showed a statistically significant higher level of satisfaction than did their colleagues in the face-to-face classes, although there were no significant statistical differences between the student evaluation ratings of the online and regular teachers. Such a finding goes against the grain of much research on online and distance-education. For this reason, we looked within the classes for evidence to support the statistics. In this chapter, Christy Desmet (as first-year composition director), Alexis Hart, and Robert Cummings (both as teachers of online classes that participated in the year-long study) respond to the survey findings by analyzing the construction of student–teacher relations in their classes.

TEACHER–STUDENT RELATIONS

For a long time, research into teacher–student relations has recognized the teacher's importance to student learning. The teacher's impact on students

---

[1]Although the scope and mission of the Deans' Forum is outside the subject of this chapter, a description of the group and its projects is available in Mewborn et al. (2002).

goes by different names. Communication studies, for instance, debates the importance of "teacher immediacy behaviors," both verbal and nonverbal, to students' cognitive growth (Christensen & Menzel, 1998; Golish & Olson, 2000; Gorham, 1988; Hess et al., 2001; and Myers & Knox, 2001). Educator David Hansen (1999) defined the teacher's concern more broadly as an *attentiveness* to students' intellectual and moral growth. Others describe the influence of "affective behavior," "affective exchange," and "empathy" on students' learning and motivation (Hess et al., 2001; Lepper & Cabray, 1988; Rodriguez, Plax, & Kearney, 1996). Only a few researchers define student–teacher interactions as occurring between actual persons (Frymier & Houser, 2000). Further complications follow when these definitions are extended to teacher–student relations in online educational settings. The cognitive vocabulary of much scholarship, which focuses on "teacher behaviors" or "affect," by definition privileges face-to-face interaction. Second, general definitions of *good practice* inevitably involve physical proximity and oral exchange between students and faculty.[2] In this chapter, we agree that teaching, and most especially online teaching, rest on a relationship between persons. Yet implicit in both terms—*person* and *personal*—is the notion that identity, from both sides of the virtual desk, is performed. Persons must be person-ated and even, at times, impersonated. In the absence of verbal exchange, physical proximity, and bodily expression, performing identity and relationships becomes more rather than less important. The personal is performative, to revise a feminist proverb.

PROBLEMS WITH THE PERSONAL

The role of the personal in the composition class has been much debated, both as subject matter for writers and as a way to authorize both readers and writers. This debate has been focused most sharply by feminist com-

---

[2]A Web site constructed by the BYU Faculty Center builds a list of specific recommendations for increasing student–faculty contact based on the first of Chickering and Gamson's "Seven Principles for Good Practice in Undergraduate Education." All of the recommendations involve physical proximity or verbal exchange, and often both. Some also involve organized social interaction ("Seven Principles for Good Practice in Undergraduate Education," available online at: *http://www.byu.edu/fc/pages/tchlrnpages/7princip.html*).

Pedagogical Performances in the Online Writing Class 25

positionists. Teachers from Florence Howe (1971) to Pamela Annas (1985) have argued not only that students should write from experience, but that women writers in particular benefit from writing from their position as *women*. By confronting the politics of identity, they can gain an authentic voice and sense of self. Although both Howe and Annas are careful not to sentimentalize or essentialize "Woman" as a category, over time the paradoxes that haunt the notions of both "experience" and "personal" have been taken up and teased out by the feminism-and-composition community. Min-Zhan Lu (1998), for instance, argued that "in validating the authority of the personal, academic feminist readers need to reflect on their privileged social location and be vigilant toward the tendency to invoke experience as an inherent right that erases differences along lines of race, class, gender, or sexual identity" (p. 239). Laura Brady (1998), examining key theoretical texts about "women's" experience, also concluded that often such examinations reify the binaries they set out to disrupt. Feminist theorists offer a range of solutions to the problem of essentialism. In the context of feminist research, for instance, Gesa E. Kirsch and Joy S. Ritchie (2003) proposed that researchers must carefully consider the politics of location. Laura Brady (1998) offered Judith Butler's equation of "identification practices" with "performatives," speech acts that enact what they say, as another corrective to essentialism (p. 40). In Brady's formulation, space is wedded with time, so that "identity construction" is not a state, but a performance. This concept of "identity-as-performance" suggests a way to define both teacher and students as "persons" rather than as "bundles of attributes" (a formulation from communication theory; O'Keefe, 1990, p. 184) and as disembodied "text" (as in postmodern theory).

IDENTITY AND PERFORMANCE THEORY

Performance theory, in conjunction with speech act theory—whence comes the notion of "performative" utterances—can help define the various relations that take place among teachers and students online. In particular, performance theory combines an understanding of interactions in time with textual relations that, according to Butler, are citational or iterative (Brady, 1998, p. 40), and therefore fixed in time by their placement on the page (or screen). Thus, performance theory helps us understand the fine line between (written) text and (oral) utterance that characterizes online discourse—a hybrid mode sometimes called Interactive Written Discourse (IWD) (Ferrara, Brunner, & Whitemore, 1991). For this reason in particular, performance theory provides a useful model for analyzing textual relations that unfold in real time through synchronous interfaces.

Performance studies, the discipline that takes seriously actions in everyday life as well as in art, ritual, and the social sphere, recognizes that repeated behaviors are by definition performances of both formal and informal kinds (Schechner, 2002). Among the thinkers cited by performance theorists is Erving Goffman (1959), whose *Presentation of Self in Everyday Life* chronicled the ways in which the life-as-theater metaphor is played out in common social interactions. Goffman defined *interaction* as the "reciprocal influence of individuals upon one another's actions when in one another's immediate presence" (p. 15). Within these encounters, individuals perform to influence the behavior of other participants. When interactions are repeated—that is, "when an individual or performer plays to the same audience on different occasions, a social relationship is likely to arise"—these relationships are governed by "rights and duties" attached to the different roles assumed by individuals (Goffman, 1959, pp. 15-16).

Performance theory also relies on more recent writers to define explicitly the discursive foundation of performed identity in different dramatic, social, and technological environments. Judith Butler (1990), most famously, explored the ways in which gender identity exists only to the extent that it is performed; she wrote that "the effect of gender is produced through the stylization of the body and, hence, must be understood as the mundane way in which bodily gestures, movements, and styles of various kinds constitute the illusion of an abiding gendered self" (p. 140). As a *"stylized repetition of acts"* (italics original), identity as performance involves repeated behaviors and utterances and the cultivation of belief in roles. Sherry Turkle (1995), in her study of emerging relationships in the MUD, applied Butler's analysis specifically to relationships that are constructed exclusively through discourse at a distance.

Performance theory can help us recognize the textual/discursive interface separating teachers from students online as a condition of pedagogical identity rather than merely as a hindrance to interpersonal relations. Because most online classes (particularly writing classes) consist primarily of text on screens, the teacher must create an appearance of presence discursively. So must the students. In discussing the results of the study, our online teachers speculated that the prominence of synchronous rather than asynchronous communication in our program may account, in part, for the students' elevated level of satisfaction. As W. Webster Newbold

Pedagogical Performances in the Online Writing Class 27

(1999) argued, "asynchronous modes of study lack the essential ingredient of immediacy—the actual, not virtual, presence of a human being at the other end of the wire." Yet synchronous chats, like face-to-face meetings, bring the teacher and students together in space and time and thus into a personal presence that is missing from the typical "any time, any where" autodidactic distance-education course. The following sections focus on two ways in which teachers and students in an online class create a virtual presence: by performing the personal (as evidenced in Alexis Hart's class), and by maintaining visibility online (as evidenced in Robert Cummings' class).

PERFORMING THE PERSONAL

In their evaluations of the class that had participated in our study, Alexis' students did not consider their teacher to be "not applicable." To the contrary, they wrote that she was "well organized," "available at all times," "effective," "encouraging," and "always had everything updated on time." In the online class, Alexis projected a personable ethos that was consistent with her self-representation in other courses. Yet in this case, she had to do so by exclusively discursive means.

Discursive performativity, according to Judith Butler (1993), is "not a singular or deliberate 'act,' but the reiterative and citational practice by which discourse produces the effect that it names" (p. 2). Alexis began the first iteration of her pedagogical performance during the very first class meeting. Of the 15 students who were present at that initial face-to-face meeting, only 2 of them raised their hands when she asked if they understood that they had enrolled in an online class. Alexis quickly assured those who worried about their lack of technological expertise that the class would not only increase their facility with computers (the practical lure), but also provide more *personal* attention because online classes at UGA are smaller than regular ones. How can we characterize this classroom moment? Alexis offered her class what speech act theory would call a "performative" utterance—a promise of attention disguised as a fact. In truth she had yet to lavish much time and attention on the students themselves; they had barely met! Yet, as Goffman (1959) described, this was a piece of "impression management," by which the teacher—with the best of motives—solicited the loyalty of her team for the upcoming semester (pp. 212-216 and passim).

A second "reiteration of the personal" was also set into motion on that first day. In lieu of having each student introduce him or herself aloud, Alexis asked the class to post an introductory paragraph to the class discussion list. Unlike more ephemeral verbal introductions, these posted introductions remained accessible throughout the duration of the course, as did the responses to them. As peer review groups shuffled members throughout the semester, students often went back to these personal descriptions to remind themselves of their peers' backgrounds and interests—not only to gain insight into each others' writing choices, but also to promote social activities such as concerts and parties.

By performing the personal in her online class, Alexis believes, generally she was able to avoid what Christyne Berzsenyi (1999) characterized as a "hierarchical interlocutor relationship" between teacher and students. Hierarchical relationships, as defined by Berzsenyi, "include a plentitude of information, criticisms, corrections, and prescriptions" (p. 233). The teacher's knowledge comes to the foreground so that advice *from* the teacher *to* the students takes center stage. Empathetic relationships, by contrast, "consist of active interaction among most or all interlocutors in a conference group. Praise of one another's viewpoints is common, as are invitations for elaboration of one's expressed viewpoints." In this way, empathetic interlocutors—teachers in common parlance—"promote a more *personal* relationship among computer conference participants" (Berzsenyi, 1999, p. 234; italics added).

Alexis' chatroom transcripts show her as engaging often in empathetic interactions with her students. She offers brief, but pointed, phrases of encouragement that single out students by name. Some characteristic interjections include: "Great!"; "Good!"; "Excellent!"; "Interesting point _____"; "_____, can you tell us more?"; "Say more about that _____"; "Right, _____!"; "Exactly, _____!"; "Go ahead, _____, tell us why you think that." Harriet Wilkins (1991) describes enthusiastic hyperbole of this nature as "devices that express the speaker's lively interest in the subject matter," and by extension, the writer herself (pp. 68-69). The students soon began to pick up the teacher's rhetoric, responding to one another's contributions in the chat discussions with "well said, _____"; "good _____"; "I agree with _____"; "well put, _____"; "I see where you're going with that"; "good point"; and "I like that answer, _____." Aware that "[o]nline learning environments often cannot support demonstration that the teacher is a decent human being by a smile and direct eye contact" (Ragan & White, 2001, p. 404), throughout the semester Alexis reiterated her performance as a personable and approachable teacher. The class came to be dominated by empathetic communica-

Pedagogical Performances in the Online Writing Class   29

tion as teachers and students evolved a common rhetoric of praise and encouragement.

As the course progressed, these performances solidified into what Goffman (1967) called a "social relationship." In the following exchange, Alexis apologizes for not returning papers and refers to her upcoming Ph.D. orals:[3]

Miss Hart	I'm sure you all are wondering when I'll get your graded papers back to you, right?
Nathan	Yes.
Alice	Yes.
Miss Hart	I typically try to return papers within a week, but I'm going to have to ask for your patience and understanding on this first one.
Alice	Okay.
Nathan	That's okay.
Miss Hart	I have my Ph.D. orals on Thursday, so I won't start grading papers until probably Sunday.
Clyde	Just as long as we get patience and understanding from you.
Alice	Good point, Clyde.
Calvin	Lol.
Bethany	Hehee nice, Cldye.
Bethany	Clyde.
Miss Hart	I plan to try to get grades back by a week from Friday.
Nancy	Lol.
Bethany	Deal.
Sarah	Just concentrate on your Ph.D. orals.
Bethany	Yeah . . . don't you worry about a thing.

Alexis asks for the students' understanding, evoking her dual role as both teacher and student to encourage empathy. The students, in turn,

---

[3]Student names have been changed.

30   *Desmet, Cummings, Hart, & Finlay*

offer moral support, but humorously remind their teacher that she "owes" them an equal degree of sympathy in the unspecified future. Communication theory would describe Alexis' ethos here in terms of attributes that make her audience receptive to her message. In this message, for instance, she demonstrates credibility by projecting a sense of trustworthiness and expertise. The responses of Alexis' students confirm that she is likeable (O'Keefe, 1990, pp. 181-184, 196-197). Such an analysis, by no means incorrect, nevertheless neglects the negotiation among parties that this exchange foregrounds. Teacher and students acknowledge having both rights and responsibilities to one another. Furthermore, the exchange highlights the social context that research tells us computer-mediated communication tends to ignore (Kiesler, Siegal, & McGuire, 1984). Finally, the transcript records evidence of a "social-emotional exchange," which generally has been shown to be more prevalent in face-to-face than in computer-mediated relations (Hiltz, Johnson, & Turoff, 1986). In this instance, at least, we have moved beyond an affect of empathy to a more complicated relationship by virtue of the teacher's and students' willingness to "perform" their respective roles, and therefore to enunciate and play with the power relationship between them.

Alexis' performance of the personal, she concludes, encouraged the students to take on themselves more of the class' intellectual work, combining praise with constructive criticism. For one assignment, students were asked to identify a strength of the evidence supporting their own arguments and then offer advice for improvement to one another. In an initial posting, for instance, a student named Darren defended the credibility of his sources: "The arguments that I am working on for Paper 2 require a great deal of data to back up my statements. I am getting this data from the articles which I have found. Most of the data is from the EPA, which is a government agency which has a good reputation, and is known as a credible and a unbiased source." Darren's use of the first-person pronoun shows a high-level of "ego involvement" (Wilkins, 1991, pp. 67-68). In the next exchange, other students praise Darren's argument, reinforcing his self-assessment by opening their responses with his name and repeating his language (e.g., "credibility"; Wilkins, p. 67). Yet Darren's interlocutors also go on to suggest further rhetorical criteria that he might consider (italics added below):

> *Nathan*   Darren, do not forget to appeal emotionally by showing exactly how the environment is affected, bird, etc. dying, and explain your data in terms of relative arguments that were seen firsthand. *You have a good*

Pedagogical Performances in the Online Writing Class 31

> *argument to write about*, but remember to relate to audience on their level.
>
> Sarah   Darren, *I think you have an excellent topic for your paper*. It seems like you have the factual side of your paper fairly solid, but remember to try and include emotional appeals in your paper as well. Maybe use of an enargeia [rhetorical vividness] would be appropriate.
>
> Melissa   *I think it's good* that you are using a lot of facts and data from credible sources, but you should also write some things that would evoke the audience's emotions. You can include info. about how animals are affected by people in the environment, and how nature is affected by humans if this is relevant to your paper.

Nathan, Sarah, and Melissa modulate from warm praise into a more hierarchical voice that offers advice. The students have begun to perform academic discourse with confidence by reinforcing the positive, supportive tone initiated by the teacher even as they have learned to critique one another.

Yet the effect of "performing the personal" is never monolithic. In some instances, paradoxically, the "completeness" of the teacher's online ethos encouraged more traditional classroom exchanges. Tharon Howard (1997) cautioned that, "far from being sites that enable free and open discussions, classroom computer conferences continue to exist within larger social and institutional frameworks and, thus, are at least partially influenced by them" (p. 114). Some of Alexis' pedagogical choices reinforced traditional hierarchies even as they strengthened the ethos of classroom immediacy. The instructor was referred to consistently as "Miss Hart" and the students by their actual names. Teacher and students knew one another by the names that appeared on student papers and by the names they would use to address one another in face-to-face meetings. In this way, Alexis and her students acknowledged the institutional divide between them.

The power of the teacher's persona, reinforced by the etiquette of address observed in Alexis' classroom, created other problems as well. Usually the online exchanges successfully highlighted the students' voices, as in the following example (italics added):

Miss Hart	Other than support, what kinds of things do you need to consider when writing to persuade?
Renee	I always seem to go to pathos and logos first.
Alice	Background of the people you are writing to.
Brianna	Can someone understand, fully, your ideas.
Darren	You need to consider who you are trying to persuade.
Calvin	To hit a common vibe.
Darren	The audience.
Kelly	*I agree, but how do you know when to use a certain type of persuasion?*
Melissa	Who your audience will be.
Nancy	The people you're talking to.
Brianna	The audience.
Darren	And how to go about persuading them.
Sarah	How the reader is taking it. who the reader is.
Nathan	Start with facts and work in your opinions.
Renee	Your audience. If you're writing to a group of mothers on drunk driving, use pathos.
Darren	And when trying to persuade doctors, use logos.
Clyde	You have to please the audience.
Miss Hart	Exactly—the audience!
Alice	We're such a smart class.

Here, in the terminology of Wilkins (1991), the participants "validate" one another by lexical repetition and by using terminology from composition theory that demonstrates a shared "cultural knowledge" (pp. 65–67). Text is exchanged rapidly, but equitably, among teacher and students, and all parties speak with the empathetic voice of encouragement and praise. (It is Alice, not Miss Hart, who concludes that "We're such a smart class.") Furthermore, one student, Kelly, accepts the teacher's role as interlocutor, prompting further discussion. In some exchanges, the teacher's voice, so resonant with phatic encouragement at other times, began to dominate. In the next exchange, by contrast, Alexis takes center stage as the classroom expert on rhetoric and effectively silences student contributions:

Pedagogical Performances in the Online Writing Class 33

Miss Hart   The book discusses four types of examples.

Miss Hart   The first is historical or examples drawn from history.

Miss Hart   Kelly began her last paper about athletes and drug use this way by giving the example of the basketball player Len Bias.

Miss Hart   Clyde used the example of Vietnam to argue that American troops shouldn't get involved in a war in Columbia.

Miss Hart   So, these examples can be quite persuasive.

Brianna   Yes.

Miss Hart   Of course, you have to consider your audience. The effectiveness of examples is a lot like the effectiveness of emotional appeals.

Miss Hart   You have to consider the distance in space and time.

Miss Hart   If Clyde's audience consisted primarily of young people, his example of Vietnam would not be as effective as if he were arguing to the generation who experienced it firsthand.

Miss Hart   Kelly's example might fall short if no one in her audience remembers Bias' death and the splash it made in the headlines.

Miss Hart   Am I putting you all to sleep yet?

Nathan   zzzzzzzzzzzzzzzzzzzzzzz.

Calvin   Lol, no we were already sleepy.

Alice   Sort of.

Kelly   Haha . . . no.

Evan   Heh.

Melissa   Kind of.

Nancy   Haha . . . kind of.

In this case, the instructor's humor mitigates, but does not upset the hierarchy of student–teacher roles. On reflection, Alexis found that she also tended to abruptly cut off student responses by asking questions ending in "right?" (e.g., "We all use rhetoric everyday, right?"). In almost every instance, once that type of rhetorical question had been asked, not a single student disagreed, deferring automatically to the teacher's assumed expertise instead.

It is difficult to determine just what ingredients of synchronous conversation worked occasionally against Alexis' quite successful performance of the personal as a classroom strategy. We might reiterate the belief of Howard (1997) and others that technology may mask, but never eradicate, institutional hierarchies. We might also cite the physical dimension of Alexis' performance; as an expert typist and active communicant, she covertly reestablished the dominance that her classroom had challenged by simply producing copious and competent discourse (Bordia, 1997). In any case, the "performance of the personal" can work to both enfranchise and silence students who, faced in the online writing class with a powerful pedagogical persona, respond by constructing textual selves of their own.

MAINTAINING ONLINE VISIBILITIES

In his response to our investigation, Robert Cummings focuses on how students interact with one another and teachers within the structures established by synchronous communication. In this instance, the theatricality of classroom performances may also be related to the dynamics of the MOO, as opposed to the chatroom, as the instructor's chosen medium for synchronous conversation. As Juli Burke (1998) described, even educational MOOs are "platforms" for virtual scene-painting, role-playing, and crossdressing that evolve into a truly theatrical event: "Entering a MOO is not unlike entering a theater building. One travels to the site, a space that exists within society for the purpose of a specific activity that is both part of and apart from the real world around us" (p. 235). The MOO therefore functions as "a sphere of theatrical interaction" (p. 239).

In the MOO as educational theater, online identity is and must be constructed through discourse. If online identity is discursive, it follows that online students must write to participate in class discussion. In fact they must write simply to exist in the electronic environment; if they fail to write, they literally disappear from view, becoming invisible not only to the instructor, but also to their classmates. For this reason, Michael Joyce (1998) referred to the MOO as a "mortal space," in which persistence is necessary to combat the ephemeral quality of written expression that rolls forward relentlessly on the screen: "We fill this moral space with the living of our lives, although like a hole in the sand it is never filled, or rather ever

Pedagogical Performances in the Online Writing Class 35

filled, since we do so in recurrence, wave upon wave" (p. 321). Students in a brick-and-mortar classroom simply do not have to face this imperative to combat invisibility; their very faces create for them a presence in the classroom. Students in the MOO, by contrast, must engage in what Erving Goffman (1967) called "face-work."

Goffman's analysis of ritual interactions in social institutions begins by analyzing the importance of face-work. In a dense definition, Goffman (1967) defined having face as a moment when a person successfully presents a self-image "that is internally consistent, that is supported by judgements and evidence conveyed by other participants, and that is confirmed by evidence conveyed through interpersonal agencies in the situation" (pp. 6–7). Although the social face described here may seem solid and immutable, a person's face is "not lodged in or on his body, but rather [is] something that is diffusely located in the flow of events" (Goffman, 1967, p. 7). As Butler (1990) argued much later, identity is citational and constructed through stylized, reiterated acts within a fluid, ongoing context. Face-work, in fact, becomes most intense when the integrity of the social self is threatened (Goffman, 1967, pp. 12-13). Establishing face, in Goffman's vocabulary, approximates what Robert here called "maintaining visibility" online.

In the MOO, because writing is linked to existence—the performance and maintenance of an online identity—students experience a powerful compulsion to write. According to Robert's analysis, they conduct facework in two rhetorical modes: either by jumping into the conversation with sporadic placeholder remarks, expressing assent with a "yeah" or "I agree," or by constructing longer, argumentative, and more polished responses that follow the conventions of written or published text more than they do the rules of conversation. Both strategies create online visibility through textual means.

In establishing a collective online ethos through praise, a strategy that Alexis analyzed earlier as part of performing the personal, Robert's students also engage in what Goffman (1959) called "impression management" (pp. 208–237). In other words, students may use short phrases not simply for rhetorical purposes (i.e., to establish community with the teacher and fellow students), but to establish for themselves a textual lifeline and to claim a place in the conversation. The findings in this case contradict two conclusions of the literature on computer-mediated composition (CMC): first, that "normative social pressure" decreases in CMC groups (Bordia, 1997; Hiltz et al., 1986); and second, that CMC encourages remarks saturated with and exerting "social pressure" (Bordia). Establishing a textual lifeline in the online classroom-as-theater involves an ongoing dialectic between social release and social conformity. The MOO as theater provides actors with a space for self-definition, but as happens so often in Shakespearean drama, the audience retains power over the actor's fiction by conferring or withholding its belief and approval.

We can see the drama of MOO interactions in one typical example from Robert's class. As revealed by the MOO transcript, in this session, students discussing Janisse Ray's (2000) *Ecology of a Cracker Childhood* predominantly employ conversational place holders to claim their place in the conversation. Ray's book, a work of creative nonfiction, addresses environmental issues based on her experiences living in Georgia. Ray alternates chapters of autobiography with investigations into the natural world, often citing quantifiable data about environmental loss. The students had an overwhelming dislike for Ray's highly elaborated environmental chapters, the first sign of which surfaced when Robert (Uncle_Ike) asked whether the book was autobiography or creative nonfiction. The MOO transcript for this transaction reads as follows:

Sarahz says,	"I'm the opposite I thought some of the description was a little too much."
Ceeps464 says,	"Janisse ray came to speak at my high school once-good times . . . the book is auto-biography/ecological."
Uncle_Ike says,	"Which chapters seem autobiographical?"
Yjm0408 says,	"She puts all those random statistics in."
Sophie says,	"It's a shame."
Yjm0408 says,	"Yea."
LaurenEJ says,	"Yea."
Sarahz says,	"Yeah."

Rather than address the question of literary genre posed by the instructor, the MOO participants focused instead on their emotional reactions to the text, discussing explicitly the fact that they did not appreciate those chapters that interrupted the author's ongoing narrative with dense facts or random statistics. Interjections of "yeah" from several students who had otherwise remained invisible indicate not only their intent to second "Sarahz's" statement that the text's description "was a little too much," but also their need to establish a textual presence in the MOO. Yjm, LaurenEJ, and Sarahz claim a space in the textual conversation by phatic

Pedagogical Performances in the Online Writing Class 37

utterances of agreement. They may play bit parts in the overall drama of class discussion, but at least step momentarily into the spotlight. Sarahz actually seconds a statement that she had authored, suggesting again that the string of expletives represents not a broad class consensus, but rather evidence of an underlying need to maintain visibility. Through such strings of affirmation, the students engage in repeated and stylized acts—to use Butler's terms—by which they perform their online pedagogical identities.

Although many students resorted to expletives, at least one writer—a student who initially found the online approach so intimidating that he almost dropped the class—took advantage of the textual nature of online discussion to craft more lengthy responses. Again the example comes from an exchange about Janisse Ray's text and specifically about the timber industry's practice of cutting and replanting trees:

> *Wisp* says, "What Ray's said is that even though they replant, they don't replant in God's image with trees like the Longleaf pine, they remake it in the utilitarian image of their need, with the trees that will be most functional on the timber market."

Another lengthy statement from the same student appears during a discussion of man as omnivore hunter in the metaphorical food chain (a question raised in Ray's book through the presence of a character named Charlie):

> *Uncle_Ike* says, "But it does raise some questions, if you work out the analogy of being the coon hunter: Charlie hunts coons, using dogs. The adult turtle has exactly 3 predators: humans, dogs, and coons."

> *Wisp* says, "So what is the conclusion based on that parallel, that man kills himself?"

> *Wisp* says, "He does only if you see Charlie as the 'cracker everyman,' and he is also viewed through the metaphor of the tortoise, then one could see how Charlie, and the cracker in general, is hunting himself through his over-utilization of his natural environment."

Certainly these statements could have been made in class. Yet the textual nature of the synchronous online environment allows the writer greater expansiveness; he poses a question that not only invites others into the discussion, but also allows the questioner to develop his own point.

The compulsion to maintain visibility and participate in an online synchronous classroom, as Wisp's experience suggests, can be channeled into fuller, more comprehensive statements than is possible within a traditional classroom environment. Wisp's response is no less stylized than that of other students, but the iterations of his performance are more lengthy. His behavior might be described, in Goffman's (1967) terms, as "dramaturgical discipline," an actor's ability to "remember his part" and move from one situation to another without becoming confused (p. 216). He becomes a star because online, much more so than face-to-face, individuals who occupy screen space and scrolling time can determine the direction and pace of the pedagogical drama. The literature comparing face-to-face with computer-mediated communication suggests that the speed and frequency of online communication creates not just a global "lack of awareness of the social context" (Bordia, 1997), but, more specifically, a higher level of "private self-awareness" that occurs in tandem with a decrease of "public self-awareness" (Bordia, 1997; Matheson & Zanna, 1988, 1989). Within this context, Wisp not only takes center stage by dominating the screen, but he also constructs a self by exploiting the virtues of writing that have been extolled, in a much different context, by Janet Emig (1977)—that is, writing's ability to record thought and invite the recursive process of revision.

To follow the "virtual-classroom-as-stage" metaphor, both choric iteration (short expletives) and soliloquy (extended text) become more prominent in online classrooms than Goffman's model, based as it is on face-to-face encounters, might suggest. Regarding the students' contributions to class discussion as "performances" therefore complicates the assessment of online conversation, because only especially brief and particularly lengthy statements stand out in the flow of discourse. In the context of the class' collective performance, individual writers balance a compulsion to maintain online visibility against the desire to express complex thoughts in a number of ways. Sometimes writers may feel the need to blurt out immediately a short statement; at other times, they may value the comprehensiveness of a longer statement. In truth, every online statement by a student writer reflects an *ad hoc* balance of brevity and depth.

Yet this balancing act is not always handled successfully. Students who, in a traditional classroom, will raise their hands and wait for acknowledgment before asking administrative questions, can no longer depend on this disciplinary mechanism. Thus, intense, probative, and often exhilarating discussion must develop among tangential outbursts, questions such as "How long does this paper have to be again?"; "When are your office hours?"; or, worse yet, "When do we get our essays back?" The detached, disembodied, if not truly anarchist nature of synchronous conversation

Pedagogical Performances in the Online Writing Class 39

online was captured by Lester Faigley (1992) as he recounted a particularly disturbing online session: "The messages seemed like they were coming from outer space: that beyond the giggly, junior-high-school-bus level of the discussion of sexuality, it had a ghostly quality, an image of the dance of death on the graves of the old narratives of moral order" (p. 196).

Thus, one of the chief challenges facing instructors in synchronous online classrooms remains the ability to manage chaos—a contingency not anticipated adequately by either older or newer accounts of identity as performance. Intelligent discussion cannot only survive in the online classroom, but also thrive. Still intelligence must thrive amid unintelligent and disruptive utterances. Underlying Faigley's fear that students are dancing "the dance of death on the graves of the old narratives of moral order" is the potential for chaos in the structure of the synchronous conversation, which not only creates a threat of invisibility and the attendant compulsion to write, but grounds discursive identity in text that scrolls continually off the screen into oblivion (buffers notwithstanding). The fleeting nature of line-by-line communication tends to flatten traditional hierarchies by collapsing teacher and students into a single audience—or at least into a collective audience in which the voice of the authority figure rolls past at the same pace as those of other class members. This flattening of hierarchies and collapsing of audiences—what Beth Kolko (1998), following Mary Louise Pratt, called the creation of a "contact zone" peopled by virtual travelers (pp. 262-263)—is often praised as a liberating feature of experimental online writing and hypertext, but virtual tourism of this nature also poses particular challenges for the virtual teacher.

The instructor leading a synchronous online discussion not only faces what Marilyn Cooper (1999) labeled "student 'underlife'" (p. 141), but must also address how his or her reduction from classroom human to an electronic metaphor alters the rhetorical paradigm. One undeniable benefit is that the online teacher becomes, at least for the length of any given MOO session, less of an authority figure and more of a true audience for student writers. In "The Writer's Audience Is Always a Fiction," Walter J. Ong (1975) imagined the writer's audience as a distant, disembodied object to which the writer must strive to give form based on an intimate and culturally shaped understanding of text:

> If the writer succeeds in writing, it is generally because he can fictionalize in his imagination an audience he has learned to know not from daily life but from earlier writers who were fictionalizing in their imagination audiences they had learned to know in still earlier writers, and so on back to the dawn of written narrative. (p. 11)

The online student must, in some important ways, still imagine his or her audience, but clearly not according the same sort of solitary, skillful game of intimate conjecture that Ong attributed to writers such as Ernest Hemingway. Online writers have an audience that, in the MOO, occupies the same metaphorical space and real time that the writer does. Nevertheless, the material layout of synchronous environments also places structural constraints on author–audience or student–teacher relationships. All discussion that occurs in the synchronous online classroom—be it MOO, MUD, or chatroom—is shaped by the line-by-line textual interface. The thoughts of each writer, student or teacher, are given the same priority and appear and disappear at the same rate: Once any given writer's message appears at the bottom of the screen, it becomes the "latest word," but only until the next writer hits "send." As Faigley (1992) put it, "Networked writing displaces the modernist conception of writing as hard work aimed at producing an enduring object. Acts of networked writing are most often quickly produced, quickly consumed, and quickly discarded" (p. 191).

Although Alexis found that performing the personal reified her pedagogical persona in traditional ways, Robert draws a different conclusion. In the competitive environment of synchronous chat, old hierarchies based on pedagogical status and formal education are flattened by a new temporal hierarchy that values the "last" (but never final) word. In one further twist, however, the flattening of hierarchy in synchronous communication does reinstall the habits and relationships of the traditional classroom. Against a steady flow of phatic communication, more thoughtful statements can stand out and acquire added value; synchronous online classrooms therefore can influence students to become insightful readers and writers in a fast-paced environment.

We have now come full circle. Alexis began by describing how online teachers can reclaim a personal relationship with students; Robert ends by showing how students can metamorphose into teachers. As Newbold (1999) and others have stressed, institutional hierarchies never fade away. Yet in the virtual spaces of the synchronous classroom, pedagogical identities can metamorphose, be exchanged, and take off in new directions.

IN CONCLUSION

Regarding relations between students and teachers as a matter of "performance" offers a useful perspective on pedagogical interchanges within

Pedagogical Performances in the Online Writing Class 41

the online environment. First, the analogy allows for closer comparison between computer-mediated communication and the face-to-face rituals on which most pedagogy is based and against which online education is often compared unfavorably. Second, the metaphor of "virtual classroom as stage" allows us to see drama as a condition of human relations that foregrounds, rather than obscures, the power relations so endemic to life in the academy. When we look at human relations in terms of *impression management*, to return to Goffman's term, we become particularly aware of both the actor's power to project a persona and the audience's power to either confer or withhold a favorable judgment on that person-ation. Furthermore, under the rule of performance, no affective state—not empathy, trust, or liking—can be seen as socially innocent, free from hierarchies and invitations to conform (Clark, 1994). In this way, an understanding of identity as performance, which is so thoroughly embedded in online communication, can inform and support what Kirsch and Ritchie (2003) called the "politics of location." Finally, the dramatic metaphor for online relations highlights the ongoing and elastic nature of pedagogical discourse. In many of the examples of student writing offered in this chapter, the students seemed to agree readily with one another and with their teachers, chiming in with expressions of agreement or succumbing to and merging with the teacher's voice. Yet the ability to see these textual traces as performance mitigates against the sense that they represent any stable and abiding characteristics of the writer's self. Iteration is the condition of selfhood, but not its end. In this way, an understanding of online identity as performance can be useful in contesting the idea that discourse in the public sphere must lead to consensus (Roberts-Miller, 2003).

In this chapter, we assumed that the mere *fact* of synchronous communication made possible the dramatic performance of pedagogical identities, both by evoking the traditional classroom and its rituals and by disrupting those rituals. What remains to be examined is the question of whether the material conditions that structure a synchronous classroom *produce* these pedagogical effects or operate as a master metaphor for *contextualizing* pedagogical performances. In other words, the synchronous classroom seems more homey only if we can already see chat as more familiar than asynchronous discourse; it seems radical if we associate classroom discourse online with other anti-institutional uses of chatroom space. As Susan Miller (2001) commented, although some evidence shows that communication at a distance can produce close relationships and triumphant performances by individuals, to this point these experiences have not been successfully "narrated" as personal experiences. Miller's distinction between relationships that "are" personal and those that are "narrated" or "constructed" as personal is an important one. This chapter offers one attempt to frame synchronous communication among teachers and students as a performance that stages pedagogical intimacy and a shared intellectual discourse against a backdrop of choreographed chaos. Performing the personal to maintain visibility online, for both teachers and students, can provide one alternative to the virtual isolation that many opponents of distance-education fear must inevitably operate in the online classroom.

REFERENCES

Annas, Pamela. (1985). Style as politics: A feminist approach to the teaching of writing. *College English, 47*, 360-71. Reprinted in G E. Kirsch et al. (Eds.). (2003). *Feminism and composition: A critical sourcebook* (pp. 61-72). Boston and New York: Bedford/St. Martin's and NCTE.

Anson, Chris. M. (1999). Distant voices: Teaching and writing in a culture of technology. *College English, 61*(3), 261-280.

Berzsenyi, Christyne A. (1999). Teaching interlocutor relationships in electronic classrooms. *Computers and Composition, 16*, 229-246.

Bordia, Prashant. (1997). Face-to-face versus computer-mediated communication: A synthesis of the experimental literature [Electronic version]. *Journal of Business Communication, 34*. Retrieved February 24, 2004, from http://global. factiva.com/

Brady, Laura. (1998). The reproduction of othering. In S. C. Jarratt & L. Worsham (Eds.), *Feminism and composition studies: In other words* (pp. 21-44). New York: Modern Language Association.

Brady, Laura. (2001). Fault lines in the terrain of distance-education. *Computers and Composition, 18*, 347-358.

Burke, Juli. (1998). The play's the thing: Theatricality and the MOO environment. In C. Haynes & J. R. Holmevik (Eds.), *High wired: On the design, use, and theory of educational MOOs* (pp. 232-249). Ann Arbor: University of Michigan Press.

Butler, Judith. (1990). *Gender trouble: Feminism and the subversion of identity.* New York: Routledge.

Butler, Judith. (1993). *Bodies that matter: On the discursive limits of "sex."* New York: Routledge.

BYU Faculty Center. *Seven principles of good practice in undergraduate education.* Retrieved on July 4, 2003, from http://www.byu.edu/fc/pages/tchlrnpages/7 princip.html

Chickering, Arthur W., and Gamson, Z. F. (1987). Seven principles for good practice in undergraduate education. *AAHE Bulletin, 39*(7), 3-7.

Christensen, Laura J., and Menzel, Kent E. (1998). The linear relationship between student reports of teacher immediacy behaviors and perceptions of state motivation, and of cognitive, affective, and behavioral learning. *Communication Education, 47,* 82-90.

Clark, Gregory. (1994). Rescuing the discourse of community. *College Composition and Communication, 45,* 61-74.

Cooper, Marilyn. (1999). Postmodern possibilities in electronic conversations. In G. E, Hawisher & C. L. Selfe (Eds.), *Passions, pedagogies, and 21st century technologies* (pp. 140-160). Logan: Utah State University Press.

Emig, Janet. (1977). Writing as a mode of learning. *College Composition and Communication, 28,* 122-128.

Faigley, Lester. (1992). *Fragments of rationality: Postmodernity and the subject of composition.* Pittsburgh: University of Pittsburgh Press.

Ferrara, Kathleen, Brunner, Hans, and Whitemore, Greg. (1991). Interactive written discourse as an emergent register. *Written Communication, 8,* 8-34.

Frymier, Ann Bainbridge, and Houser, Marian L. (2000). The teacher-student relationship as an interpersonal relationship. *Communication Education, 49(3),* 207-219.

Goffman, Erving. (1959). *The presentation of self in everyday life.* Garden City, NY: Doubleday.

Goffman, Erving. (1967). *Interaction ritual: Essays on face-to-face behavior.* New York: Doubleday.

Golish, Tamara D., and Olson, Loreen N. (2000). Students' use of power in the classroom: An investigation of student power, teacher power, and teacher immediacy. *Communication Quarterly, 48(3),* 293-310.

Gorham, J. (1988). The relationship between verbal teacher immediacy and student learning. *Communication Education, 37(1),* 40-53.

Hailey, David E. Jr., Grant-Davie, Keith, and Hult, Christine E. (2001). Online education horror stories worthy of Halloween: A short list of problems and solutions in online education. *Computers and Composition, 18,* 387-397.

Hansen, David T. (1999). Understanding students. *Journal of Curriculum and Supervision, 14(2),* 171-185.

Hess, John A. et al. (2001). Is teacher immediacy actually related to student cognitive learning? *Communication Studies, 52,* 197-219.

Hiltz, S. R., Johnson, K., and Turoff, M. (1986). Experiments in group decision making: Communication process and outcome in face-to-face versus computerized conferences. *Human Communication Research, 13,* 225-252.

Howard, Tharon, (1997). *A rhetoric of electronic communities.* Greenwich, CT: Ablex Publishing Corporation.

Howe, Florence. (1971). Identity and expression: A writing course for women. *College English, 32,* 863-871. Reprinted in G. E. Kirsch et al. (Eds.). (2003). *Feminism and composition: A critical sourcebook* (pp. 33-42). Boston and New York: Bedford/St. Martin's and NCTE.

Joyce, Michael. (1998). Songs of thy selves: Persistence, momentariness, recurrence and the MOO. In C. Hayne & J. R. Holmevik (Eds.), *High wired: On the design, use, and theory of educational MOOs* (pp. 311-324). Ann Arbor: University of Michigan Press.

Kiesler, S., Siegel, J., and McGuire, T. W. (1984). Social psychological aspects of computer-mediated communication. *American Psychologist, 39*, 1123-1134.

Kirsch, G. E., and Ritchie, J. S. (2003). Beyond the personal: Theorizing a politics of location in composition research. In G. E. Kirsch et al. (Eds.), *Feminism and composition: A critical sourcebook.* (pp. 140-159). Boston and New York: Bedford/St. Martin's and NCTE.

Kolko, Beth. (1998). Bodies in place: Real politics, real pedagogy, and virtual space. In C. Haynes & J. R. Holmevik (Eds.), *High wired: On the design, use, and theory of educational MOOs* (pp. 253-266). Ann Arbor: University of Michigan Press.

Lepper, M. R., and Cabray, R. W. (1988). Socializing the intelligent tutor: Bringing empathy to computer tutors. In H. Mandl & A. Lesgold (Eds.), *Learning issues for intelligent tutoring systems* (pp. 247-257). New York: Springer-Verlag.

Lu, Min-Zhan. (1998). Reading and writing differences: The problematic of experience. In S. C. Jarratt & L. Worsham (Eds.), *Feminism and composition studies: In other words* (pp. 239-251). New York: Modern Language Association.

Matheson, K., and Zanna, M. P. (1988). The impact of computer-mediated communication on self-awareness. *Computer in Human Behavior, 4*, 221-233.

Matheson, K., and Zanna, M. P. (1989). Persuasion as a function of self-awareness in computer-mediated communication. *Social Behavior, 4*, 99-111.

Mewborn, Denise et al. (2002). Expanding the "Great Conversation" to include arts and sciences faculty. *Innovative Higher Education, 27(1)*, 39-51.

Miller, Susan. (2001). How near and yet how far? Theorizing distance teaching. *Computers and Composition, 18*, 321-328.

Myers, Scott A., and Knox, Rhonda L. (2001). The relationship between college student information-seeking behaviors and perceived instructor verbal behaviors. *Communication Education, 50*, 343-356.

Newbold, Webster. (1999). Teaching on the Internet: Transactional writing instruction on the World Wide Web. *Kairos: A Journal for Teacher of Writing, 4.1.* Retrieved September 6, 2002, from http://english.ttu.edu/kairos/4.1/features/newbold.

Noble, David. (2001). *Digital diploma mills: The automation of higher education.* New York: Monthly Review Press.

O'Keefe, Daniel J. (1990). *Persuasion: Theory and research.* Newbury Park, CA: Sage.

Ong, Walter J. (1975). The writer's audience is always a fiction. *PMLA, 90*, 9-21.

Ragan, Tillman J., and White, Patricia R. (2001). What we have here is a failure to communicate: The criticality of writing in online instruction. *Computers and Composition, 18*, 399-409.

Ray, Janisse. (2000). *Ecology of a cracker childhood.* Minneapolis: Milkweed Editions.

Roberts-Miller, Trish. (2003). Discursive conflict in communities and classrooms. *College Composition and Communication, 54*, 536-557.

Rodriguez, J. I., Plax, T. G., and Kearney, P. (1996). Clarifying the relationship between teacher nonverbal immediacy and student cognitive learning: Affective learning as the central causal mediator. *Communication Education, 45*, 293-305.

Schechner, Richard. (2002). *Performance studies: An introduction*. London: Routledge.

Turkle, Sherry. (1995). *Life on the screen: Identity in the age of the Internet*. New York: Simon & Schuster.

Wilkins, Harriet. (1991). Computer talk: Long-distance communications by computer. *Written Communication, 8*, 56-78.

2

AND NOW, A WORD FROM OUR SPONSOR

John G. Bryan

Few broad developments in higher education during the last 15 years have stirred more controversy among American university faculty than distance learning (DL). Even the funding crisis of 2003 to 2004 seems not to have elicited as much passionate debate perhaps because funding affects tenured faculty less than it does current students and prospective faculty. Distance education, however, affects current faculty. It questions comfortable assumptions about the role of faculty, about the relationship between faculty and students, about a faculty member's intellectual property rights, about the relationship between faculty and the institutions that employ them, and about the entire division of labor in higher education. Distance learning threatens faculty comfort. That is only one of its virtues.

ADMINISTRATORS AND DISTANCE LEARNING

Faculty sometimes see administrators who venture into the realms of curriculum and instruction (C&I) as interlopers, especially when—as with distance learning—the administrators are promoting radically different approaches. Certainly some issues peripheral to C&I also heighten faculty apprehensions about administrators' promotion and control of distance programs. For example, the creation of for-profit subsidiaries of public and private nonprofit institutions could undercut the demand for tenured faculty at an institution and could move those institutions even closer to seeing their relationship with students as that of a vendor and consumers. Institutional incentives for faculty to devote energies to developing DL courses and programs may also undercut the devotion of those faculty resources to already-enrolled students and to scholarly work.

More particular to C&I, however, many faculty fear any erosion of their traditional control of C&I and fear DL's perceived threat to faculty job security. If stand-alone DL ventures thrive or die depending on fulfillment of some administrator's business plan, will the business plan come to determine the scope and shape of the curriculum and the deployment of faculty? Will the technology's ability to record and endlessly "play back" faculty activities render some number of faculty redundant? (Since the 1960s, American higher education's steady shift of reliance—from 22% to 43%—on part-time faculty and graduate teaching assistants instead of on full-time tenure-track faculty demonstrates that socioeconomic forces do indeed reshape the profession.) At a more personal level, many faculty see DL as another step in the direction of commodification or, even worse, commoditization, making higher education a monolith of mass production with faculty as piece workers and with little distinction among various institutions' offerings of English 101 or any other course, thereby diminishing both the quality of student learning and the quality of faculty life. Administrators, who are often characterized as being more concerned about the bottom line than about quality, typically control an institution's involvement in DL and so constitute the agents of these perceived threats.

Despite these real and perceived threats, as the "sponsors" of instruction, administrators have broad, significant interests in and responsibilities for the institution, including DL. They must ensure:

- the institution's continuing solvency in an increasingly competitive, resource-strapped environment;
- integration and coherence of individual courses that compose programs;
- alignment of courses and programs with the intended educational outcomes and priorities of the institution;
- alignment of the intended educational outcomes with the demands of the institution's stakeholders: society, the

And Now, a Word From Our Sponsor   *49*

employment marketplace, taxpayers (if a public institution), people ultimately responsible for institutional success (such as legislators, regents, trustees), students, and, of course, faculty;

- efficient investment and use of the institution's resources; and
- allocation of resources consistent with the institution's priorities.

Administrators also often bring unexpected but useful interpretations of the data of faculty activity. For example, the faculty member who feels overworked and underpaid mostly likely believes that the cause lies beyond faculty control—that the cause lies in administrative exploitation of faculty. That may be true. Yet an administrator may alternatively see that the faculty member who feels exploited has the same workload as another faculty member who teaches the same courses, achieves comparable student learning outcomes, and seems not to feel beleaguered or exploited. What accounts for the difference? By pressing such issues, the administrator may stimulate the questioning of assumptions that faculty often make.

Given these responsibilities—and despite the fears and sometimes competing interests of faculty—administrators bring to DL initiatives a perspective that faculty should understand even if for no reason other than self-preservation.

ONE ADMINISTRATOR'S PERSPECTIVE

This chapter offers a perspective infrequently represented in collections on pedagogy, the perspective of an administrator—albeit an administrator who regularly teaches courses in professional writing. First, I offer a little about my administrative history as it pertains to DL and related technology-assisted pedagogies. In addition to holding a full-time, tenure-track position in the English Department at the University of Cincinnati (UC), since 1989: I have held three relevant administrative positions at UC: 4 years as director of the department's computing, 3 years as associate dean of UC's College of Arts & Sciences (with direct responsibility for technology as well as other issues), and 6 years as dean of UC's University College, a college that was the university's second largest, had the highest saturation of computer resources on campus, and enjoyed a faculty heavily committed to the use of technology in the classroom. As dean of that college in 1999, I led creation of what would become the university's largest program delivered by distance learning. Over those 13 years, I recognized an interesting pattern of faculty members' engagement of instructional technology, typically beginning with fear and resistance before growing into acceptance, embracement, and innovation.

ASPECTS OF CONTROL

In 1992, I was experimenting with what I called the *silent classroom* in my own technical writing classes. I conducted them entirely online using the Daedalus Integrated Writing Environment (DIWE), although all of the students and I were in the same networked DOS lab. At the same time, I was promoting the use of another program, Aspects, in composition classes that were taught in a networked Macintosh lab. The classes were not what we would characterize today as DL, but they were beginning to simulate computer-based DL that would follow. Aspects, a program produced by Group Logic, but now defunct I understand, facilitated collaborative writing. Each user of the software joined an online group, and multiple group members could simultaneously open two windows on their computer screens. One window functioned much like a chatroom, enabling users to converse with other group members. The second window held a text submitted to the network by any of the group members. All users in the group could simultaneously see and move through the document, use pointers to highlight or point to parts of the document, and edit the document—although no two users could simultaneously edit a particular paragraph. Using the chat window, members could discuss the document and its editing.

The ambitious design of Aspects was unusual, insightful, and progressive for that period because the program so cleverly promoted collaboration and negotiation of editorial control among peers. Rather than relying on prompts and the tunneling of communication between instructor and student, Aspects recognized and promoted the social character of much workplace writing. It shifted responsibility for learning and product from instructor to student, and it encouraged peer mentoring in the fulfillment of that responsibility. At the time, the program seemed to me conceptually better than DIWE and other collaborative writing software, and it established a model for parts of later programs like CommonSpace, and even later for

And Now, a Word From Our Sponsor 51

important modules of courseware like Blackboard. The program's simulation of a professional work environment was no accident. Education, in fact, was a secondary market for the software, which had been designed to facilitate workplace collaboration. (For a useful comparison of the collaborative writing software of the 1990s, consult Sands, 1997.)

Unfortunately, the software could not fully exploit its laudable design because it was buggy. The system often froze, forcing students to repeatedly reboot, log back in, and reload the shared document—activities that typically caused other users' systems to hesitate, capriciously teetering on the edge of failure. Wasted time in class, work lost into the ether, students' distraction, and the faculty's need to always have a back-up plan in the case of system failures all were understandably objectionable, and some of our faculty elected either not to use Aspects or not to teach in that lab because they did not wish to deal with such problems. They had a choice, unlike instructors in a true DL program.

Despite their gravity, the technological problems with Aspects were not as tough to address as other issues related to the role of faculty. When I introduced the software to one reluctant composition teacher, she had a list of concerns. She talked about the rapport she establishes with her students, about the importance of body language and eye contact, and about being able to associate a name and a face. I knew just what she meant. Having observed her teaching, I admired her interaction with the students, the way she leaned toward them when they spoke, her animated facial reactions to the class discussion. "Just try it," I suggested—and she reluctantly agreed. Yet when she discovered that the software would force her students to form at least two groups (Aspects limited groups to 16) and that she could join only one online group at a time, she asked me, "But how will I *control* the students if I can't be in both groups at the same time?"

Set aside questions of why one would ever compose a collaborative writing group with as many as 16 members. Set aside, if you will, the quick assumption that I was encountering the typical "sage on the stage." That was not her model. Assigned to a traditional classroom, this faculty member conducted interactive classes, skillfully leading discussions among those students willing to participate, and she used small groups for peer collaboration and review. Nor had I merely encountered a traditional teacher-centered classroom. No, it went beyond that. This instructor wanted *control* because she assumed that the orderliness of her traditional classroom, punctuated only by dyadic exchanges between herself and the various students, signified the students' attentiveness and learning. When she used small groups and floated about the room from group to group, the students acknowledged and responded to her periodic presence, indicating to her satisfaction that they were on task. To her, all this meant that she had created an environment conducive to student learning. As my engagement with her class waned, so did her use of Aspects.

During the same term, another composition teacher let me know that she had already tried Aspects and judged it a disaster. The class had quickly spun out of control, she said. Students in one group had begun using vulgar language that she would never have permitted in her traditional classroom. Another group, she said, had turned on one of its members and had attacked her so viciously that the young woman had left class. Frantically trying to restore order, she at first leaped in and out of the online groups, demanding that they maintain decorum and focus on their assignments. That many of the students ignored her directions shocked her. What had happened, she wondered, that the quiet orderliness of the students before her had gone anarchic under the influence of this software? Unable to restore control online, she stood up in the classroom and demanded that all of the students log out and shut down their computers. She would never use Aspects again.

Had I known in 1992 what I now know, I would have prepared the faculty for what they would encounter online, but I was not yet aware of the burgeoning body of literature on the issues of authority and control in the classroom—and especially in the online environment, nor had I yet experienced for myself such online rebellion. That would come 2 years later when I arranged an online meeting of my students with a New Mexico State University technical writing class in a MUD. That meeting spun "out of control" just as my university's president appeared in the classroom to observe, as part of a planned departmental visit, this transcontinental coupling of English classes. Fortunately, he found the idea of connecting across the country more interesting than the chaotic text scrolling across the projection screen.

Although the technological problems with Aspects were considerable, they could be solved by improving the technology. However, Aspects exemplified what faculty so often find objectionable in instructional technology: its inherent inflexibility—or, at least, an inability to adapt to the sometimes idiosyncratic desires of individual faculty (such as having a collaborative work group with 25 members). The technology, some would argue, takes precedence over the faculty, forcing them to reshape their curriculum and instruction to accommodate the technology. That is an understandable objection, but too often, in my experience, the greater inflexibility occurred in the faculty member whose years of classroom success had resulted in little desire to explore alternative approaches that just might yield greater success.

FROM LAN TO SATELLITES AND INTERNET

Flash forward to the creation of a true distance program at UC. In 1999, as dean of UC's University College, I began collaborating with faculty and other administrators to extend our associate degree program in early childhood education to students outside the Cincinnati area. The initiative was prompted largely by Congress' 1998 bill reauthorizing Head Start, the large federal program aimed at improving the long-term academic and social success of economically disadvantaged preschool children. In short, the legislation meant that, to keep their jobs, at least 55,000 Head Start teachers nationwide would have to get an associate degree. Most would face that prospect without being able to change their complicated life circumstances (children at home, marginal educational backgrounds, limited access to colleges, cultural environments that did not encourage higher education, full-time jobs at which they made little more than the minimum wage, limited opportunities for other jobs). Traditional college programs offered few options except to students who lived close to a campus. Most DL programs targeted people on the sunny side of the digital divide: highly motivated, middle-class, technologically savvy students who were looking to upgrade their professional careers. By contrast, our design assumed that students would never set foot on campus, would have limited funds, would have neither home computers nor sophisticated computer skills, would be long out of high school with ages in the mid-30s, would have decent reading skills but marginal writing skills, and would be overwhelmed by a delivery format that depended entirely on asynchronous, text-based communications. All of those assumptions later proved correct and held significant implications for the delivery format. (For a full discussion of the students and the complications of serving a population across the digital divide, see Holstrom & Bryan, 2003.)

Planning of the program initially relied heavily on several faculty in early childhood education; a video production company, RISE Learning Solutions; and administrators like me who had backgrounds in education, business, marketing, and educational outreach. We all met through the summer of 1999 and developed curricular and business plans. In addition to courses in early childhood education, the degree program of 27 courses would include standard core courses plus two developmental courses, one each in writing and math.

As is often the case with new initiatives—and especially with DL—the business plan looked infeasible at first. Transplanting the traditional, on-campus, live model of instruction to the DL format would prove too expensive, both in labor and communication costs. We knew that we were entering the DL market—with our first course offering scheduled for spring 2000—later than many leaders in the field (such as the University of Maryland's University College and the University of Phoenix), yet we also knew that DL had not yet reached maturity and much remained unknown about the softness of the market. Bold ventures from some universities looked interesting and promising. Other ventures, both public and private, nonprofit and for-profit, looked as dangerous as the then-still-luminous dotcom bubble, and many such ventures suffered fates similar to the dotcoms, either failing outright or being put on long-term life support. Western Governor's University, California Virtual University, Arizona Learning Systems, NYU online, and Harcourt Higher Education were among those for whom the bubble seemed to burst (Clayton, 2001; Horowitz, 2000/2001). As the dean of the college developing the program—a program that would cost more than $2 million before it generated any revenue—I knew that the life of the program would rely on approaching its delivery in some other way.

To make the plan work, we devised what seemed to us to be an educationally responsible, financially feasible model that relied on professionally producing and video recording major portions of each course. (The typical undergraduate course at UC has 30 classroom contact hours per quarter.) All but the writing courses would have 20 hours of video; the writing courses would have from 10 to 15 hours recorded. Using this model, each course would repeat major elements each term during an estimated shelf life of 3 years. Meanwhile the remainder of each course would be conducted live each term in an online format using Blackboard; the faculty who would conduct the live course segments would not necessarily be the same as those who produced the corresponding video. The video production would enjoy far higher production values than the typical telecourse, using three or four cameras on a real sound stage, professional producers, directors, technicians, and even a make-up artist. The production crews were there to help plan and execute the faculty's marriage of technology and pedagogy. We would even hire "studio students" for the videotaping, providing the faculty with a simulation of a real classroom. This was another concession to the financial exigencies of the project. Taping the 20 hours of video for two entire courses would occur mornings and afternoons over 2-week periods to efficiently use the very expensive facilities and crew.

From the beginning, I knew that faculty compensation would be an important piece of making the enterprise work. Without fair compensation and acknowledgment of traditional faculty rights to intellectual property,

And Now, a Word From Our Sponsor

nothing could move forward. Even so, financial feasibility meant costs had to be controlled as did ownership of the courses. We could not permit a faculty member simply to withdraw a course on which the degree depended and for which the university had invested $75,000. To make all this work, we planned to pay faculty for both the development of courses for the video format and for "performing" in the video productions. Significantly, we also offered royalties to those faculty for as long as their videos were used, even if the faculty moved to other universities, in exchange for their explicit agreement that the videos and course materials they produced were legally "works-for-hire" and were owned by the university. The provision of course materials beyond the video (syllabi, online activities, assignments, exams, etc.) by the faculty who developed the video was conceived as an important element in maintaining continuity in this unconventional division of labor. (For a full discussion of the intellectual property issues in this case, see Bryan, 2003.)

Faculty who conducted the online portions of courses each quarter (the online faculty) would also be paid or would receive the online assignments as part of their normal teaching loads. For most courses, the online faculty members' compensation would be about 70% of the normal compensation for a course because the prerecorded video, constituting about two thirds of the course contact hours, would not be the responsibility of the online faculty. They would be expected to adhere to the course materials provided by the faculty course developers. They would have responsibility for all student contact pertinent to the course, for grading exams and assignments, for ensuring the engagement of the students, for referring students to support services (advising, tutoring), and for assigning final grades each term. In bureaucratic terms, they would be the "instructors of record."

Because writing instruction tends to be labor-intensive and involve little lecture and much one-to-one and small-group instruction, the writing courses would involve less recorded video and more online interaction. We also planned appropriate shifts in faculty compensation to recognize this different sharing of the total labor.

As an administrator, I was proud of what we had planned: We had found a means of re-conceiving courses to achieve more efficient use of resources while not eliminating vital interaction between individual faculty and individual students. (Indeed the student population we envisioned would need the focused attention of faculty even more than many on-campus students.) We would be serving a population for whom the program would not merely be a convenience, but rather would mean the difference between job security and possible unemployment. We had a plan for periodically changing the program to reflect ongoing assessment of learning outcomes. We found a compensation formula that recognized the delicate balance between those who create enduring intellectual property and those who must adapt that property to the changing circumstances of student learning. We found a formula for avoiding exploitation of those who create intellectual property without ever permitting any of those individuals to hold the program or institution hostage. We knew that our faculty and production company would create programs to which we and UC would gladly claim ownership. We felt confident that the program would not become the financial boondoggle that so many other DL programs had become. We knew students could succeed using this approach.

WE DO NOT LECTURE

Unfortunately, some of that pride proved premature. When we drew more faculty—especially faculty from the liberal arts—into the process, we suddenly faced skepticism about the unconventional division of labor. Among the most skeptical were a few English faculty who initially saw no possibility of creating content that could be recorded and substituted for major portions of courses in succeeding terms. One kept telling me, "We don't lecture," as if I, also a teacher of writing, somehow did not get it. "Our classes aren't like those in history or sociology or philosophy. Our classes are all about process." They described the interactivity of their classes, the orchestration of in-class discussion, the conferences they held with individual students—all the familiar protocols of English, and especially of composition, classes. Therein lay a revelation not just about some unfortunate perceptions of the limited options for teaching history, sociology, and philosophy, but about the limited options that many English teachers conceive for their own pedagogy. The reaction reinforced my perception that many faculty accept and emulate the models they have witnessed, often not departing far from those models unless pressed to set aside their assumptions about pedagogy, to imagine new approaches. In the case of our DL program— both the video productions and the online technology—we had at our disposal some unusually sophisticated technological opportunities and support staff who were waiting and eager to help the faculty's imagination come alive, yet the initial reaction of some faculty suggested they had no desire to exert their imaginations. Fortunately, the story does not end there.

In defense of this initial reaction of faculty, let me also explain some elements of the political context. At that time, University College was the

And Now, a Word From Our Sponsor 57

low-status unit on the main campus with heavier teaching loads and lower pay than the research units and with an open-admissions student body. Perennial budget cuts had cost numerous full-time faculty positions and increasing dependence on adjunct faculty. Over the decade preceding my arrival in the college from A&S, the college had seen a succession of four deans, two of whom were forced to resign by the central administration. A faculty strike for the first week of spring term in 1993 had followed a vote of no-confidence in the university president. Twice since then, faculty contract negotiations have led to strike authorizations before reaching agreement. Faculty distrust of administrators could not have been much more intense—at least not at this university, where the initial response of faculty to any administrative directive or request tends to be autonomic: *You can't make us do that; it isn't in the contract.*

A few faculty beyond those in English joined the debate, citing the most common objections to DL—that it just is not as good as the on-campus experience, although those sounding that argument had no supporting evidence. They talked about the learning that goes on outside the classroom, on campus sidewalks, and in their offices. Like the instructor to whom I was pitching Aspects a dozen years ago, they talked about body language, eye contact, and associating names and faces.

Ultimately, however, they all came around, even the English faculty. My administrative ego whispers in my head that my leadership skills brought them around. Countering that view are the fainter whispers of my cynical side, which says that the money was just too enticing for them. Yet every other voice in my head argues that they did it for the students—without giving up any of their values or beliefs. We discussed the options facing Head Start teachers given the congressional mandate and constraints on their lives. They were not going to quit their jobs and move to Cincinnati to enroll. Few lived sufficiently close to public, low-cost, open-admissions colleges with programs in early childhood education. No other credible DL program in the field existed. Those many thousands of students needed this program.

The English faculty in particular stepped back from the assumptions that had initially caused them to question the pedagogical feasibility of teaching their courses through DL. Indeed because the lecture format could be fairly easily adapted to video performance, the non-English liberal arts faculty tended to take that easier route, adding Power Point and some other bells and whistles, but not fundamentally exploiting the technology. The English faculty examined the medium, considered the audience's relationship to the medium, and exploited the medium in various and ingenious ways. Some used a talk-show format, emulating a mass-media approach that would look familiar and feel comfortable to the student population. Another instructor went to the opposite extreme, creating a kind of intimate basic-writing tutorial with two students (see Chap. 4, in this volume). Feedback from students enrolled in the courses suggests they all work.

STOP ME BEFORE I KILL MYSELF (TEACHING)

Most of the program's course sections are not taught by the same faculty who recorded the video materials developed for those courses. Whereas the faculty charged with developing the videos and other course materials finally arrived at pedagogical solutions with which they were generally satisfied, the online faculty with ongoing responsibility for the offering of those courses were also initially dissatisfied. Despite our assignment of a full-time DL specialist to work with faculty on these and related academic issues, the online faculty have not, for the most part, adapted to the division of labor inherent in the program design. Our first inkling that something was not working as intended came in the form of complaints about compensation. The pay for the online portions of the courses, we heard, was far too little. Teaching the courses online, the online faculty said, was more work than teaching them on campus. When we investigated the reasons, we found multiple causes. First, the faculty did what most faculty new to DL do: too much. They checked their e-mail hourly, wrote exhaustive replies to each student inquiry, and imposed no limits on themselves for virtual office hours. Just as the novice instructor of composition typically marks student papers as if copyediting, so these faculty looked at communication with students as if they held sole responsibility for every student's success and that success depended on—to return to the issue broached before, and years earlier—*controlling* all communication with and among students. For example, using Blackboard discussion groups, some faculty felt they had to respond to every student posting, correct student misstatements, and even reinterpret for everyone a clumsily expressed idea from a student. We regularly dealt with such issues and helped faculty understand both the value of students hashing through their mistakes on their own and with their peers and the need for limiting students' access to and expectations of their instructors.

That was not enough. Most of the online faculty were still feeling overwhelmed. Further inquiry found that most of the online faculty were treating the video—by design, the centerpiece dominating all of the nonwriting

And Now, a Word From Our Sponsor 59

courses—as if it were ancillary material, like articles on reserve at the library. The faculty had turned the pedagogical design on its head, putting the online portions of the course at the center, which naturally put themselves at the center—in control. Conscientious professionals that they were, they were killing themselves with the work. They were still unhappy about the pay in relation to the work. At that point, we enjoyed few options. We could heavy-handedly clean out the nonconformist faculty to be replaced with more compliant faculty, could pay more while reducing their teaching loads, could work more with the faculty to influence their understanding of their more limited roles, or could shrug our shoulders and hope that their unhappiness did not spill its effects into the virtual classroom. In the end, we chose a combination of these options. While increasing the rate of pay for online instruction, we worked with the faculty to reshape their understanding of their more limited roles. Although their understanding of the pedagogical design's intentions grew, I doubt many scaled back their involvement to the levels originally envisioned. Most still work harder than they should, but they know that and their pay has improved. For now, anyway, the problem has gone away.

Today, the program launched in spring 2000 with eight students is growing at an average rate of 13% per *quarter*. It enrolls students from 38 states and four countries. Its first graduates—some of whom did travel to Cincinnati for commencement—received their degrees in spring 2003. In FY04, its net revenues began repaying the start-up capital. More important, student retention and academic success in the program are, on average, higher than in the same program offered on campus.

CONCLUSION

Several years ago, I wrote a long article on the distortion of data that the creators of charts and graphs introduce, wittingly or not, by adding decorative elements (such as 3D effects). Such practices have become so common that the distortions are now built into much of the software used to automatically generate charts and graphs, especially spreadsheet programs. Introducing data distortion has become as easy as picking a chart style from a menu of style options—and usually neither the author nor the reader is aware of the distortion. That is one of the simplest illustrations of technology's subtle role in reshaping communication and learning. (Of course we should be careful not to anthropomorphize technology; it was some software engineer, not the software, that defined Excel's range of styles.)

Technology will similarly try to shape and channel instructors' roles, whether in the on-campus computer classroom or across the Internet via DL. Technology will push faculty toward the roles envisioned by the creators of the technology. Yet technology does not trump all, not even in DL. Faculty push back, sometimes asserting the immutability of their long-established pedagogical approaches, sometimes letting the resistance channel them into new ways of considering their pedagogy. In that regard, technology and administrators are a lot alike. Whether faculty and administrators will productively exploit DL technology depends on their imagination, their funds, their ongoing adaptability, and their will to collaborate and succeed for the students' benefit.

REFERENCES

Bryan, John G. (2003). Your, theirs, mine: Just who owns those distance courses? In S. Reisman (Ed.), *Electronic learning communities: Current issues and best practices.* Boston: U.S. Distance Learning Association.

Clayton, Mark. (2001). A life raft year for higher education [Electronic version]. *Christian Science Monitor.* December 26, 2001. Retrieved July 17, 2003, from http://www.csmonitor.com/2001/1226/p20s1-lehl.html.

Holstrom, Lisa, and John G. Bryan. (2003). A different practice: Spanning the digital divide through distance learning. In S. Reisman (Ed.), *Electronic learning communities: Current issues and best practices.* Boston: U.S. Distance Learning Association.

Horowitz, Ellis. (2000/2001). Charting the future of distance-education [Electronic version]. *Faculty Forum: The Newsletter of the USC Academic Senate.* Retrieved July 17, 2003, from http://www.usc.edu/academe/acsen/resources/newsletter/0001v2n34 /0001vol2num34article02.shtml.

Sands, Peter. (1997). *Writing software comparisons.* Retrieved July 19, 2003, from http://english.ttu.edu/kairos/2.2/reviews/sands/comparison.html.

II PROCESSES

A Language All Its Own:
Writing in the Distance-Learning Classroom

Ellen H. Hendrix

Trying to Connect:
A Distance-Learning Basic Writing Course for Nontraditional Students

Stuart Blersch and Carolyn Stoll

Anyone? Anyone? Anyone? Leading Discussions in Cyberspace:
E-Journals and Interactivity in Asynchronous Environments

Debbie Danowski

3

A LANGUAGE ALL ITS OWN

WRITING IN THE
DISTANCE-LEARNING CLASSROOM

Ellen H. Hendrix

"How would it look if [English teachers] assumed . . . that people write
. . . in order to be accepted, to join, to be regarded as another member
of the culture or community that constitutes the writer's audience?"
Doing so, [. . .], would change "pedagogical attitudes and classroom
practices."

—Bruffee, 1997 (p. 411)

About 12 years ago, the staunchly Protestant citizens of Georgia found
themselves faced with a dilemma: continue losing lottery dollars to Florida
or create a lottery of their own. Although many never believed a lottery ref-
erendum would pass a statewide vote, Zell Miller, then governor of Georgia
and subsequently U.S. senator, made an offer that many Georgians found
hard to refuse: Every dollar generated by the lottery would go toward the
education of Georgia's citizens, including the creation of the HOPE scholarship, which would guarantee every qualified graduate of a Georgia high
school a postsecondary education. No one ever imagined how much

money the lottery would generate. After building up the pool to support Georgia's HOPE scholars, the state legislators began to look for other ways to spend the money to "improve education."

Many legislators equated improvements in education to increased use of technology, and consequently distance-learning classes were one improvement funded by lottery dollars. Unfortunately, some administrators were hard pressed to find faculty willing (much less qualified) to teach in the distance-learning classroom. The Department of Writing and Linguistics (at that time part of the English Department) of Georgia Southern University was among the first asked to offer distance-learning first-year composition classes to high school seniors who qualified for early admission to GSU, but did not live close enough to campus to attend classes in the traditional sense. In the Georgia Southern model of distance-education, up to 10 students would attend class on campus in a technologically enhanced classroom. In addition, up to 10 students would attend through a technologically enhanced remote-site classroom. Using GSAMs, Georgia's two-way audio and video interactive environment, distance-learning students would be able to see each other on TV monitors and talk to each other simply by cueing their microphones.

Almost immediately, the addition of such technology to the composition classroom affected the way students talked to each other and to their professors. Experience has shown that students grow as writers, people who are able to write for a specific purpose or achieve a certain goal, through collaboration, but interaction with other writers has to be supportive and consistent. As Gere (1987) explained, "Collaboration that effectively reduces alienation appears in groups where no one individual constantly dominates, where all members are supported, and where individual contributions are developed upon by other members" (pp. 68–69). Active participation among all members of the group is essential for developing learners engaged in the writing process, for "[p]articipants in collaborative groups learn when they challenge one another with questions, when they use the evidence and information available to them, when they develop relationships among issues [. . .] when they assume that knowledge is something they can help create rather than something to be received whole from someone else" (Gere, 1987, p. 69). Although finding successful ways to encourage and reward collaboration in traditional classrooms is not usually difficult, simulating the same activities in the distance environment proved much more challenging.

Teaching via distance learning means having to work hard, as Selfe (2000) suggested, to "[think] about what we [as teachers] are doing" and

A Language All Its Own   65

"to understand and make sense of, *to pay attention to*, how technology is inextricably linked to literacy" (p. 193). Distance-learning composition teachers, therein, need "to understand and make sense of" the impact technology has on their classes, their students, and their students' styles of learning. Composition teachers cannot simply assume that a distance-learning environment is one where students can share and grow as collaborators, thinkers, and writers. In fact sharing and responding to writing in the GSAMs distance-learning environment at GSU proved a bit awkward. Students would fax drafts and written responses to each other when collaborating between sites; then they would respond to each others' writing using the system's interactive communication tools. There was a moment's delay between the time the students pressed their microphones and the time the sound was relayed to the other site—a delay that became less noticeable as the term continued. Nevertheless, students' oral responses were broadcast over room-wide speakers at the alternate site, so even with modifications technology affected the students' collaborative activities. Although all students at GSU are asked to complete an end-of-term course evaluation, distance-learning composition teachers wanted more specific feedback from their students to gauge the impact of technology on the students—an issue not addressed in the university's standard evaluation form. Therefore, at the end of the semester, distance-learning composition teachers asked students to reflect on the distance-learning environment and how it had impacted their growth as writers. To better ensure that such reflections were unbiased, they were administered in cooperation with the standard evaluation, collected by facilitators, and not released to the instructors until after the semester had ended and final grades had been assigned. Students had the option of composing their reflections anonymously, but no one exercised this option.

After one semester of freshman composition in the distance-learning environment, the responses of both the on- and off-campus students were alarming, yet honest. Robbie, an on-campus student, responded, "I relate distance learning to a class with a brick wall separating some students in the class from others. The separate sides never group up, barely talk, and have very little interaction." Although the students had collaborated in theory, the students obviously felt otherwise. Joshua, an off-campus student, wrote, "I have to admit that talking to a television screen was different than talking to a teacher. After a while, though, I got to know the television screen." Responses as such indicated that students had not felt part of a learning group, at least not outside of their own site. If the teacher were perceived as no more than a TV screen, then how could he or she have motivated students to be active participants in the writing classroom? In other words, effective learning could not possibly have taken place. Such student comments forced the distance-learning teachers to seriously reflect on the possibility of teaching freshman composition successfully in the distance-learning environment.

LOOKING FOR ANSWERS

Such seemingly negative comments, however, did not lead to the conclusion that technology cannot be used effectively. Instead the responses have led to a search for new ways to improve interaction among students, although students may be separated physically. As Selfe (2000) suggested, *"Deciding whether or not to use technology in our classes is simply not the point—we have to pay attention to technology"* (p. 194; italics original). Thus, distance-learning teachers have to pay more attention to how technology impacts student–student and student–teacher discourse and begin to consider activities that will work in the distance-learning environment.

With the onset of these technological complications, distance-learning theory has remained similar in many ways to composition theory. In *Building Learning Communities in Cyberspace*, Palloff and Pratt (1999) admitted that teaching and learning change when they are taken out of the traditional classroom setting; however, they added that in the distance-learning environment, "there is a great deal of room for students to explore the content collaboratively or to pursue their own, related interests" (p. 5). However, Anson (2000) warned that, "While these technologies offer an endless array of new and exciting possibilities for the improvement of education, they also frequently clash with some of our basic beliefs about the nature of classroom instruction, in all its communal richness" (p. 170). Anson added that "sustaining our pedagogical advances in the teaching of writing [. . .] will be to take control of these technologies, using them in effective ways and not [. . .] substituting them for those contexts and methods that we hold essential for learning to write" (p. 169). In short, the composition teacher's job is to find pedagogically effective ways to use technology.

Anson (2000) also suggested that some of the concerns with technology stem from early uses of multimedia where students were presented information via technology rather than taught to use technology: "In all their activity as creators of their own knowledge, students remained relatively passive [. . .] receiving deposits of knowledge from automatic teller machines that

A Language All Its Own   67

supplemented the more direct, human method" (p. 172). Freire (1972), a well-known and respected learning theorist, argued that students should be more than mere "receptacles for received knowledge." Gardner (1993), a psychologist who has identified seven distinct types of intelligence, added that intelligence goes well beyond knowledge and includes the potential to find or create solutions for problems and the ability to gather new knowledge. Palloff and Pratt (1999) then built on Freire's and Gardner's theories when they asserted that "many students are concrete-active learners, [. . .] they learn best from concrete experiences that engage their senses. Their best learning experiences begin with practice [. . .]" (p. 5). Anson (2000) added that "the new capabilities emerging from multimedia technology offer many alternatives for teaching and learning, and for assigning and responding to writing" (p. 173). He went on to show how technology has "enhanced students' experiences," including increasing "participation among marginalized groups" and argued that "electronic innovations [. . .] integrated into the existing curriculum in principled ways [. . .] do not erode the foundations on which the teacher-experimenters already base their instructional principles" (p. 176). Nevertheless, Anson cautioned, although technology may offer increased social communication, it also contributes to a physical isolation that leads to different types of interaction among members of the class.

Because "the teaching of writing [. . .] is founded on the assumption that students learn well by reading and writing with each other, responding to each other's drafts, negotiating revisions, discussing ideas, sharing perspectives, and finding some level of trust as collaborators in their mutual development" (Anson, 2000, p. 177), many believe that distance-education is contrary to the goals of teaching writing because students cannot learn to write in isolation and "computers [are] poor substitutes for old-fashioned human interaction" (p. 179). Anson felt that our roles as educators "—as those who create opportunities and contexts for students to write and who provide expert, principled response to that writing—must change in the present communications and information revolution" (p. 184). Hence, instead of being threatened by technology or allowing technology to "take over," teachers need to make thoughtful decisions about how to put technology to good use in terms of what they know "about good teaching and sound ways of working" (p. 184) and how technology can provide access to strategies to meet multiple learning styles or accommodate Gardner's types of intelligence.

Composition teachers also have to acknowledge Gere's (1987) warning: "Teaching does, of course, imply guiding and shaping students' activities, but it does not require limiting students' access to language" as the distance-learning environment obviously does (p. 94). Therefore, teachers have to find ways to provide concrete experiences for all students and engage their senses in such ways that everyone in the classroom becomes more than just a TV personality. Once such an environment is created, students can, as Bruffee (1997) suggested, engage "in conversation among themselves at [. . .] many points in the writing and reading process [. . . because] the way they talk with each other determines the way they think and the way they will write" (p. 642). Before students can begin to see themselves as writers, teachers have to find ways for students to converse, talk about both their reading and their writing, and become members of a learning/writing group even though all members of the group may not be in the same physical environment. Because student comments indicated that "talking" between sites did not seem to work in the GSAMs environment, other means of communicating between sites needed to be explored. The most logical alternative to talking was writing, but could writing be an effective substitute when students are much more comfortable with talking?

According to Gere (1987), "Writing can succeed only when it adheres to the conventions of 'normal discourse' for a given community, and writers can learn this discourse through using it in the kinds of conversations that occur in collaborative learning" (p. 73). Following Gere's (1987) logic, given the right tools, student writing could take the place of "normal discourse"; the problem facing GSU's distance-learning writing instructors lay in finding the right tools.

In "The Shared Discourse of the Networked Computer Classroom," Irvin (2000) examined the way discourse changes in a technologically advanced classroom. Although the concept of "talk" changes when technology is used, learning can still occur. Irvin (2000) explained his own discovery as follows:

> I realized that shared discourse in the networked computer classroom has three levels [. . .]. These levels form a continuum of interactivity from students sending messages "AT" each other, to students sending messages "TO" each other, to students sending messages "BETWEEN" each other. (p. 220)

Irvin (2000) argued that the "greatest value of [the 'AT' level of shared discourse] for the student is comparability" (p. 220). Because students gather knowledge through their own actions and at their own pace, this level allows them more ownership of the knowledge they acquire. At this stage,

A Language All Its Own 69

all students have equal voice, and the classroom is clearly student centered because the students are learning from each other.

Meanwhile, in the "TO" level of shared discourse, students develop "a clearer purpose" and begin to write for "a more defined audience" because the "TO" level is "rhetorically more sophisticated" (Irvin, 2000, p. 223). At this stage, students "implement judgments and knowledge they have gained" because messages often "contain peer comments and evaluations" (p. 223). Irvin also claimed that the "TO" level allows students "to be more objective and honest in their discourse" than the traditional classroom setting allows because students are not face-to-face with the person whom they are addressing. He added that the physical "distance, coupled with the power and confidence computers encourage in students, seems to help students write more and better responses" (p. 223).

Finally, in the "BETWEEN" level of shared discourse, students "dialogue back and forth among themselves" (Irvin, 2000, p. 224). "Out of the crucible of discourse," Irvin added, "meaning forms, explodes, takes shape again. [. . .] Students feel a real sense of audience in this environment because the rest of the class is reading and can respond immediately" (p. 224). He claimed that, at this level, "more students get involved in the discussion and each has an equal 'voice' since all messages appear in the same way on the computer screen" and that "students [. . .] engage more with each other rather than direct their discourse toward the teacher, as in the traditional classroom" (p. 225). Real learning takes place at this level because "students make conclusions and evaluations on their own, rather than the teacher making them for the students" (p. 225).

Having students fax responses between sites is one means of conversing through writing. What seemed to be missing from such correspondence in the GSAMs environment, however, was the immediacy that sparked within Irvin's students. GSU's distance-learning students needed an environment where writing could be exchanged as freely as conversation is exchanged in the traditional classroom. Limited access to computer technology at distance-learning sites made synchronous online communication impossible, yet asynchronous communication offered possibilities.

WHY TECHNOLOGY WORKS

Although online communications media offer many alternatives for communicating (chats, listservs, MOOs, etc.), Georgia Southern invested in

WebCT, an integrated software program designed to enhance online course work. WebCT offered possibilities for simulating a free exchange of ideas by enabling students to use various forms of communications media without having to learn or use different computer programs. Distance-learning students needed only basic Internet access, which was readily available in Georgia through local schools and libraries. Online communications activities, particularly chatting and posting questions and responses about drafts to a bulletin board, significantly improved students' ability and willingness to interact. Such activities assigned through WebCT Tools enabled students a "great deal of room to explore the content collaboratively" (Palloff & Pratt, 1999, p. 5) and to progress from "normal discourse" as members of a class to writers/composers, those engaged in creating with language. To that end, "writing constitute[d] the task of collaboration, the process of working together [that] enables writers to use language as a means of becoming competent in the discourse of [their] community" (Gere, 1987, p. 75). As writing became the "normal discourse" for the online community, students quickly became more competent in its use. Although online activities greatly improved the collaboration between students and increased the opportunities for collaborating in distance-learning classes, understanding why is essential.

Language acquisition and use theory offers a possible explanation. Focusing on the work of Edward Sapir, Britton (1997) broke the act of communication into three categories moving from informal to formal: transactional, expressive, and poetic. He defined *transactional* as the form of discourse used most often in carrying out day-to-day activities. *Expressive*, in contrast, is more formal and informative in that it allows the speaker/writer to express his or her views of the world. The *poetic*, meanwhile, allows a speaker/writer to make something with language—to create a world rather than express views of the world (Britton, 1997, pp. 136–137). Online communications media offer tools that facilitate all three categories of communication: A chatroom meets the transactional needs of students, in that they become "participants in events" (Britton, 1997, p. 136). The bulletin board allows students to be "expressive," to assume "an interest in the writer as well as in what he has to say about the world" (p. 136). Likewise, the bulletin board allows all students to be writers in whom other students take interest. Finally, a student-created Web page becomes a forum for poetic discourse, allowing students to "[make] something with language rather than [do] something with it" (pp. 136–137).

Many have come to share Irvin's (2000) excitement for the communication that takes place in the online environment and support his claim that, "What becomes exciting is when the shared discourse, and thus the social knowledge of the group, gets extended. This extension occurs as a repeated sequence of *invention, reflection,* and *reinvention*" (p. 226; italics original). In fact this extension of shared discourse indicates a connection between language acquisition and development in young children and the increased use of writing as language in the technologically advanced classroom. As Irvin (2000) suggested, "[U]nderstanding the characteristics of the 'talk' in the networked computer classroom" (p. 228) can help students become more effective writers and communicators.

In *The Language Instinct,* Pinker (1994) argued,

> Language is a distinct piece of the biological makeup of our brains. Language is a complex, specialized skill, which develops in the child spontaneously, without conscious effort or formal instruction, is deployed without awareness of its underlying logic, is qualitatively the same in every individual and is distinct from more general abilities to process information or behave intelligently. (p. 4)

In *How the Mind Works,* Pinker (1997) added that mankind's instinct for language evolved as language became valuable: "[L]anguage is a means of exchanging knowledge. It manipulates the benefit of knowledge, which cannot only be used but exchanged for other resources" (p. 130). Therefore, the instinct for language, according to Pinker (1997), evolved "because the value of having better information multiplies when a group is involved; information becomes a commodity that can be given away and kept at the same time" (p. 192).

Perhaps Pinker's theory offers a seed to understanding how students in technologically enhanced classes develop writing skills. When all meaningful communication between students takes place through writing—even transactional discourse—students come to see themselves as writers because writing is their primary means of communicating. Writing then, like talking, becomes socially constructed, "the center of knowledge because it constitutes the means by which ideas [are] developed and explored" (Gere, 1987, p. 73). It becomes a commodity—a thing of value. Those who write successfully, who create an effective product, realize Gardner's (1993) claim that intelligence is not a uniform cognitive capacity as they develop as intelligent, productive members of the group. Student writers, like children acquiring language, take advantage of opportunities to experiment with and develop their skill. The less formal means of communication (transactional and expressive) allow writers to try out their ideas and explore new ways of communicating.

Through chatroom and bulletin board interaction in GSU's distance-learning writing classroom, students not only exchanged ideas, but also experimented with new ways of writing. The change in students' reactions to the class after integrating computerized communications media suggests that when students use writing as their primary means of communication, their use of writing is enhanced, and they learn to write more effectively in both formal and informal settings. More important, they begin to value writing as a means of communicating. According to Rose (1997), "Writing seems central to the shaping and directing of certain modes of cognition, is integrally involved in learning, is a means of defining self and defining reality, is a means of representing and contextualizing information [. . .]" (p. 533). Rose implied that students' thinking and knowledge of the world around them is likewise enriched. Experience with using online communications media in the distance-learning composition classroom certainly supports Rose's assertion.

In WebCT-enhanced classes, the greatest amount of writing and sharing takes place on the bulletin board. The process begins with the teacher posting prompts related to reading assignments. Students then respond to those prompts and also read what other students have written. The conversation truly begins when students begin to respond to each other's responses. In this way, students use the bulletin board as a means to discover and share ideas, and they come to consider it a place where they can share without fear of being judged as writers or thinkers. On the bulletin board, what students have to say is important; how they say it is not. The bulletin board also enables students to "talk" to each other, much as students talk to each other in traditional classroom discussions or small groups. For example, in one assignment, students used the bulletin board to interview each other about the impact of distance learning on student interaction. By asking each other questions and responding to each other's questions, students were better able to determine how their classmates felt about using technology in the writing classroom and to share ideas. More significantly, the bulletin board technique for peer response proved useful in that it allowed students time to think about what their classmates posted and to reflect before responding—a luxury that in-class peer response often does not allow. However, it also means that discourse exchange may be delayed a day or two—a delay that disconcerts many students who seek more immediate feedback.

Although the bulletin board enables the students to "group up" and "have interaction" that the GSAMs classroom alone obstructs, students often want more one-on-one interaction, and they want it more immediately (and sometimes more privately) than the bulletin board allows.

Therefore, students are encouraged to schedule regular individual and small-group chatroom visits with the teacher and with each other. Chatting, as such, often serves to allay fears more than it serves to develop ideas. The students simply want to know that someone who cares is willing to listen to them. Chatting also allows students to "talk" to each other in an informal manner, just as students "talk" to each other before a traditional class begins. For example, when two or more students join the teacher for a writing conference in a chatroom, students fax drafts of essays in progress and plan to discuss those drafts in the conference. However, these sessions often begin with students asking questions about each other, where they are located, what their interests are, and so on. After a few personal exchanges, students begin to feel more comfortable responding to drafts of essays because the personal exchanges help them respond to a person rather than simply a name on a draft. In this sense, the chatroom allows for immediacy and spontaneity—a dialogue much closer to face-to-face communication and Irvin's "AT" level of shared discourse. Likewise, chatroom interaction transfers into the GSAMs classroom as students become less paralyzed by the microphones and TV monitors once they have a sense of "knowing" the face on the screen. Thus, after chatroom visits with small groups of students, teachers are more likely to come into the GSAMS classroom and find students willingly and freely talking between sites despite having to use microphones to do so.

To truly view themselves as writers, students have to write for a larger audience, not just for the teacher. The bulletin board and chatroom require students to write transactionally and expressively, whereas effective, poetic discourse is the ultimate goal of GSU's first-year composition sequence. As Britton (1997) explained, "[Distinction] between transactional and poetic discourse is by reference to the way a reader grasps the message. If what a writer does when he draws from all he knows and selectively sets down what he wants to communicate is described as 'decontextualization,' then the complementary process on the part of the reader is to 'contextualize,' interpreting the writer's meaning by building it into his existing knowledge and experience" (p. 140). In other words, before students will see themselves as writers, they have to know that their message has been meaningfully received and interpreted by readers. Formal student writing, therefore, needs to be shared among members of the class if students are truly to develop confidence in themselves as writers, people who are able to realize a purpose or achieve a goal through their writing. Accordingly, online communications media offer opportunities for students to "publish" their essays for all members of the writing community to share and enjoy. In WebCT, individual student pages or a teacher-created publications page becomes the place for publishing. In addition to expanding the writers' audience, being published gives students a feeling of accomplishment and satisfaction. Britton (1997) concluded that the world students create through their writing "is a world they control and [. . .] a source of deep satisfaction" (p. 147). If students write essays "for the teacher" and have their writing evaluated as such, they will never come to see themselves as writers because they may never sense the "deep satisfaction" to which Britton alluded. When students' writing is "published" for other students in the class to read and respond to, then they know that their message has been received and interpreted by other members of the community. Likewise, the students' knowledge is often confirmed by responses other members of the class post to the bulletin board in response to the published essays. The essays also help develop a sense of connectedness because each of the published essays grows from other online interaction, and students other than the writer have had input in their development.

ONLINE WRITERS RESPOND

Since adding WebCT to the distance-learning classes at Georgia Southern, students have supplied the answer to Bruffee's (1997) question: "How would it look if we assumed [. . .] that people write in order to be accepted, to join, to be regarded as another member of the culture or community that constitutes the writer's audience?" (p. 411). When asked how the use of technology has affected their participation in class and growth as writers, the students have responded more positively on reflections offered as part of their end-of-semester course evaluation:

> *Loraine*   When [I am] on the computer, [I am] interested in that person's words and what [he/she is] saying, which connects me with that person on a personal level.

> *Laura*   I feel I get much more honest and constructive results when I post on WebCT. Evaluating face-to-face can be somewhat awkward. I think that the computer created a comfort zone that is much easier to work in, thus resulting in my becoming a more productive writer.

Ali	I feel that it is easier to write an essay using WebCT because I get to write at my own pace and I still get feedback from my classmates and my teacher.
Tracy	I think that [technology] does improve my writing because it takes away any excuses [I] may have about getting feedback or not having the opportunity to participate.
Mitchell	I find that using WebCT not only includes my creativity, but I can also incorporate the thoughts of others, improving my paper as well.

Distance-learning classes have continued at Georgia Southern University, and most students enrolled in these classes indicate that their freshman writing experience has been a positive one. In fact one student published an essay in WebCT during the semester and used her distance-learning experience to draw the following conclusion:

> Just as technology revolutionalized communication with the telephone in the 1800's, it has and will continue to revolutionalize written communications now and into the future. By embracing such advancements, these students are not only reaping the educational benefits that it offers, they are also preparing themselves for a world that is becoming increasingly progressive. Those who are equipped with the right tools and experience will be the ones that succeed as technology emerges into every aspect of our advanced society. (L. Collins, personal communication, November 22, 1999)

Students enroll fully realizing that they will be using technology, so the search for pedagogically effective ways of using technology to enhance teaching and learning continues.

CONCLUSION

For students who are ready to embark on the journey toward learning to write, of becoming writers, and of viewing themselves as writers, the distance-learning class can help them in ways that the traditional classroom cannot because, as a member of the distance-learning class, they will have to write "in order to be accepted, to join, to be regarded as [a] member" of a writing community (Bruffee, 1997, p. 411). In addition, the students will reap the additional benefit of learning technology. As Horner (2000) suggested, "Modern technology is not revolutionizing language; it is merely continuing the revolution begun many centuries ago by writing" (p. 173). Horner acknowledged that the technology is developing rapidly, and composition teachers must expand their thinking to keep up with its development. They must adapt their pedagogy "to fit around the expanding technology" (p. 175).

If online interaction allows group members to use writing in various ways, to understand writing as language used for a purpose, then the class members will begin to value writing in the same way that they value speech. They will also develop confidence in themselves as writers, and opportunities for meaningful online communication will enable them to use written language just as they use spoken language as a means to express themselves and what they know. Although not all writers will develop at the same pace or to the same level, they will all have the opportunity for using language—more specifically, writing—to create meaningful discourse.

REFERENCES

Anson, Chris M. (2000). Distant voices: Teaching and writing in a culture of technology. In *Trends and issues in postsecondary English studies* (pp. 167-189). Urbana, IL: NCTE.

Britton, James. (1997). Spectator role and the beginnings of writing. In V. Villanueva (Ed.), *Cross-talk in composition theory* (pp. 129-151). Urbana, IL: NCTE.

Bruffee, Kenneth A. (1997). Collaborative learning and the conversation of mankind. In V. Villanueva (Ed.), *Cross-talk in composition theory* (pp. 393-414). Urbana, IL: NCTE.

Freire, Paulo. (1972). *The pedagogy of the oppressed.* Hammondsworth: Penguin.

Gardner, Howard. (1993). *Multiple intelligences: The theory in practice.* New York: Basic Books.

Gere, Anne Ruggles. (1987). *Writing groups: History, theory, and implications.* Carbondale: Southern Illinois University Press.

Horner, Winifred Bryan. (2000). Reinventing memory and delivery. In M.D. Goggin (Ed.), *Inventing a discipline: Rhetoric scholarship in honor of Richard E. Young* (pp. 173-183). Urbana, IL: NCTE.

Irvin, L. Lennie. (2000). The shared discourse of the networked computer classroom. In *Trends and issues in postsecondary English studies* (pp. 219-228). Urbana, IL: NCTE.

Palloff, Rena M., & Pratt, Keith. (1999). *Building learning communities in Cyberspace: Effective strategies for the online classroom*. San Francisco: Jossey-Bass Publishers.

Pinker, Steven. (1994). *The language instinct*. New York: Morrow.

Pinker, Steven. (1997). *How the mind works*. New York: Norton.

Rose, Mike. (1997). The language of exclusion: Writing instruction at the university. In V. Villanueve (Ed.), *Cross-talk in composition theory* (pp. 525-547). Urbana, IL: NCTE.

Selfe, Cynthia. (2000). Technology and literacy: A story of the perils of not paying attention. In *Trends and issues in postsecondary English studies* (pp. 190-218). Urbana, IL: NCTE.

4

TRYING TO CONNECT

A DISTANCE-LEARNING BASIC WRITING COURSE
FOR NONTRADITIONAL STUDENTS

Stuart Blersch
Carolyn Stoll

In 1998, as part of the Head Start Reauthorization Act, Congress set a goal that by the year 2003 at least half of the Heat Start teachers in the United States would have an associate, baccalaureate, or advanced degree in Early Childhood or a related field (U.S. Department of Health and Human Services, 1998). Suddenly, in Head Start centers across the country, thousands of teachers of young children were faced with the prospect of doing something they had perhaps never dreamed of: They were going to earn a college degree.

The abrupt enactment of this new requirement meant that as many as 30,000 Head Start teachers would need associate degrees (Fuller, 2000). Where would all these people find the coursework they needed? Degree programs in Early Childhood Education are relatively rare, and chances were small that all the Head Start teachers would be near enough to a college that offered such a program. It would be impossible for those who did not live near a college to pack their belongings and travel en masse to a college that did offer such a program. These are not 18-year-old high school graduates, but adult men and women with families and established lives.

The answer was not to bring the students to the school, but rather to take the school to the students. Distance learning was not only ideally suited to this unique situation, it was perhaps the only answer to a pressing need. So the University of Cincinnati set about to develop an associate degree program, offered via distance learning, for Head Start teachers: the Early Childhood Learning Community (ECLC). ECLC would be housed in the Early Childhood Education program of UC's University College, a 2-year open-admissions college on the main campus.

Because many University College students, especially nontraditional students, begin their English composition sequence in basic writing, this course was one of the first that had to be in place for this new distance-learning program. We anticipated that our population of distance learners was not going to be some new breed of student that we had never seen before and for which we would need to reinvent the pedagogical wheel. Like the nontraditional on-campus students we have been teaching for decades, they needed help learning how to be students, remediation in academic areas where they were underprepared, and support to help them achieve their goals. These were services we knew how to deliver on campus. The question became, how do we deliver them online?

We needed to adjust to the loss of some critical components. The personal link between on-campus student and teacher was one such loss that had to be addressed. We also had to learn how to work from an area of weakness (the basic writer's lack of writing, reading, and computer skills), instead of an area of strength (the basic writer's oral communication skills) to teach. Finally, we had to find a way to re-create the writing workshop and learning community online .

The two English professors most involved with this DL course (Stuart Blersch, who designed and videotaped it, and Carolyn Stoll, who has done most of the online work with the DL students) have written this chapter to reflect on the experience of designing and delivering a basic writing course via distance learning. Of the many issues that arose in this effort, those involving the personal aspects of the course and the use of technology, both in curriculum design and day-to-day interactions with students, emerged as the most challenging.

STUART: FOOLS RUSHING IN

In January 2000, when my department head asked me to create an online basic writing course for ECLC, I said no. My 25 years in the basic writing

Trying to Connect: A Distance-Learning Basic Writing Course 81

classroom have convinced me that a strong personal working relationship with students is indispensable, particularly with nontraditional students like those who would enroll in ECLC. She agreed, and then clarified her request. Because ECLC students would have only two options—either take a basic writing course via distance learning or take no basic writing course at all—our department *must* create and be prepared to deliver this course by September 2000. With the realistic (I hoped) goal that my course be better than no course at all, I agreed.

My on-campus basic composition classes include a generous amount of personal writing. Students begin by writing personal narratives, which become texts for further reading, exploration, and analysis later in the term. The student narratives are not simply stand-alone assignments, but texts that get braided into the curriculum. This approach starts with the language strengths that students already have and then works from there in the direction of academically respected writing. Students write personal narratives relating to a particular issue, read published narratives also relating to this issue, and then read expository texts that "theorize" the experiences in the narratives (an approach similar to that presented by David Bartholomae & Anthony Petrosky [1986] in *Facts, Artifacts and Counterfacts,* except for the introduction of expository texts, an innovation advocated by Marcia Dickson [1995] in *It's Not Like That Here).*

To adapt this curriculum to distance learning, I wanted to make it as personally meaningful as possible to Head Start teachers. I decided to begin with narratives about a personal experience when someone did something that served as a positive or negative example. While planning, drafting, revising, and editing this chapter, we would read Maya Angelou's (1970) *I Know Why the Caged Bird Sings* (amazing as it seems, hardly anyone in these courses has read it before). Students would post their completed narratives on our course's Web site, and then everyone would read each other's papers. This activity, in addition to encouraging students to see themselves and each other as writers with a real audience, leads to Paper 2, where students pick two incidents, one from a classmate's narrative and one from Angelou's autobiography, and write an expository paper focusing on the most important similarity.

While working on this paper, students would read an expository text by Gail Sheehy (1986), "The Victorious Personality," which explains a number of personality traits that help people overcome personal obstacles. Sheehy illustrates each trait with personal narratives from the lives of a Cambodian refugee, a single teen-age mother, and two Holocaust survivors. For Paper 3, students would choose two characteristics presented by Sheehy, define and explain them, and then use specific incidents from

Caged Bird as evidence to argue whether Maya Angelou exhibits a "Victorious Personality" in *I Know Why the Caged Bird Sings*. When the students complete Paper 3, they would then submit their "e-portfolios" for review and, we hope, move on to English 101.

By using these particular texts and topics, I aimed at making the course's reading and writing assignments personally meaningful for the Head Start teachers. I hoped that the curriculum would ultimately lead them to a deeper appreciation of their roles as Head Start teachers. Specifically, I hoped that Paper 1 would encourage them to relate to Maya Angelou's girlhood experiences first from a child's point of view and then, later, as Head Start teachers (and, in many cases, mothers)—to relate to and appreciate the behavior of the pivotal adults in Angelou's life. Finally, I hoped that Sheehy's article would give Head Start teachers a new lens for looking at Angelou's experiences, their own childhood experiences, and their current roles as influential adults in the lives of Head Start children.

I was satisfied with the personal content of the curriculum, but what about the personal working relationship between a professor and a student? In their *Journal of Basic Writing* article, "'It's the Way that They Talk to You': Increasing Agency in Basic Writers Through a Social Context of Care," Joan Piorkowski and Erika Scheurer (2000) confirmed the importance of this relationship. After studying exit interviews with students in four basic writing classes, the authors concluded that, "students' perception of a context of care in the classroom is a crucial factor in building their confidence as writers and is inextricably linked to their assuming agency and responsibility for their own progress as writers" (p. 75). Similarly, in their paper presented at the 2002 International Reading Association conference, Missy and Chet Laine reported that all of the basic reading and writing students in their study credit the encouragement of their professors as a key element in their academic success.

My next task, then, was to figure out how to make the all-important professor–student relationship possible via distance learning. The format for ECLC courses had already been determined: Each professor was to prepare 20 one-hour lectures that would be videotaped for broadcast via satellite over a 10-week period to students at Head Start centers. I needed to design the course so that someone besides me, the "online professor," would work with the students via the Internet as they do the assignments and go through the process of writing papers. The students would never see their online professor in person.

At the point when I was ready to take my newly planned curriculum into the classroom—to roll up my sleeves, sit down with the students, and get to work—I was led into a TV studio.

Trying to Connect: A Distance-Learning Basic Writing Course 83

As part of my preparation for this course, I visited the studio to watch one of the first ECLC courses being taped. The TV cameras were focused on a professor lecturing in front of Power Point slides while two paid "students" listened and took notes. This was not the way I teach; it was not the engaging, personal model that I wanted.

Searching for a TV model, I thought *Oprah*. Here the medium of TV is particularly good at creating a feeling of intimacy for the viewer. With our budget, I could not invite Maya Angelou and Gail Sheehy to appear on *Stuart's Book Club*, but I could have real students who would participate in my class and create an interactive hands-on writing class. I recruited two bona fide basic writing students to take the class with me in the TV studio. Like many of the Head Start teachers who would be taking the course, both were nontraditional female students.

Each session was unrehearsed; the three of us talked extemporaneously as the tapes rolled. I had a laptop computer linked to the TV monitor, and the students brought in their journals and drafts on floppy disks so we could brainstorm, write, revise, and edit together. We modeled all the activities that the Head Start teachers would do as they worked their way through the course. I felt like the French Chef of composition.

These studio sessions, once we got past the initial "out-of-body" sensation of being taped, met my goals of being personal. The two women were thoughtful and articulate as we discussed their experiences (and mine), connected them to Maya Angelou's, and compared and evaluated these experiences in light of Gail Sheehy's article. We used the cooperative give-and-take communication style that Deborah Tannen (1990) described in *You Just Don't Understand* as female-friendly "rapport talk."

The curriculum and taped sessions met my goals for being personal, but one important personal aspect of a good writing course remained to be created—the relationship of the students in the class to each other. The ECLC plan was to broadcast each tape at a specified time to small groups of students watching together at their Head Start center. I envisioned each group of viewers replicating the group dynamic of my two students and me in the studio. Several times during each taping, therefore, I posed an open-ended question and paused for several minutes to give the Head Start teachers time to discuss it among themselves. We usually began with a question for their reader-response journal entries posted each week to the class' discussion board. Then the camera came back to the studio and my two students would give their thoughts. Similarly, while we were discussing our progress on a paper, my studio students and I would go over their work together on screen, and then we would break for a few minutes so the Head Start teachers could form small groups and go over their work together. I was trying to create learning communities at the Head Start centers, just like the one that we were modeling on tape.

As the time neared for the first tapes to be broadcast, I felt satisfied that I had done as well as I could under the circumstances—that this course would be better than no course at all. However, I could not stop recalling a line from *New York Times* columnist, Natalie Angier (1995): "Nothing ruins a good idea like the real world."

The weekend before the term began, when we saw that we would need to add a section of the course, we recruited Carolyn Stoll, my most computer-savvy colleague, to be an online professor.

CAROLYN: AGREEING IN HASTE AND REPENTING AT LEISURE

When the ECLC director explained the program, I thought it would be just my thing. I learned that our Early Childhood Education degree program is the only one in the country offering all the courses completely online, with no on-campus component. Our students never need to set foot on campus. The combination of satellite broadcasts and Internet delivery is also unique to our program. I also learned that, to attract students, the technology expectations were kept low. Students were not even required to own a computer as long as they had access to the Internet through the library, WebTV, or some other means. The platform for the Internet part of the delivery system, Blackboard, was chosen because of its relative user friendliness. Because I often teach nontraditional students who are not comfortable using computers, I was no more worried about the ECLC students using this technology than I was my with on-campus students.

When we took the curriculum online, the use of personal narratives as a starting point, and the primary text for the course, *I Know Why the Caged Bird Sings,* engaged the students immediately. Angelou is a consummate storyteller, and her autobiographical tale of adolescence in Stamps, Arkansas, with its theme of persevering and overcoming obstacles, struck a chord with our students. Like Angelou, they cope, often unprepared, with circumstances not of their choosing.

Once students got their own narratives posted online for use in the second paper, they saw their own writing become part of the course. What begins as pre-academic storytelling suddenly becomes evidence for theories applicable to their own and Angelou's narratives. The final step, examining

Trying to Connect: A Distance-Learning Basic Writing Course 85

Angelou's narratives in the light of Gail Sheehy's text, clinches the transformation. For taking on the twin obstacles of college and distance learning, the students can, without exaggerating, make the claim that they too are "victorious personalities." This idea often comes up in either the conclusion of their third paper or in their letter to the portfolio committee. The curriculum was clearly a success online. If only that had been the end of it.

CAROLYN: "SHIPS PASSING IN THE NIGHT"— CREATING A BASIC WRITING WORKSHOP ONLINE

Stuart's reservations about even trying to develop an online English course for basic writers are understandable, considering all the personal interaction in such a course that cannot be done the same way online. Working with his two students on the tape, he modeled the kinds of activities we wanted our online students to do and hoped for the best. We did not know then, but would learn later, how wrong our assumptions were. These students were alone.

A survey of ECLC students showed that 100% of the students taped the broadcasts for "later reference," but less than half of the students watched the tape or broadcast as a group. What this meant for our basic writers is that not only did they not have a live professor, but they also did not have each other. Because much of the work demonstrated in the videotaped lesson was group oriented, they could not do much of it; they could only watch.

This reality created some difficult situations that forced us to rethink the role of the online professor. As a believer in revision, I naturally encouraged my students to revise their drafts. Because we did not have the benefit of working in small groups as we do on campus, at first I allowed an unlimited number of revisions for each paper. I was not prepared for how enthusiastically most of my students took advantage of that offer. Most wanted to do well; they wanted to get their papers right. They wanted and needed the personal attention that we provide on campus. They rained drafts down on me, sometimes sending a revision back to me in less than a day. Eventually, I realized that instead of creating a workshop, *I* was the workshop. Whereas on-campus students might ask a tutor for help with their essay's opening paragraph, my ECLC students sent me a draft with a new introduction. On-campus students might work on sentence boundaries in a small group, whereas my students sent me their draft they just edited. Whereas on-campus students might talk with a partner to focus their thesis, my students sent me a draft to try out their new idea. It was not unusual for me to read six or seven drafts of a paper from one student.

Not only was I their only source for feedback, but without the time structure of regular class meetings they translated the immediate nature of e-mail and Internet access into expectations for immediate responses to their questions and return of graded work. Just as they would often resubmit a revised draft to me on the same day, they expected that I would do the same. Because we did not meet at a regular time, they assumed I was just always there, 24 hours a day, 7 days a week, living on the Internet and waiting for a paper to grade.

I eventually solved some of that problem by establishing Friday noon as the cutoff for a paper to be submitted to me, with the promise of a return by Monday. Yet their need for personal connection popped up in other ways too. Blackboard always confirms the success of any action the student makes, including submitting a file into the Digital Dropbox. However, because the confirmation is not from me personally, they often do not believe Blackboard. So they e-mailed me as soon as they submitted a file, wanting to know if I got the file. If I did not get back with them right away, they grew worried and persistent. The worst example was a woman who e-mailed me throughout the night, unable to sleep for the worry of not knowing whether I got her file. Of course, I was not online all night, so I did not get her e-mails until the next morning, and by then she was clearly beside herself. She was so unsure of herself and so in need of human response that she nearly made herself ill wondering whether I got her work.

What I would not have given at times for 10 minutes in person with some of my students. For example, one woman was struggling with quotations. She kept mixing up paraphrasing with quotations, often putting quotation marks around indirect or paraphrased dialogue. My comment to her was, "This person wouldn't have said this in this way." I meant he would not be paraphrasing himself and using "that" or third-person pronouns and verbs. My student interpreted my comment to mean that I was trying to challenge what he actually said. Her e-mailed response was a heated: "How do you know what he would have said?" It actually took me a minute to understand what she meant. It took considerably longer to get *her* to see what I meant. I do not like to rewrite students' texts for them, so I tried every explanation I could to avoid writing out her quotation in first person, but finally I was forced to do just that. This frustrating exchange of e-mail messages happened over the course of 2 days—2 days to explain a point that I could have explained in 2 minutes in person.

Trying to Connect: A Distance-Learning Basic Writing Course 87

Lack of computer experience was another problem that I could have handled much more easily if I had been with my students in person. At first most students treated their word processors like typewriters. Each time they worked on a draft, they started over, typing it from scratch. When I pointed out to one student that she could add and delete text, or rearrange text that had already been written, it was a revelation. "Wow," she exclaimed in our chatroom one night, "I can't believe how much easier that is!" Although that comment caused me to chuckle at the time, the problem of constantly retyping a paper is actually quite serious because it causes a frustration and fatigue that inhibits the learning that revision fosters.

Starting in the winter of 2001, we piloted online tutoring for the ECLC program. In her study of the barriers to learning in distance-education, Jill Galusha (1997) noted that distance learners feel tutors are a key component to success in an online course, so the addition of tutors was a major, and overdue, advance in the program. Now students could send their drafts to a tutor assigned to our class and get feedback, much like on-campus students do in the Writing Center. This arrangement was not as beneficial as having tutors actually come to class 2 days a week, as they do in our on-campus basic writing classes, but it was a step in the right direction. Our tutor was trained to help basic writing students and was comfortable with computers. He promised and delivered a 24-hour turnaround on papers and even took part in our class' chatroom, which allowed him and me to help individual students in real time.

The creative use of the technology and the addition of a tutor made the movement toward a writing workshop for online basic writers possible. Without the burden of reading and commenting on draft after draft of their papers, I could make my comments more comprehensive and then direct the work they would do with the tutor before submitting another draft to me for grading. In this setup, students actually got more and, more important, *better* feedback on their papers—a crucial component for any basic writing curriculum. Yet there was still one more hurdle to overcome.

CAROLYN: "TAKE MY HAND, I'M A STRANGER IN PARADISE"—COMMUNITY AND THE STUDENT–TEACHER RELATIONSHIP ONLINE

Creating a writing workshop for basic writers online required more than just the use of technology and providing tutors. As Stuart realized, the ECLC basic writers would also need to be part of a learning community. Nontraditional students in general and basic writers in particular need lots of reinforcement, and the learning process with these students can be shut down by even a small frustration. Because distance learners work in isolation from the teacher and each other, the need for "cheerleading" and reinforcement of their efforts becomes even more important, sometimes critically so. I have had many late-night e-mail exchanges with students who for one reason or another wanted to chuck the whole thing and give up. They needed to be convinced that their failures are part of the learning process, that the online classroom community is a safe place for the risk taking that is necessary in learning to write, and that they are not alone. However, when we learned that over half of the ECLC students watched tapes of the broadcast by themselves, we realized that the ability of the teacher to form a relationship of trust, and therefore community, with the students was compromised. We would have to rebuild that connection.

We were kept apart by virtue of having only computers to communicate. What we eventually learned is that it would be those same computers that would bring us back together. We had some students who were comfortable with computers, who read well, who were articulate in their language skills, and who thrived in our course. Yet these students were a minority. Despite being teachers, and therefore presumably skilled problem solvers, many ECLC students reacted like many basic writers do when confronted with obstacles: They quit. Unlike in a live class, where students can be helped by both the instructor and the interaction of the whole class, these students must have felt bereft. Their only lifeline was their online professor, and the tether of that lifeline was the technology we were using.

Stuart's situation as both online professor and broadcast professor made things somewhat simpler for his students. At least they did not confuse him with me. In my section, at least one of my students did not quite understand that I was not Stuart or that the broadcasts were tapes that had been made months earlier. She requested in one e-mail that I quit standing in front of the Power Point slides during the broadcasts. I always get a laugh when I share that story with colleagues, but in truth it is rather poignant. Unused to communicating with a disembodied "text" instead of a person, she made the assumption that the teacher she saw in the tapes was also the typist who spoke to her on her computer. She needed help, and she reached out for the only "person" she saw—the man on the tape.

The loss of this personal link in a distance format carries serious consequences. Jill Galusha (1997) cited the disruption of the student-teacher relationship as one of the top five reasons for failure and attrition in any

Trying to Connect: A Distance-Learning Basic Writing Course   89

online class (p. 5). Another reason the personal component is so important to our population has to do with gender differences in communication. Our demographic studies show that 98% of the ECLC students are female. Deborah Tannen's (1991) research into the way males and females communicate has shown that females and males often bring different expectations to the classroom. Females typically try to find common ground by sharing experiences and working to create rapport, whereas men are more inclined to see the classroom as a competitive arena for challenging and debating others. To form a community and establish a student–teacher connection with female distance learners would require using that typically female communication style.

It is certainly not original in distance learning to hold "virtual office hours" or require real-time attendance at class chat sessions. What is original is the need it fills for this population of students. Scheduling problems make it nearly impossible to find a chat time that meets the needs of all students, but for those who do come, the benefits are enormous. The second time I taught a composition course online, I scheduled online office hours, and suddenly I was not just an e-mail message; I was a real person at the other end of the wire responding to them in real time. By encouraging them to use the technology of the chatroom, I created a way for them to begin to get to know me, and they got to know one another better. They found out they were not the only one who did not understand quotation marks or had trouble posting their journals to the Discussion Board.

I went back and examined the chatroom archives of an online class from a year ago. These students were then in my online English 101 class, but had taken the basic writing course the quarter before. I looked at two chat sessions—one very early in the quarter and the other the very last one at the end. The differences are striking, and they show how nontraditional female students used the chatroom to create a learning community. They needed to create a community before they could become a learning community.

The initial discussion centered almost entirely on nuts-and-bolts issues such as figuring out where to type and how the white board worked. Next, the students moved the conversation into Tannen's "rapport talk," the give and take of personal information to discover a common ground. With this group, it was our children. One student, who I call Jane, enters late and apologizes because she has been putting her daughter to bed.

"I hear ya. I got my two down a while ago," I reply. Then, trying to get down to business, I type, "Any problems or questions?"

"I have 6 to get in bed," writes Jane.

"Six???!!!" I type.

Jane then acknowledges my efforts to focus on class business, but apparently she is not finished establishing our relationship as mothers: "I haven't figured out the how to do the Drop Box. Yep, 6—ages 4, 5, 7, 8, 9, 10."

I make another stab at being serious. "Wow," I say, "You're a busy lady. You say you've been trying the Drop Box?"

Jane, however, reaches for another connection, this time a mutual acquaintance. "Do you get to talk to Stuart about how we did in Prep Comp Class?" she asks.

"Oh, yes," I reply. "In fact we helped each other with portfolios. He told me you were a hard worker and a good student."

Jane types, "Cool! Tell my buddy I said hi. I miss writing to him. Really, he said that! You're kidding, right? He was a big help to me. Well, I've got to do my lesson plan for my class and I'm calling it a night too. Hey, thanks for being here. :)"

For Jane, the most pressing need was for personal connection. We quickly achieved rapport concerning Stuart, and then she went on to mention the need to do lesson plans, another area that she and I share. With that, the chat ended for that week. In her effort to establish rapport with me, Jane seems to have forgotten her question about the Digital Drop Box, which at the time I, as a teacher, thought was the real point of the conversation.

What is interesting to me about this first chat is the "first date" quality. It was clear that this was a new way of communicating and that it was taking some getting used to. It was also clear that, although we were only able to type to one another, the chatroom was allowing us to get to know each other in a new way. The discussion about kids and the references back to the previous quarter were all attempts on our parts to form a new community on the foundation of what we already had in common. Jane does not know me well enough to trust me at this stage of the game, but she remembers Stuart and refers to him almost as a comforting technique. All the areas that we discussed were safe topics. It was important to get through these preliminaries, but as with many first dates, no one was particularly interested in sticking around long.

Five weeks after beginning our regular weekly chatroom time, the dynamics of our cyber meeting have changed dramatically. The students have formed a learning community.

Student 2 (who I call Mary) enters several minutes before the scheduled starting time, followed closely by Student 3, (who I call Helen).

Helen begins with, "Hi, is anyone here?"

Mary replies, "I am."

Trying to Connect: A Distance-Learning Basic Writing Course   91

"I know it's early, but I'm glad I found you here."

"Why is that?"

"Because at least you can talk to someone. It gets good when there are at least six or more."

"I can't wait. While we are talking, are you done reading the book?"

"Yes, thank God, and I didn't enjoy it at all. I read it before Christmas."

"I didn't like the book either."

"If I pass the class I'll be thankful, forget the dean's list."

To read this exchange, you might think it is a transcript of a conversation between two students waiting for their teacher to arrive in a regular "live" class. They even feel safe enough to criticize the novel we are reading, Breena Clarke's *River, Cross My Heart*, as if I would never "hear" what they say. One is also helping the other. Mary has not been to a chat before, having had technical problems all quarter. Helen is enthusiastic about the whole chat experience and tries to encourage Mary. At this point, we were piloting online tutoring, and this evening the tutor joins the chat, with some additional aspects of a community emerging.

The tutor, who I call Fred, says, "This is our last chat."

"I hope not," protests Mary, "It can't be."

"You've missed them all," Helen reminds Mary.

"Don't remind me," answers Mary.

Helen says, "At least you got to meet Fred before it was all over."

Fred types, "He-he."

Helen explains, "Those are Fred's famous words."

Fred asks, "What about our field trip to Red Lobster???"

"You guys never talk about the book or homework," points out Mary.

"When C. Stoll gets on you will," answers Helen.

As the tutor and other students join, Mary is told about two running gags—that we will all meet at Red Lobster in Columbus one night for chat time, and that our tutor always indicates laughter with "he-he." It is clear that a community has been formed here with its own culture of inside jokes, shared communication codes, and familiar personas.

By this point in the quarter, I had made the chat time more structured. Over the course of the quarter, we looked at examples of effective writing and talked about why they were effective. We looked at problematic sentences in their writing and discussed ways to improve them. We discussed the texts we were reading. Later in this session, for instance, after yet another student (who I call Lucy) joins, we have a particularly lively and productive discussion concerning the ending of the novel we have just finished. It was at this point that I knew we had succeeded in becoming a *learning* community.

I type, "My point is that I'm not sure that's what Clark meant to do, because she draws no attention to the difference."

Lucy replies, "I don't think she had to. As a black person that deals with racism daily when you read these type of books it is understood without saying."

"Right," agrees Helen.

Jane, who has joined us, chimes in, "I realize that, but the whole family should have considered sticking together, instead of drawing attention to their family by sending her away. (If they would have followed through.) I understand what you're saying, Lucy."

Lucy counters Jane's point with, "It would not have necessarily drawn attention. During these times children were back and forth from North to South."

"Oh, I guess I didn't think about that. Good point," Jane admits, "See this helps me."

"My point about this whole thing," I continue, "Is that I think you may be doing some filling in for Clark that she should have done herself."

Lucy disagrees, "I think she meant it to be that way."

"Ok, Lucy," I type, "I think there's room to argue that way." Then moving on, I ask, "So what's the other kid in the pool mean?"

"I think she thought it was Clara. It was her way of finally dealing with her death," offers Lucy.

"I agree," types Helen, "I also thought Willie was henpecked."

Jane joins in with, "I thought she felt it was Clara. Not henpecked. Alice was trying to figure a way to get him to change his mind. She referred to him as too much of a rooster."

Helen says, "Ok, I'm alone in this opinion of henpecked."

Lucy adds, "I think Clara led her to where she drowned and she couldn't reach her either time. Then she led her back and helped her win the race."

Jane types, "Some roosters are henpecked. I live on a farm. I see it once in a while."

The discussion centered at first on whether White people could relate to the reaction of the Black characters in the novel. I do not shy away from controversial discussions in my classes, believing that only with the free exchange of ideas can learning actually happen. Yet when this discussion occurred, I remember being concerned about where it would go, because I had only my keyboard to guide the conversation. I remember closing the chat with the feeling that I had been successful if only because no one had "flamed" anyone else. Looking back at the archive now, over 1 year later, I realize how very well the discussion went. Although pretty much everyone

Trying to Connect: A Distance-Learning Basic Writing Course   93

held their ground, there was no hostility, and there was a range of analysis of the novel's conclusion. One student even boldly declared herself to be alone in her opinion. Another student offered a real-life example that, although not exactly relevant, did offer support to her classmate.

What I see now is that I succeeded in more than just keeping a fight from breaking out—I had successfully created an environment where the participants felt like part of the group, where they respected each other, and where it was safe to express opinion. Slowly, the learning community that Stuart was striving for when he developed the course had taken shape.

CAROLYN AND STUART: MAKING A CONNECTION

From our experiences teaching basic writing online, we gained a new appreciation for a curriculum that had served us well in the past. The choices of reading texts and the progression of writing narratives and then expository papers worked with our ECLC students just as it has for so many on-campus students. Despite the difficulties of the distance format, these components of the curriculum have been a constant positive.

In addition to benefiting from the curriculum, our students gained a technological expertise that would not have come about otherwise. We were perhaps naive and misguided when we designed our ECLC courses, the composition courses in particular, to be "technology lite." We were correct in thinking that technology would be the barrier between the students and us, but we were wrong to think that we were making too many technological demands. One of the students that first quarter used the computers at her local library, which only became a problem when she kept forgetting to save to her floppy disk instead of the hard drive on the library's computer. Another student did not have any computer at all; she used WebTV as her Internet service provider, meaning that she had just a keyboard and her TV set. She was a good student, but the difficulty of using e-mail as a word processor nearly drove us mad. As it turns out, the same thing that caused the problem was the only thing that could also solve it. Our students needed to use technology more, not less. By learning to delete, add, and move text, students revised more and their revisions got better. By communicating online with tutors, students achieved more of a writing workshop experience. By navigating the chatroom, students and teacher interacted in real time, helping to develop a learning community of trust, which is essential to basic writers.

Above all, we gained a new appreciation for the role of the personal relationship between students and teachers, as well as a sense of what a learning community can be online. Once we got over the technological hurdles, the students began to joke with each other, we talked some about our families, and we shared some things about our backgrounds—we began to create a community. It did not happen immediately, but that is to be expected. Communities are built over time. We were separated not just by physical distance, but also by the barriers inherent in the technology that is needed to take and teach a course online. Once the walls were broken down and human interaction began to occur, the vital link between student and teacher, and between student and student, started to develop. We became people linked together by computers, not people kept apart by computers.

As the ECLC program develops and expands, the next wave of technical innovation looms before us. Wireless voice and video communication, for instance, has the potential to enrich the online student–teacher relationship by greatly improving our ability to interact personally. Teleconferences in real time have the potential to transmute the online basic writing course.

As the technology of online communication progresses, more and more people for whom college has not been an option—like our ECLC students, whose locations and time constraints make going to a college campus impossible—will find that the situation has changed. For teachers, it is not a question of whether we should teach basic writing online, but rather how. Although many of us may continue to prefer teaching in person, the distance-learning option should become an increasingly workable alternative. The technology is here, and we are not asking too much of online basic writers to use it. However, we are asking too much of them if we are not creative in the ways we use technology to bridge the distance in distance learning.

REFERENCES

Angelou, Maya. (1970). *I know why the caged bird sings*. New York: Random House.
Angier, Natalie. (1995, September 5). Please say it isn't so, Simba: The noble lion can be a coward. *New York Times*, p. B5.
Bartholomae, Donald, & Petrosky, Anthony. (1986). *Facts, artifacts and counterfacts*. Portsmouth: Boynton/Cook.
Dickson, Marcia. (1995). *It's not like that here*. Portsmouth: Boynton/Cook.

Trying to Connect: A Distance-Learning Basic Writing Course 95

Fuller, Dawn. (2000, Feb. 25). Head Start teachers get jump start on degrees via distance learning. *University of Cincinnati Currents*. Retrieved January 2004 from http://www.uc.edu/info-services/headproj.htm.

Galusha, Jill. (1997). Barriers to learning in distance-education. *The Infrastruction Network*. Retrieved May 7 2002 from http://www.infrastruction.com/barriers.htm.

Laine, Chet, & Laine, Michaeline. (2002, May 2). *Literacy histories: Insights into college developmental readers*. San Francisco: International Reading Association Conference.

Piorkowski, J., & Scheurer, E. (2000). It's the way that they talk to you: Increasing agency in basic writers through a social context of care. *Journal of Basic Writing, 19*(2), 72-92.

Sheehy, Gail. (1986, April 20). The victorious personality. *New York Times Magazine*, pp. 24-25, 43-47, 50.

Tannen, Deborah. (1990). *You just don't understand*. New York: Ballantine.

Tannen, Deborah. (1991, June 19). Teachers' classroom strategies should recognize that men and women use language differently. *Chronicle of Higher Education*, p. B1.

U.S. Department of Health and Human Services. (1998, November). Head Start reauthorization approved. *Head Start Bulletin*. Retrieved May 7 2002 from http://www.headstartinfo.org/publications/hsbulletin64/hsb64_02.htm.

5

ANYONE? ANYONE? ANYONE? LEADING DISCUSSIONS IN CYBERSPACE

E-JOURNALS AND INTERACTIVITY IN ASYNCHRONOUS ENVIRONMENTS

Debbie Danowski

"Anyone? Anyone? Anyone?" The image of an instructor standing in front of the classroom begging for student participation in the film *Ferris Bueller's Day Off* exemplifies the lack of student participation many experience in the classroom. Although student participation is necessary in a face-to-face classroom, in a distance-education environment, the survival of the course depends on interactivity, yet the tendency for decreased sharing can be even greater.

This chapter offers an overview of the current literature discussing the use of student e-journals as a means to promote interactivity in asynchronous environments. A brief history of distance-education is presented prior to a summary of successful pedagogical practices highlighting the concept of interactivity. Following this, basic composition theory as related to journal writing is examined. Expanding on this, an overview of e-journals precedes a discussion of shifting distance-education pedagogy to further include e-journals. Throughout this chapter a clear distinction between the traditional expressive student journals currently used in composition and writing across the curriculum courses and a new method of interactive student e-journals is made.

Although an overview of existing literature may, at first, seem redundant, the concept of interactivity in distance-education is so vital to its success that the sheer importance of the concept substantiates the need for inclusion of this material in a work such as this. Furthermore, a review of the necessity of interactivity in distance-education assists in making certain that early practices in the field are not easily repeated.

To begin, early distance-education practices consisted of e-mail exchanges between the professor and individual students. Although students received individual attention, their experience amounted to an electronic version of mail order pedagogy that sorely lacked in interactivity. To some extent, this practice continues today, yet distance-education scholars have worked hard to promote more effective methods. As Markel (1999) pointed out in his article, "Distance-education and the Myth of the New Pedagogy,"

> As long as students have access on campus to a library and the Internet, they can respond successfully. They do not need computers in the classroom, and whether the course is offered by distance or in a classroom does not matter. The important characteristic of active, student-centered education is what students are asked to do—how they engage the material—not whether the media used are digital or analog. (p. 6)

Consequently, as the field progressed, more and more researchers began to notice the benefits of distance-education. For instance, several studies have even proved distance education to be more effective than face-to-face instruction. Jerald G. Schutte conducted a study of his Saturday Sociology 364 class at California State University–Northridge. Thirty-three students in Schutte's course were randomly divided into two groups. One group was provided with traditional face-to-face instruction, whereas, the other was given a distance-learning format.

The traditional class met every Saturday for 14 weeks as originally scheduled from 9:00 a.m. to 1:30 p.m. The "virtual class" met only twice after the first 2 weeks to take midterm and final exams. In addition to this, the virtual class was randomly assigned groups of three students and required to take part in weekly virtual discussions. Homework and questions were submitted by forms on the World Wide Web. Traditional office hours were held for both sets of students with separate times for each (Schutte, 1998).

Anyone? Anyone? Anyone? Leading Discussions in Cyberspace 99

"Results indicate the virtual students scored an average of 20 points higher on the 100 point midterm and final exams," according to Schutte. "It was hypothesized that face-to-face professor-student interaction is crucial to test performance. However, the data indicate the reverse, that virtual interaction produces better results" (Schutte, 1998, p. 3). Before continuing, it is necessary to present a brief overview of distance-education theory regarding the concept of interactivity as the key to the success of Schutte's virtual class—it lies within the use of weekly virtual discussions and group assignments. In distance-education environments, these pedagogical techniques are equivalent to classroom discussions in face-to-face settings.

SUCCESSFUL DISTANCE-EDUCATION AND INTERACTIVITY

Perhaps one of the most significant theories in relation to interactivity in the distance-education classroom is the equivalency theory. As Simonson, Schlosser, and Hanson (1999) pointed out, this theory requires an examination of the learning paradigm in both face-to-face and distance-education classrooms:

> Central to this theoretical approach is the concept of equivalency. Local and distant learners have fundamentally different environments in which to learn. It is the responsibility of the distance educator to design learning events that provide experiences with equal value for learners. Just as a triangle and a square may have the same area and be considered equivalent even though they are different geometrical shapes, the experiences of the local learner and the distant learner should have equivalent value even though these experiences might be very different. (p. 71)

The fact remains that classroom interactivity is vital in successful pedagogy. The most effective means to achieve interactivity in computer-based distance-education is through the use of Internet bulletin boards. Holmberg's theory of distance-education, named Guided Didactic Conversation, centers around the emotional as well as the communicative aspects of the learning process. He offered seven background assumptions for his theory:

1. The core of teaching consists of interaction between the teaching and learning parties. Simulated interaction through subject matter presentation in preproduced courses can subsume part of the interaction by causing students to consider different views, approaches, and solutions and generally to interact with a course.
2. Emotional involvement in the study and feelings of personal relations between the teaching and learning parties is likely to contribute to learning pleasure.
3. Learning pleasure supports student motivation.
4. Participation in decision making is favorable to student motivation.
5. Strong student motivation facilitates learning.
6. A friendly, personal tone and easy access to the subject matter contributes to learning pleasure, supports student motivation, and, thus, facilitates learning.
7. The effectiveness of teaching is demonstrated by students' learning of what has been taught. (Simonson, Schlosser, & Hanson, 1999, p. 67)

From these seven assumptions, Holmberg developed his theory, which he stated as,

> Distance teaching will support student motivation, promote learning pleasure and make study relevant to the individual learner and his/her needs, creating feelings of rapport between the learner and the distance-education institution (its tutors, counselors, etc.), facilitating access to course content, engaging the learner in activities, discussions and decisions and generally catering for helpful real and simulated communication to and from the learner. (Simonson, Schlosser, & Hanson, 1999, p. 67)

Holmberg, feeling that the theory was incomplete, later refined his ideas to include a listing of the essential elements conducive to learning. He later added the following:

- All learning concerned with the acquisition of cognitive knowledge and cognitive skills, as well as affective learning and some psychomotor learning, is effectively provided for by distance-education.

- Distance-education is based on learning as an individual activity.
- Learning is guided and supported by noncontiguous means.
- Distance-education is open to behaviorist, cognitive, constructivist, and other modes of learning.
- Personal relations, study pleasure, and empathy between students and those supporting them (tutors, counselors) are central to learning in distance-education. Feelings of empathy and belonging promote students' motivation to learn, influencing learning favorably.
- Although it is an effective mode of training, distance-education runs the risk of leading to mere fact learning and reproduction of accepted "truths." However, it can be organized and carried out in such a way that students are encouraged to search, criticize, and identify positions of their own. (Simonson, Schlosser, & Hanson, 1999, p. 68)

From this theory as well as the previously mentioned one, it is clear that success in this area depends greatly on "personal relations" between fellow learners and the instructor. According to Eisenberg (1998), the present higher educational design was originated in the Middle Ages where today's technological advancements were never conceived. He said:

> The new technology, and delivery of material at a distance, brings the possibility of great and positive change for higher education. It makes possible highly specialized classes—a seminar in Whitman, or a class in Korean—that only the largest institutions can presently offer. In a text-based environment, the instructor need not worry about students' gender or physical appearance influencing grading. (p. 3)

This being so, it seems clear that interactivity is necessary, yet methods of achieving this have been varied and sometimes ineffective. Although requiring students to participate in real-time discussions appears to be a solution to establishing greater interactivity in a distance-education classroom, for the most part this contradicts the spirit of distance-education.

As Eisenberg (1998) noted, "With asynchronous instruction, scheduling problems all but disappear. Within limits—a 24-hour period, say—professors can teach when they want, and students can 'attend' when they want. The disabled can be more easily accommodated" (p. 3). Although as Hiltz (1997) pointed out in her 2-year study of asynchronous learning networks (ALN), "The data thus do support the conclusion that ALN is 'as good

102   *Danowski*

or better' than other modes of course delivery in terms of enabling students to master course materials" (p. 8), there are several benefits to this type of learning environment.

Owston (1997) pointed out that one of the major advantages of Internet-based learning is the flexibility:

> When you browse through courses listed in the World Lecture Hall, you'll discover many courses where faculty have dramatically reduced the amount of face-to-face contact between instructor and student, or in some cases, entirely eliminated it. In lieu, they provide Web based study projects and online activities that students can access at their convenience. (p. 6)

Expanding on this, a brief examination of basic composition theory is necessary prior to discussing the need for e-journals and a paradigm shift in distance-education practices.

JOURNAL WRITING AND COMPOSITION THEORY

For decades, composition theorists have lauded writing as a means of self-expression and a way to increase learning (Anson & Beach, 1995; Fulwiler, 1987). Fulwiler noted that, "human beings find meaning in the world by exploring it through language—through their own easy talky language, not the language of textbook and teacher" (p. 1). Similarly, Emig (1997) noted that, "writing is often our representation of the world made visible, embodying both process and product, writing is more readily a form and source of learning than talking" (p. 10). In addition to this, Berlin noted that writing

> is an art, a creative act in which the process—the discovery of the true self—is as important as the product—the self discovered and expressed. . . . Discovering the true self in writing will simultaneously enable the individual to discover the truth of the situation which evoked the writing, a situation that, needless to say, must always be compatible with the development of the self. (p. 688)

In a like manner, some theorists point to the academic value of journal writing. "Given the recursive nature of the writing process, in which stu-

Anyone? Anyone? Anyone? Leading Discussions in Cyberspace 103

dents continually cycle between generating and organizing ideas in drafts, the journal can provide an excellent place for them to work out their thinking informally, during and even after their drafting" (Anson & Beach, 1995, p. 44).

Similarly, Arbuthnot (1993) pointed out, "Private [informal] writing enables students to discover the intellectual and emotional pleasures of creativity; it promotes critical thinking by encouraging them to explore issues in depth; by freeing their minds from the specters of misplaced modifiers and run-on sentences, it helps them write with greater ease and grace" (p. 1).

Furthermore, the importance of journal writing was emphasized in a study by Patton, Woods, Agarenzo, and Brubakeret during a senior practicum nursing class. The authors discovered that journal writing helped develop critical thinking skills and aid in honing observation skills. Both of these elements are vital to critical thinking and academic success.

Additionally, journal writing is also a method of enhancing formal writing to meet the challenge of rigorous academic work and research necessary to both undergraduate and graduate curricula. Smagorinsky (1997) documented a southwestern high school student's experience in developing meaning through writing. Although a good portion of the student's writing was for academic purposes, his experience with personal writing proved invaluable in his classes. "I believe that this stuff (his senior year writing) helped me in the fact that when I got in there and it was time to write a paper, it was very easy for me . . . I had a very easy time thinking it through in my head, and the essay just came flowing out," the student said (Smagorinsky, 1997, p. 17). As Smagorinsky's study proves, practice with personal writing provides students with necessary skills for academic writing. In other words, the more practice students have with expressing their ideas informally, the more effective learners they will eventually become.

Similarly, after an extensive review of observations regarding the relationship between journal writing and the thinking process, Zacharias (1991) concluded that there is "a connection between the upsurge of interest in the processes of journal writing and thinking processes. The connection is that journal writing assists the development of thinking processes" (p. 5).

Consequently, it is clear that journal writing is a valuable pedagogical technique in any discipline. Building on this foundation, it next becomes necessary to synthesize traditional composition theory with current distance-education pedagogy resulting in a more effective means of instruction.

DISTANCE-EDUCATION AND E-JOURNALS

Although composition theorists have historically noted the academic value of expressive writing, or writing that allows free expression of thoughts and feelings, making the connection in a distance-education format is vital to interactivity in the classroom. Considering that, as Holmberg pointed out, "distance-education is based on learning as an individual activity," engaging students in electronic discussions about course material is essential. The use of e-journals or electronic journals is ideal in achieving this interactivity. Yet using this pedagogical method requires a shift in the way instructors currently view journal writing. Requiring students to post weekly or biweekly messages responding to assigned readings and then further requiring replies to student postings promotes in-depth interaction with both course material and other students, yet at the same time this type of pedagogy makes these journals public.

The difference in e-journals lies in the fact that this type of journal is open to all students in the classroom at all times. Unlike Fulwiler's personal emphasis in traditional journals, e-journals are used as a means to increase understanding of course material and generate responses, rather than promote highly personal emotional reactions. The benefits of this type of journal are clear. By forcing students to interact with both classroom material and each other, instructors are provided with lively, high-quality online discussions allowing for varied, interesting student interactivity.

The challenge in using e-journals lies within making students feel comfortable enough to post their journals to electronic bulletin boards. Similar to face-to-face instruction, quality distance-education teaching practices generally consist of creating a comfortable learning environment for all students. Cheryl Doran, a Ph.D. graduate from Capella University (formerly The Graduate School of America) in Minneapolis, Minnesota, describes her learning experience in online tutorial courses:

> These courses are offered on a quarter basis [12-week period] and are taught by faculty members [called tutors] who assign reading material and discussion topics. Students participate in online discussions with each other and with the tutor. A term paper or project is required, too. Online courses offer structure and peer interaction whereas tutorial courses offer a great deal of independence. In both cases, expectations regarding quality of work are very much like those found in a traditional university setting. Truthfully, this has been the best educational experience in my life.

Anyone? Anyone? Anyone? Leading Discussions in Cyberspace   105

Doran's enthusiasm for her learning experience reflects the level of interactivity she was required to achieve. At Capella University, depending on the program of study, professors require students to post responses to directed questions a minimum of once a week. In addition to this, students are required to respond to three of their peers' responses. Often this results in even further discussion of course material.

Building on this idea, in English distance-education, e-journals written in response to directed questions about readings allow students the opportunity to reflect on both the compositional and narrative structures of readings. For instance, in introductory composition courses, students preparing to write papers on summary or paraphrase may practice these techniques via their e-journals while offering responses to the narrative structure of readings.

The hallmark of e-journals involves requiring directed student responses that are broad enough to allow for diversity in replies yet focused to provide in-depth interaction. Using electronic classroom bulletin boards, instructors can post weekly or biweekly questions. Providing students with deadline and length requirements as well as evaluating the quality of responses allows for assessment of journals.

Additionally, e-journals can be used to track student progress and understanding of course material. This is especially true in upper level literature courses. Instructors worried about student understanding of material are provided with an easily accessible means to assess students' comprehension of readings. Furthermore, by requiring responses to students' writings, instructors are promoting in-depth understanding of the material. To effectively utilize e-journals, however, an element of interactivity needs to be present. Following is a discussion of methods to achieving this.

E-JOURNALS AND A SHIFT
IN CURRENT PEDAGOGY

Although e-journals use electronic bulletin boards, the nature of their content separates them from standard classroom postings. In e-journals, students are asked to synthesize their own life experiences with course material, allowing for increased understanding. Rather than restating compositional rules, narrative elements, or literature history, in e-journals students are asked to interact on a personal level with course material, synthesizing life events with academic discourse.

For instructors accustomed to evaluating students either with traditional journal writing assessment criteria or strict compositional structure, the use of e-journals requires a shift in thinking. Rather than relying on highly personal journal writing or highly academic formal writing, e-journals combine both elements to introduce a hybrid mix of the two. For instance, students in introductory composition classes can be asked to relate their experiences to those found in readings while being asked to mimic the narrative structure of the original piece in their responses. With e-journals such as this, instructors are asking students to synthesize material on several different levels while employing sophisticated narrative techniques.

For instructors using e-journals, the benefits are many. In addition to producing generally more interesting student readings, e-journals allow for public responses from several students as well as the instructor, which can potentially eliminate the repetitive nature of instruction. Students needing similar assistance with course material can be directed to read previous instructor or student responses to further assist in their learning process. Furthermore, instructors can easily provide struggling students will concrete examples of superior classwork by pointing to superior e-journals.

Additionally, when students are asked to write formal papers, previous e-journal work will allow instructors to assess academic growth as well as help prevent plagiarism. The public nature of e-journals provides instructors with easily accessible examples of previous student writings, thus making plagiarism more difficult.

Although these benefits are important, perhaps one of the most important, and sometimes underrated, benefit of using e-journals is the connection students make both to each other and to their lives. Katula and Threnhauser (1999) credited Dewey with advocating that students be allowed to make a "real" connection between classroom abstractions and their lives. They noted that,

> Dewey urged that education in the classroom be focused on helping students make sense out of their experiences. He called for a pragmatic education, one that linked knowing to doing. The role of the teacher went beyond preparing lessons to structuring experiences that actively engaged the child in developing practical usable knowledge. 'I take it,' Dewey (1938) wrote, "that the fundamental unity of the newer philosophy is found in the idea that there is an intimate and necessary relation between the processes of actual experience and education." (p. 3)

Furthermore, the quality of the experience was also a major factor for Dewey when evaluating the educational effectiveness. As Katula and

Threnhauser (1999) further pointed out, "Teachers were charged by Dewey (1938) with creating experiences for students that were agreeable and that would prepare them for future problem-solving and decision-making. Thus, it was not simply experience, but rich and structured experiences, to which students were to be exposed, and upon which they would reflect and learn" (p. 4).

The use of e-journals in distance-education English classes provides students with the rich and structured experiences Katula and Threnhauser advocated as being necessary to successful educational environments. As Barrett, one of the first in his area to begin teaching online, pointed out, "Working online is often better for students because there is a much greater opportunity to write, to read what others have written and to respond interactively with each other" (cited in Gabriel, 1998, p. 3). What Barrett failed to point out is that the use of e-journals in online English courses makes working online and teaching better for instructors as well.

REFERENCES

Anson, Chris M., & Beach, Richard. (1995). *Journals in the classroom: Writing to learn*. Norwood: Christopher-Gordon.

Arbuthnot, Lucie. (1993, March 10). Ethics and the "personal writing" of students. *The Chronicle of Higher Education* [online]: 4 pp.

Berlin, J. A. (1997). Rhetoric and ideology in the writing class. In V. Villanueva, Jr. (Ed.), *Cross-talk in comp theory* (pp. 678-699). Urbana: National Council of Teachers of English.

Eisenberg, Daniel. (1998, August 21). College faculty and distance-education. *Virtual University Journal* [online]. Available: < http://www.openhouse.org.uk/ virtualuniversitypress/vuj/Issue2/ > .

Emig, J. (1997). Writing as a mode of learning. In V. Villanueva, Jr. (Ed.), *Cross-talk in comp theory*. Urbana: National Council of Teachers of English.

Fulwiler, Toby. (Ed.). (1987). *The journal book*. Portsmouth: Boynton/Cook.

Gabriel, Michele. (1998, August 17). Earn Degree@Home. *Business Journal Serving San Jose & Silicon Valley* (EBSCOhost), 5 pp.

Hiltz, Starr R. (1997). Impacts of college-level courses via asynchronous learning networks: Focus on students. Sloan Conference on Asynchronous Learning Networks. *Journal of Asynchronous Learning Networks,* 10 pp.

Katula, Richard A., & Threnhauser, Elizabeth. (1999, July). Experiential education in the undergraduate curriculum. *ProQuest Direct*, 15 pp.

Markel, Mike. (1999, April). Distance-education and the myth of the new pedagogy. *Journal of Business & Technical Communication* (EBSCOhost), 12 pp.

Owston, Ronald D. (1997). The World Wide Web: A technology to enhance teaching and learning? *Educational Researcher* 26.2 [online.] 11 pp. Available: < http://www.edu. yorku.cal ~ rowston /article.html > .

Patton, June G., Woods, Stephanie J., Agarenzo, Tina, & Brubakeret, Cynthia. (1997). Enhancing the clinical practicum experience through journal writing. *Journal of Nursing Education 36.5* [online], 5 pp.

Schutte, Jerald G. (1998). Virtual teaching in higher education: The new intellectual superhighway or just another traffic jam? [online] Available: < http://www.csun.edu/ sociology/virexp.htm > .

Simonson, Michael, Schlosser, Charles, & Hanson, Dan. (1999). Theory and distance-education: A new discussion. *The American Journal of Distance-education, 13*(1), 60-75.

Smagorinsky, Peter. (1997). Personal growth in social context: A high school senior's search for meaning in and through writing. *Written Communication 14*(1) [online], 24 pp.

Zacharias, Martha E. (1991). The relationship between journal writing in education and thinking processes: What educators say about it. *Education 112*(2) [online], 7 pp.

III COMMUNITIES

Rhetorical Violence and the Problematics of Power:
A Notion of Community for the Digital Age Classroom

Lori E. Amy

Critical and Multicultural:
Pedagogy Goes Online

Lesliee Antonette

Feminist Civic Engagement and the Role of the Bureaucrat:
Graduate Education, Distance Learning, and Community Action

Debbie Danowski

6

RHETORICAL VIOLENCE AND THE PROBLEMATICS OF POWER

A NOTION OF COMMUNITY FOR THE DIGITAL AGE CLASSROOM

Lori E. Amy

> If the political is not dissolved in the sociotechnical element of forces and needs (in which, in effect, it seems to be dissolving under our eyes), it must inscribe the sharing of community . . . a community consciously undergoing the experience of its sharing. To attain such a signification of the "political" does not depend, or in any case not simply, on what is called a "political will." It implies being already engaged in the community, that is to say, undergoing, in whatever manner, the experience of community as communication: it implies writing. We must not stop writing, or letting the singular outlines of our being-in-common expose itself.
>
> —Jean-Luc Nancy (1991, pp 40–41)

ELECTRONIC CONTACT ZONES

Mary Louise Pratt (1992), in her ground-breaking *Imperial Eyes: Travel Writing and Transculturation*, coined the term contact zones to refer to "the social spaces where disparate cultures meet, clash, and grapple with each other, often in highly asymmetrical relations of domination and subordination" (p. 4). She critiqued the "utopian quality" that underlies "much of the thinking about language, communication, and culture" (p. 4) in the academy and argued that utopian notions of "community" fail to understand the real contest over meanings and representations that mark relations among heterogeneous cultural groups. Pratt's work has proved especially helpful to English and composition/writing instructors working with students from diverse backgrounds, with a range of cultural knowledges, literacies, and values. Indeed several important studies such as Karen Fitts and Alan W. France's (1995) *Left Margins: Cultural Studies and Composition Pedagogy* and Gerald Graff's (1992)[1] *Beyond the Culture Wars: How Teaching the Conflicts Can Revitalize American Education,* have expanded on and elaborated Pratt's early work. In particular, a contact zone perspective has helped many instructors work toward educational spaces in which "dominant" voices and perspectives are de-centered, in which "unsolicited oppositional discourse, parody, resistance, [and] critique" are valued (Pratt, 2002, p. 616), and in which the "community" of the classroom is, far from a harmonious, consensual space of commonality, intentionally figured as a space of struggle and contest over meanings and representations.

As influential as Pratt's work has been to teachers in traditional classroom settings, it is even more significant for those of us working with "virtual" communities. Following the 1994 privatization of the Internet and the 1996 Telecommunications Act,[2] the move to incorporate increasingly sophisticated technologies into our traditional classrooms and move more and more of our classes into the field of the World Wide Web mandates an ongoing rethinking of our notions of "classroom" and "community." As one of the first group of graduate students to pioneer uses of the World Wide Web with composition and English classes in the University of Florida's

---

[1]See also Phyllis Van Slyck (1997) and Gregory Jay (1994).
[2]For a cautionary analysis of the global implications of the United States' technology euphoria and the 1996 Telecommunications Act, see Selfe (1999).

Networked Writing Environment (NWE),[3] I have been immersed in this continual rethinking as I moved from graduate student teaching in the NWE to combinations of traditional classroom, computerized classroom, and online teaching in my professional career.

Like many of my peers, I began teaching in UF's NWE with idealistic visions of the Internet and virtual classrooms as spaces of radical equality, as sites of oppositional discourse through which students could subvert the power position of the traditional teacher, develop their own voices, and establish their own positions of authority. Although my peers and I understood the myriad problems that differential access to technologies of writing posed for our students and the ways in which America's technological "literacy agenda" fails to redress the social injustices and structural inequalities that mark our students' lives before they enter our classrooms (Selfe, 1999), most of us thought of our actual *practices* with students as "liberatory." We had good reason for our optimism: We were seeing an increasing number of students who were "speaking," and their proliferating discourses were emerging in new forms (from ironically subversive emoticon "speech" to the elaborate construction of discursive space in a MOO to the relatively straightforward e-mail or discussion board post).

These early dreams of radical equality, however, were quickly problematized by the frequently contentious, sometimes hostile, and always unpredictable discourse practices we have come to expect from students interacting in MOOs, discussion boards, chatrooms, and on e-mail lists. We all had to navigate the kinds of "outbursts" of verbal violence among students that Lester Faigley (1992) described in "The Achieved Utopia of the Networked Classroom." Despite the common occurrence of such outbursts in transcripts of MOO conversations among students in my NWE classes at the University of Florida between 1995 and 1997, I failed to understand these outbursts as instances of epistemic violence—instances of rhetorical violence to personhood and subjectivity, such as racist, sexist, and homophobic insults. Especially when such insults were rebutted by members of the identity groups attacked, I could explain the *exchange* as productive: I saw the articulation of a position derogatory to an identity group as afford-

---

[3]Established in 1994 with a "$992,000 hardware grant from the IBM Corporation," The University of Florida's Networked Writing Environment represents one of this country's first large-scale efforts to pioneer teaching with Internet technologies and "remains one of the largest computerized writing environments in the world" (http://web.nwe.ufl.edu/writing).

ing the opportunity to contest, challenge, and potentially revise the derogatory position.

Although I still maintain the importance of oppositional discourse and the value of pedagogies that enable students and teachers to confront and negotiate the multiple and conflicting identities and relations of power defining us, I have come to believe that a laissez-faire attitude toward students' rhetoric in our courses' online communications does far more harm to students than good. In much of the work addressing the hostility and verbal violence that can erupt in electronic discussions, teachers' analyses of "what goes wrong" involve rendering our own struggles with issues of power, authority, and control in the classroom. In the same gesture in which we recognize that these discussions can get "out of hand," we recuperate "out of hand" as the inevitable, even necessary, agonistic experience of entering the contact zone and engaging difference. From this perspective, we have understood electronic eruptions as students' appropriation of power away from teachers. This is highly problematic: Figuring "out of control" only in terms of the student–teacher relation obscures the potentially oppressive exercise of power *between* students and acquiesces to rhetorically violent exchanges as appropriate ways to relate to each other and in the world. This allows us to gloss the epistemic violence that some discussions, sometimes, with some groups of participants, can entail. Without naming "out of hand" as epistemic violence, we get away with paying surprisingly little attention to the potential effects of these exchanges on students in our classes.

We must rethink the "equalizing" power of the Internet and digital technologies to account for the "electronic contact zones" created when reading, writing, and teaching online. Understanding electronic discourse as spaces of struggle and contest over meanings can help us with this. Whether we are teaching a completely online distance-education course or working face to face with students in networked writing environments, we need to develop what Pratt (2002) called the "arts of the contact zone," including methods for establishing "ground rules for communication across lines of difference and hierarchy that go beyond politeness but maintain mutual respect" (p. 618). To "establish ground rules" does *not* require teachers' oppressive imposition of power over students or a notion of "discourse community" as nonconflictual or consensual. Rather our ground rules can foreground a politics of "co-presence and interaction" as well as highlight the "asymmetrical relations of power" in which we come together and the means by which "subjects are constituted in and by their relations to each other" (Pratt, 1992, p. 7).

RHETORICAL VIOLENCE

Early visions of the electronic classroom as an equalizing space that could erase the power differentials of race, gender, class, and physical appearance lulled us into hoping that our students would be universally empowered when we went online. Yet students do not, in fact, enter our online classes as equal players on an equal playing field. Students enter online classes with varying degrees of sociocultural power (technological literacies, access, linguistic competency in the dominant language, etc.), and their online conversations frequently chart struggles among them to establish the dominance of their particular social/subject position. Drawing on sociolinguist Pierre Bourdieu's (1991) analysis in *Language and Symbolic Power* of the economy of practice in social fields, I understand students' struggles to establish dominance in terms of a competition for cultural capital. Within the social field of the online classroom, students are at one level competing for the cultural capital structured by the class (a grade, linguistic proficiency, to stand out to the teacher, etc.). Yet, as a social field, online exchanges mimic other and different social fields of which students are a part. For example, the discussion lists and bulletin boards we ask students to use mimic virtual social spaces, such as the Internet chatrooms in which many students "hang out." Similarly, the demand to informally "discuss" a topic unconstrained by the voice and presence of a teacher mimics the social spaces in which college students come together informally to talk (such as residence halls, bars, social events), as well as the traditional classroom in which they are accustomed to discussing assignments. Each of these other spaces structures a field of interaction and a value system according to which specific behaviors are rewarded and valued. Each is governed by an economic logic according to which those who have more of what is valued in that particular field have greater power than those who have less.

We have yet to adequately theorize the ways in which virtual classrooms mimic multiple social spaces with different economic logics. This mimicry, which conflates spaces with competing systems of valuation, inevitably poses structural difficulties for both teachers and students. For example, vulgar insults are valued in Internet chatrooms as a form of verbal jousting, and exaggerated performances of gender are valued in the residence halls, at athletic events, and in bars, yet neither of these performances are particularly valued in traditional classroom spaces. Our virtual classroom spaces conflate these competing social fields and invoke the contradictory habits, behaviors, and strategies for interacting conditioned

116   *Amy*

by them. Indeed as contact zone theory shows us, much of the struggle that occurs among participants in a class is the struggle between students from different and competing social fields to establish the value of the economic logic of the social spaces in which they are primarily staked.

From this perspective, we can understand students' struggles for dominance in online classrooms in terms of the struggle to establish the symbolic value of one social field over another. Given the conflation of competing social fields, it is hardly surprising that much of this struggle for dominance manifests in rhetorically violent ways. Jacqueline Lambiase's (2001) analysis of online communications as rhetorical situations maps some of the most common rhetorical strategies for gaining dominance, including posting "inflammatory messages," "'misunderstanding' previous discussions in order to appropriate them for one's own agenda, . . . and overloading the group with multiple postings on one topic" (p. 112). Although many instructors are aware that these common rhetorical strategies are methods of gaining dominance, we frequently overlook the linguistic violence inherent in these strategies (including the ways in which such strategies alienate and silence some students) and disregard their potentially harmful effects on students and our learning environments. In short, we and our students are frequently witness to and participatory in violences that are "enacted through enunciatory and discursive practices, or else in the interstices of language, in traumatic and enforced silence" (Hanssen, 2000, p. 174). To fail to analyze these linguistic violences common to Internet discourse and electronic exchanges is to "normalize these ways of communicating" and hence to "accept exclusion and conformity" (Lambiase, 2001, p. 123).

Before looking at some of the more obvious instances of rhetorical violence with which analyses of online pedagogy have struggled, I would like to unpack one instance of a conceptual paradigm that can support epistemic violence in even the most careful, conscientious online pedagogy. Webster Newbold, a lucid advocate of online teaching and proponent of transactional theories of writing, invited students to evaluate their online exchanges in his spring 1997 online freshman composition class. One student commented that, although she "felt really comfortable with several people in the class," others "seemed to take offense at honest comments" (Newbold, 1999). In response, Newbold (1999) explained: "Having been involved in conferencing for about 10 years now, I've noticed that it's easy for people who are inclined to be irritated with others to BE IRRITATED [sic] with others in electronic discussions." Instead of engaging this student and her comment further, Newbold glossed it. In contrast, a careful critical analysis of this comment would ask: What does "to take offense" mean?

Who is offended? At what? What are the ways in which different participants hold different degrees of power and how is the power differential related to the "offense" that some students take?

This dismissal of what it means to be offended as a character flaw, and hence the fault of the offended party, is also apparent in Newbold's analysis of the barriers to student learning in online environments. Newbold (1999) argued that:

> Novices may have trouble avoiding the pitfalls of terseness or skewed implications in their comments on others' work, while experts are usually comfortable exchanging thoughts and feelings with peers. And as in traditional settings, the general maturity level of students is the main determiner of their peer interactions. With the less mature students who are unsure of both their technical expertise and writerly status, gaps of silence are common where we think there should be useful peer interchange. (online)

This quick dismissal of offended students ignores the possibility that some of the problems with students' online exchanges may be related to the ways in which these exchanges replicate the sociocultural inequalities and tensions that students bring with them to the online classroom. In Newbold's analysis, students who are offended in the electronic interchange are "inclined to be irritable," and/or they are immature novices. This explanation implicitly rules out the possibility that an online communication could *be* offensive: Rhetorically, the problem is with the offended student, not with a potentially offensive transaction. Hence, a personality characteristic (irritability, immaturity, insecurity) is to blame for problem exchanges, not the language, dynamic, content, or culture out of which the offense emerges. In each case, the experience of the offended or nonparticipatory student is glossed as *her fault*.

Attributing being "offended," silence, and nonparticipation to irritable, immature, and insecure students too easily allows us to overlook the complicated and unequal power and identity positions from which students enter into online exchanges. Academia's steady move toward teaching in online environments demands that we confront these issues of inequality and develop ethical methods for facilitating students' negotiations in the electronic contact zones of their online classes. If we want to create effective online learning environments for *all of our students*, we can no longer afford to gloss the ways in which our online classes mirror the cultural "differences and asymmetries created by an unequal distribution of power" in our society (Hanssen, 2000, p. 175).

118   *Amy*

Even in our discussions of those things we acknowledge as rhetorical violence—racist and hate speech, homophobic insults, profane name-calling—we have hesitated to directly intervene in students' exchanges. Admirably, many of us have been trying to create electronic communication spaces as sites of "healthy conflict" (Craig, Harris, & Smith, 1998, p. 131), in which honest communication "may reveal the differences that we frequently ignore" and thereby "educate one another in active, engaged discussion" (Craig et al., 1998, p. 124). Yet we too frequently take a hands-off approach to students' communication, abdicating our responsibility to structure and guide effective exchanges. In "Rhetoric of the Contact Zone: Composition on the Front Lines," Craig, Harris, and Smith (1998) went so far as to argue that "teachers can inhibit genuine debate and honesty" and that, in fact, students involved in hostile exchanges can nevertheless forge a productive bond "founded on [their] hostile reaction[s] to the hegemonic authority of teachers and their politically correct ideas" (p. 142). Although it is true that "community identity is often formed by identifying some group as hated" (Roberts-Miller, 2003, p. 552), this is at best a shaky and at worst a destructive community-forming strategy, and certainly not one I want to encourage in my classes. The creation of a hated out-group and the multiple violences that ensue from uncritical us–them polarizations destroy the possibility of copresence and mutual respect and are not effective "arts" of the contact zone (Pratt, 2002).

Although many instructors would find it difficult to value us–them polarizations as productive, healthy conflict, even the most conscientious of us has struggled with how to respond to blatant verbal violence in students' online communications. Lester Faigley (1992), in one of the earliest analyses of rhetorical violence in electronic communications spaces, struggled with how to interpret and respond to an overtly hostile exchange between students who met both face to face and online. The exchange was characterized by a high degree of gender warfare and permeated with "insults" and "homophobic accusations" (p. 197). Faigley explained the rhetorical violence of this exchange as, in part, an extension of the classroom dynamic, where he wondered whether one participant is "paying back" fraternity members for previous insults or if students who were unhappy with their midterm grades were writing him out of the conversation. He ended by deciding that the pseudonyms participants chose (such as butthead and arm pit) suggest that students entered the conversation with the "intention to fight," and he understood the violence of this exchange as, at least in part, students claiming and using classroom space "for their own purposes" (1992, p. 197).

Rhetorical Violence and the Problematics of Power   *119*

Although Faigley (1992) acknowledged that participants in the rhetorical violence of electronic exchanges can all too easily distance themselves from any responsibility for "racist, sexist, and homophobic slurs" (p. 198), he went on to wonder whether exchanges such as the one he critiqued do not support "Lyotard's assertion that agonistics is the inevitable condition of contemporary life and that the best we can do is to allow everyone to speak" (p. 199). Although he insisted that we cannot draw "any easy conclusions about the politics of pedagogy arising from electronic discussions" (p. 199), the move to understand the rhetorical violence that exploded in his class as the inevitable condition of agonistic inquiry unnecessarily equates the "struggle" and "conflict" characteristic of the clash of cultures in the contact zone (Pratt, 1992, p. 4) with abusive rhetoric. On the one hand, in "an agonistic, pluralistic democracy" that can "only aspire towards a 'conflictual consensus'" there will inevitably always be "dissensus on the interpretation of its constitutive principles" (Hanssen, 2000, p. 162).[4] Yet *dissensus* and *healthy conflict* are *not* the same as verbal violence or explosions of homophobic, racist, sexist, and hate speech.

"Dissensus" and "healthy conflict" *are* crucial arts of the contact zone, and we *do* need to structure spaces in which we engage one another in open, honest exchanges that engender "active, engaged discussion" capable of sustaining passionate disagreement through which we can "educate" one another (Craig et al., 1998, pp. 131, 124). Yet a productive discussion of our different experiences and positions *cannot* occur in an environment of violent communication that polarizes groups, entrenches participants in preconceived stereotypes, intimidates students out of the conversation, and shuts down any real possibility for exchange. Indeed such rhetorically violent exchanges work against the transformations that contact zone theory advocates. As Carstarphen and Lambiase's semester-long study of online student communication shows, violent exchanges typically follow a pattern in which "an initial situation occurs and harassment is initiated, next comes resistance to harassment and then escalation of harassment, after which the 'targeted participants drop out and/or targeted participants accommodate to dominant group norms'" (cited in Lambiase, 2001, p. 118).[5] In the conversations Lambiase (2001) tracked, "several flame wars included sexist and racist speech," and

---

[4]For her discussion of dissensus, Hanssen drew heavily on Mouffe's (1997) analysis of conflictual.

[5]Quoted sections from Lambiase (2001) drew heavily on a previous study by Carstarphen and Lambiase (1998).

120   *Amy*

students had vastly different perceptions of the discussion, depending on whether they felt comfortable with the topics discussed and with the tone of the discourse itself. Some students never participated in the discussion after the flame wars because, as one woman stated, "the environment was hostile . . . I don't need the negativity nor does anyone." (p. 130)

TOWARDS AN ANALYSIS OF POWER

Clearly, then, a thorough analysis of electronic contact zones has got to be able to account for the "many versions that silence or nonparticipation in democratic discourse can take" (Hanssen, 2000, p. 178). Up until now, many of us have been celebrating the possibilities for online environments to help us overcome the power politics of a teacher-dominant classroom. For instance, Rena Palloff and Keith Pratt (1999) argued that, by changing "the roles of students and faculty," online classes "facilitate more learner-centered personalized education" (p. 3). Like Palloff and Pratt, many of us have applauded online classes as empowering for students. From the empowering students point of view, students have the ability to control their own time and speak with more freedom than in traditional classrooms. Indeed Palloff and Pratt extended the freedom position so far as to argue that there "should be few rules" for online classes; in their discussion with teaching groups, the only real rules they proposed are about "norms, meaning how much and how often" students are required to contribute to online discussions (p. 36). Yet, as encounters with rhetorical and epistemic violence are showing us, we can no longer afford a laissez-faire attitude toward online class communications. We have got to think through "how to balance the democratic right to freedom of speech" with an equally necessary resistance to verbal and epistemic violence (most clearly denoted by hate speech)" (Hanssen, 2000, p. 178).

Although I understand that an aversion to rule setting stems from the laudable desire to create a space in which students are freed from the teacher's exercise of oppressive power over them, it is seldom the *teacher* who hostilely or oppressively engages with students in online discussions. The power-free zone argument too narrowly understands power as a unidirectional teacher-over-student relation and pays too little attention to the potential for embattled exchange to function as a participant's or group of participants' problematic exercise of power over other participants. Moreover, as Cooper (1999) argued, online discussions do not constitute a

Rhetorical Violence and the Problematics of Power   *121*

"giving or sharing of power with students" (p. 146). We are still structuring assignments, requiring and evaluating writing, and assigning grades. In short, as teachers we *cannot avoid* exercising power over our students. Moreover, the "actions that students take in electronic conversations—and the actions that teachers take in the resulting conversations—constitute relations of power" (Cooper, 1999, p. 146). After a lengthy analysis of the now infamous case of virtual rape at LambdaMOO, Cooper (1999) concluded that "the lesson that postmodern ethics suggests for writing teachers faced with what they see as inappropriate behavior in electronic conversations" is that they "should engage in electronic conversations in such a way as to enable students to take up the challenge to consciously consider and take responsibility for the effects their actions have on others" (p. 157).

To "consciously consider and take responsibility for the effects" of our actions on others requires a "more diversified reflection on how power is deployed concretely in various registers of language politics" (Hanssen, 2000, p. 177). From this perspective, our online pedagogy *should* ask students to analyze and take responsibility for their language: insults, name-calling, derogatory stereotyping, hate speech, and verbal threats are acts of linguistic violence that can have harmful effects on others, and our online pedagogy needs to confront this. As Kathleen Welch (1999) argued in *Electric Rhetoric: Classical Rhetoric, Oralism, and the New Literacy,* "our students need careful, intense instruction in the production of discourse as a way of negotiating unpredictable issues—such as judgment, passion, and sensibility—that confront human beings throughout life" (p. 70). Frequently, students come to our classes without having developed the capacity to critically reflect on their emotional responses or work through the feelings of defensiveness, anger, or shame that frequently arise from discussions of controversial issues. As teachers, then, it is our *job* to provide the "careful, intense instruction"—including guidelines and structures— that can enable students to enter the electronic contact zone of their online classes in ways that consciously work against eruptions of epistemic violence and toward a dialogic space of meaningful exchange.

Working against rhetorical/epistemic violence and toward meaningful exchange is especially difficult given that our virtual classrooms conflate genres and invoke competing logics. For example, the electronic discussion—whether conducted as a threaded bulletin board exchange, on a listserv, or interactively in MOO or chatroom spaces—is a standard component of any online communication. Yet the electronic discussion closely overlaps other social spaces, such as social Internet chatrooms, instant messaging, and personal e-mail exchanges with family and friends. Worse, our good intentions backfire when we frame online discussions as spaces

122   *Amy*

that liberate students to speak freely (in contrast to traditional classrooms, which may constrain students' speech). Although one of the primary arguments for online discussion is that students who would normally not speak can,[6] the desire for more equal student participation cannot change the fact that these "discussions" are *not* informal rap sessions with close friends: They are *writing assignments*, albeit informal ones, conducted in a *class* for a *grade*.

It is thus especially important that we articulate the competing economic logics and contradictory linguistic practices invoked by our synchronous and asynchronous assignments. Many instructors conceptualize MOO conversations, electronic bulletin board posts, e-mail, and instant messaging exercises as akin to traditional classroom genres such as group discussion, informal or prewriting, and journal writing. However, these assignments invoke a very different set of genres, with competing behaviors and practices, for our students. Even the demand that students "speak freely" contradictorily invokes, but is not the same as, social spaces such as recreational Internet chatrooms and candid discussions among identity-forming peer groups or families. Electronic discussions thus borrow from multiple genres, invoke competing linguistic practices, and frequently leave students unsure about the audience and purpose for their writing. From this

---

[6]As a cautionary note, we should remember that "studies on gendered interactions in cyberspace indicate that traditional gendered interactions are maintained and even magnified in cyberspace" and that traditional "gender relations persist even in virtual worlds" (Adam & Green, 1998, p. 96). As a number of postcolonial theorists have pointed out, despite our utopian vision that we "are all equal" in cyberspace and that online communications circumvent the reading/hearing of bodies, and hence voices in terms of gender, class, and race, we still confront hierarchical and power inequalities online in that language use—from spelling and grammar to vocabulary, including disciplinary language, dialect, native language and foreign language fluency, all race/class/embody and situate voices, and these embodiments are an important part of reading/hearing/responding to "voices" online. Not all posts are received equally! As Gillian Youngs (1999) argued in "Virtual Voices: Real Lives," those who argue that online communications level the playing field for participants and that those traditionally silenced can speak often overlook the fact that for the traditionally silenced to be *heard* they must speak in the language of the dominant discourse culture; they must masquerade. To masquerade—to be imaginable as another kind of body—one must own the discourse practices of the body to be imagined. For an especially illuminating discussion of the ways in which global feminist discussions have encountered the boundary-crossing stakes of power and hierarchy in electronic communications, see Lourdes Arizpe (1999).

perspective, we can see electronic discussions *as writing assignments* that fail, in large part, because they do not follow the same discourse conventions as any of the genres from which they borrow.

We see these confusions played out in sometimes violent and destructive ways. Many of our students may well bring assumptions of "appropriate behavior" to their online activities that, within the discourse community of the classroom, are not only inappropriate but counter-productive, even downright *destructive*. (Here I am thinking, clearly, of flaming.) Some of our students will be experienced with Internet chatrooms, whereas some will not; some of them will come from discourse communities that interpret verbal attacks in positive ways, whereas some will not; all of them will have identity and political alignments that lead them to interpret words in different ways. Indeed we should *assume* that the range of worldviews our students bring with them will engender conflict, and one of our primary jobs is to forge communities of discourse based on meaningfully and productively engaging this conflict.

Moving students into an online environment does not magically resolve students' difficulties navigating the rhetorical situation of the classroom. Quite the contrary, the mixed genres and overlapping discourse conventions of online discussions that are, in fact, *writing* assignments can further confuse students and contribute to the incidences of rhetorical and epistemic violence. As Patricia Bizzell (1992) reminded us, "language-using in social contexts is connected not only to the immediate situation but to the larger society, too, in the form of conventions for construing reality" (p. 87). Thus, "finding words is always a matter of aligning oneself with a particular discourse community" (Bizzell, 1992, p. 88), which is also "an interpretive community . . . whose language-using habits are part of a larger pattern of regular interaction with the material world" (p. 88). However, a random grouping of students engaged in electronic discussion for a required class cannot be easily constituted into "an interpretative" community with shared discourses and practices. On what basis, and from what frames of reference, can we expect our students to engage in the "*interpretive* activities" (Bizzell, 1992, p. 222) of electronic discussions?

POLICIES AND PRACTICES

If we want our online classes to be effective and liberatory experiences for students, we must acknowledge that "out of hand" *can* be destructive—that

124   *Amy*

the verbal fighting electronic discussions sometimes entail cannot simply be glossed as the necessary friction of the contact zone. We can no longer avoid entering into the *relation* that dialogic exchange requires out of our fear of reinscribing the power relations of a traditional classroom. To structure our virtual classroom spaces as communities of discourse that work against rhetorical and epistemic violence is not to sidestep controversial issues or painful discussions. As Pratt (2002) argued, the nature of the contact zone puts "ideas and identities on the line" (p. 617). Seriously grappling with radical differences in experience, values, and worldviews inevitably engenders moments of "rage, incomprehension, and pain" (p. 617). At the same time, it is only through the sustained confrontation with these differences and the emotions they invoke that we can reach the "exhilarating moments of wonder and revelation, mutual understanding, and new wisdom" that are part of the "joys of the contact zone" (pp. 617–618). The point of communication guidelines is not to prevent students (or ourselves) from feeling discomfort or being unsettled. The point is to make clear at the outset that we will all experience these things and to agree on strategies for meeting our emotional responses without attacking others.

Although I do not pretend to have evolved a definitive set of practices that can, in one semester, turn a random group of students into a discourse community seamlessly able to navigate the conflictual emotional currents engendered in electronic contact zones, I have developed a general framework for guiding our work. Over the last 5 years, teaching freshman through advanced composition in combinations of computerized classrooms and online environments, I have evolved the following general principles for electronic communications.

1. *Establish Ground Rules*
   The single most effective thing I have done with students in virtual classroom spaces is to say up front that I *want* them to confront controversial issues, that these confrontations will inevitably produce heated emotions, and that part of the work of the course is to find ways to negotiate our emotion and seriously engage with our classmates *without* insulting each other, using derogatory names, intimating violence, or expressing hatred for any individual or group of people. Far from being an exercise of oppressive power over my students, I see my clear articulation of the basic respect that I think is important to our interaction as part of the "careful, intense instruction in the production of discourse" for which Welch argues.

2. *Confront Power Issues*

   Especially if we do not want to use our power oppressively, we must self-reflectively analyze what kinds of power we are using and how we are using it. As a teacher, I exercise significant power over my students before they ever enroll in my classes: I choose the range of communication tools they will use, the texts they will read, and the assignments they will complete. Owning up to the kinds of power I am exercising and the ways in which I am using it allows me to ask students to think about the various ways in which they have and exercise power as well as the ways in which power is exercised over them. Confronting the different positions of power/powerlessness we occupy in different social spaces can help students think more deeply about the kinds of power their words can have, including the power to harm and the power to inspire, build, and transform.

3. *Self-Consciously Define Class as Discursive Space Working Toward "Community"*

   Although I am empathetic to the reluctance to impose controls and dictate what is "acceptable" speech, I have found exchanges between students to be far more productive and marred by far fewer episodes of rhetorical and epistemic violence when classes begin by formulating communication guidelines. In their reading and writing, my students confront sociocultural issues of power, identity, and inequality, and these are the kinds of controversial topics that frequently devolve into embattled encounters and which polarize, divide, and further entrench participants into unproductive and often destructive us–them identity constructions. Effectively engaging with such controversial issues demands that we understand our "agonistic inquiry" as "an activity that is a social process of negotiating . . . conflicts of position and power—conflicts in which students can discern that something is at stake" and that "someone is affected" by their words (Lynch et al., 1997, p. 66).

In all of my classes, I begin the semester by outlining my basic guidelines for confronting heated emotion while remembering that "someone is affected" by our words. My basic guidelines are simple: Do not insult each other, use derogatory names, intimate violence, or express hatred for

126   *Amy*

any individual or group of people. In the years that I have been experimenting with different methods for doing this, I have *never* had a student object to these straightforward rules. In fact at the beginning of the semester, before heated emotions arise, the injunction "don't call each other derogatory names" seems not only imminently reasonable, but rather obvious.

Once I define some of the rules of engagement important to me, each class then discusses and decides on their specific communication guidelines. This is a crucial community-building exercise. First, when the class is charged with defining the terms of their interactions, they have to name what they do and do not want in their relation. Besides allowing the class to define its own ethos, this public discussion inevitably gives both me and my students a more sophisticated understanding of our online audience. Second, these articulations define our online interaction as a genre of *writing* and spell out the expectations of the genre. With these definitions, students can enter online discussions with a greater sense of their purpose in the writing and with strategies for avoiding polarizations and working against tendencies to entrench in reactionary positions.

Although different classes evolve slightly different variations of communication guidelines, most of them agree on a basic set of additional practices:

- Allow a 24-hour distancing/reflecting period before responding in public to a discussion that evokes high emotion;
- Write in "I" statements, not "you" statements; and
- Imagine how somebody with a different position would feel reading your post.

Interestingly, I frequently ask leading questions to elicit students' ground rules (the "write in 'I' statements" guideline almost always originates as a suggestion from me, although students are free to reject this as a guideline), yet the rest of the guidelines almost always originate with students. In fact the first time I ever did this exercise with a class, a student immediately proffered the elegant and necessary, "Imagine how somebody else would feel" guideline (which had never occurred to me). Occasionally, a class will ask for a shorter or longer waiting period before responding in public to a heated exchange, or it will ask that students have a third party read a response before it is posted in a public forum. Perhaps I have been lucky, but so far none of my classes has simply rejected this exercise outright.

SELF-REFLECTION AND COMPOSING

In conjunction with our public discussion of how we want to communicate with each other, I ask students to undertake a private inventory: read through the syllabus, identify readings that provoke emotion, and anticipate hot spots. Our readings, which confront racism, sexism, homophobia, class inequality, nationalism, and war, inevitably hit students' emotional triggers. *Some* students *do* enter our classes hating members of different races, believing that members of different religions will burn in hell, convinced that homosexuality is a sin and that women were made to serve men. Hence, self-reflexively reflecting on our triggers is an important part of thinking through how to engage with controversial and emotional issues. I invite students to e-mail me privately with their reflections; when students anticipate difficulty with some of our topics, I offer to correspond privately with them to address their needs.

Various forms of private writing are crucial to the public discourse of the class. Personal free writes, private e-mails to me, and private e-mails or chats with friends outside of class or classmates with whom students are forming relationships—all of these can be effective tools for working through the emotion that can be triggered by our public discussions. Discussions that challenge our most deeply held beliefs inevitably feel like attacks on our identity structures, and one of the critical functions that private, self-reflective writing serves is to identify the identity stakes underlying intense emotional responses. Thus, I ask students to engage in self-reflective reading and writing practices that couple the question "what do I think?" with the questions "why do I think this?" and "what emotion evolves from this thinking?" This writing can serve as a site for asking ourselves how and why we have come to think/feel as we do, for confronting the radically different ways that others have come to think/feel as they do (Spigelman, 2001, p. 173 note), and for "reflecting on and revising [our] sense of self, [our] relations with others, and the conditions of [our] lives" (Lu, 1999, p. 173).

In addition, the private writing students do serves the double function of prewriting. In their private writing, students are not required to be conscious of or responsible for the potentially violent effects of their words on their audience. Private writing affords students a safe place to unpack their emotional responses, to consider and analyze them. As Ratcliffe (1999) argued, "we may not always choose or control the discourses that socialize us; neither may we choose or control our unconscious responses to them.

128   *Amy*

But once we consciously articulate our socializations and choose to respond to them, we become responsible for our words, our attitudes, and our actions" (pp. 207–208). Thus, private writing can provide the critical distance necessary to formulate a public articulation.

Because the coursework triggers emotional responses and hot spots, we all invariably find that observing the guidelines for communicating on which the class has agreed is not as easy as it sounded like it would be in the beginning of the semester. Many of my students have not previously been asked to simultaneously expose themselves to strong, initially negative, emotion and to write/act on that emotion in a way that conscientiously redirects angry, attacking impulses into socially responsible public rhetoric. Practicing the strategies for this kind of public discourse *is* a lot of work, both for students and myself. For my part, I am often tasked with reading students' private writing about strong emotional responses and helping them shape from it a public articulation that both tells their truth and respects others with different positions. This balance between honesty and respect is extremely difficult to maintain and requires each of us to address our adversarial emotions. When working with individual students to shape writing for our public sphere, I have found it helpful to have them respond to this set of questions:

- What specific statements, and by whom, triggered what emotion?
- What past context can you connect your emotional responses to?
- What reactions does the response elicit?
- What belief structures underlie your emotional response and your instinctive reactions?

The very things that make this labor difficult, however, yield the rewards that keep me teaching. The biggest rewards I have ever had as a teacher have come from confronting strong emotion honestly and staying with the emotion until it resolves itself into something I could not previously have imagined. I attribute these moments of meaning-making in no small measure to the fact that my students and I shape public discourse that links what we think to our lived experience. Pratt's (2002) sketch of the pedagogical arts necessary to the contact zone guide us in this effort. Among other things, Pratt cautioned that we need to develop ways for "people to engage with suppressed aspects of history (including their own histories)," ways to "move *into and out of* rhetorics of authenticity," and a

Rhetorical Violence and the Problematics of Power 129

"systematic approach to the all-important concept of cultural mediation" (p. 618).

In the best spirit of the contact zone, then, our public discourse is more concerned with *reflecting on* what we think/feel than with simply stating positions in closed terms. In the course of gaining critical distance on ourselves and our responses, we ask things like: What kinds of relationships did we see growing up? How did our parents, neighbors, church officials, and friends speak, both verbally and nonverbally, about the issues at stake? Rather than divert any real dialogue or potential growth into the verbal violence into which controversial discussions frequently devolve, I ask my students to find ways to use personal articulations to understand our own lives and thinking as "cultural, learned, [and] value-ridden" without falling into the trap of "reinscribing stereotypes and prejudices instead of challenging them" (Mutnick, 1998, p. 84). Posing these kinds of questions is far more than a simple psychologizing of emotion. Personal articulations are a way to "illuminate the self as a socio-historical subject" (Mahala & Swilky; cited in Mutnick, 1998, p. 84) and can help us make "connections between theory and practice, knowledge and experience, as we learn to participate more fully in diverse social discourses as speakers *and* listeners, as writers *and* readers" (Mutnick, 1998, p. 84). As Mutnick argued, self-reflexive writing

> encourages a theorization of experience—both of everyday life and acts of witnessing, observing, reading. . . . A bifocal perspective on writing as social act stresses a rhetorical dimension in which we situate ourselves as writers in relation to reader, texts, and context, and a phenomenological dimension in which we transmute perceptions into words. (p. 85)

A CLOSING REFLECTION

Welch (1999) reminded us that the early classical rhetoric of the sophists understood language as power out in the world and language as activity. Nancy (1991) urged us to enter into community as communication, to write as a means of "consciously undergoing the experience of" our sharing (p. 41). Our online writing pedagogy can be a means of rising to Welch's and Nancy's challenges: By conscientiously articulating the parameters of our relation, by guiding students through analyses of language and power, and by consistently linking our analyses of language and power to analyses of the larger worlds we inhabit, we can help our students understand their language use as an activity with consequences in the world and themselves as language users with civic responsibilities. If we fail to do this—if we fail to clearly articulate the audience and purpose of the writing in which they are to engage and the ways in which this writing is both similar to and different than the speaking of traditional classrooms and the social electronic-communications spaces with which they are familiar, then we send them into a language fray. The language-using habits to which we expose students in our classes will, to greater or lesser extents, become part of the language-using habits that they reproduce in the worlds they inhabit when they leave our classes. If we structure the electronic communication spaces of our online classrooms as places in which we explore language as power and as an activity with civic responsibilities and consequences, then we just may be able to show each other how to transcend our own limits instead of bludgeoning down others by imposing our limits on them.

REFERENCES

Adam, Alison & Green, Eileen. (1998). Gender, agency, location and the new information society. In Brian D. Loader (Ed.), *Cyberspace divide: Equality, agency and policy in the information society* (pp. 83-97). New York: Routledge.

Arizpe, Lourdes. (1999). Freedom to create: Women's agenda for cyberspace. In Wendy Harcourt (Ed.), *Women@internet: Creating new cultures in cyberspace* (pp. x–xxi). London; New York: Zed Books.

Bizzell, Patricia. (1992). *Academic discourse and critical consciousness*. Pittsburgh; London: University of Pittsburgh Press.

Bourdieu, Pierre. (1991). In John B. Thompson (Ed.) & Gino Raymond & Matthew Adamson (Trans.), *Language and symbolic power*. Cambridge: Harvard University Press.

Carstarphen, Meta G., & Lambiase, Jacqueline Johnson. (1998). Domination and democracy in cyberspace: Reports from the majority media and ethnic/gender margins. In Bosah Ebo (Ed.), *Cyberghetto or cybertopia? Race, class, and gender on the internet* (pp. 121–136). Westport, CT: Praeger.

Cooper, Marilyn. (1999). Postmodern possibilities in electronic conversations. In Gail E. Hawisher & Cynthia L. Selfe (Eds.), *Passions, pedagogies, and 21st century technologies* (pp. 140-162). Logan: Utah State University Press.

Craig, Terry, Harris, Leslie, & Smith, Richard. (1998). Rhetoric of the "Contact Zone": Composition on the front lines. In Todd Taylor & Irene Ward (Eds.),

Literacy theory in the age of the internet (pp. 122-145). New York: Columbia University Press.

Faigley, Lester. (1992). *Fragments of rationality: Postmodernity and the subject of composition.* Pittsburgh; London: University of Pittsburgh Press.

Fitts, Karen & France, Alan W. (Eds.). (1995). *Left margins: Cultural studies and composition pedagogy.* Albany: State University of New York Press.

Graff, Gerald. (1992). *Beyond the culture wars: How teaching the conflicts can revitalize American education.* New York; London: Norton.

Hanssen, Beatrice. (2000). *Critique of violence: Between poststructuralism and critical theory.* London; New York: Routledge.

Jay, Gregory. (1994). Knowledge, power, and the struggle for representation. *College English, 56*(1), 9-29.

Lambiase, Jacqueline J. (2001). Like a cyborg cassandra: The Oklahoma City bombing and the internet's misbegotten rhetorical situation. In Laura Gray-Rosendale & Sibylle Gruber (Eds.), *Alternative rhetorics: Challenges to the rhetorical tradition* (pp. 111–126). Albany: State University of New York Press.

Lu, Min-Zhan. (1999). Redefining the literate self: The politics of critical affirmation. *College Composition and Communication, 51*(2), 172–194.

Lynch, Dennis A., George, Diana, & Cooper, Marilyn M. (1997). Moments of argument: Agonistic inquiry and confrontational cooperation. *College Composition and Communication, 48*(1), 61–86.

Mouffe, Chantal. (1997). Decision, deliberation, and democratic ethos. *Philosophy Today, 41*(1), 27.

Mutnick, Deborah. (1998). Rethinking the personal narrative: Life-writing and composition pedagogy. In Christine Farris & Chris M. Anson (Eds.), *Under construction: Working at the intersections of composition theory, research, and practice* (pp. 79-92). Logan: Utah State University Press.

Nancy, Jean-Luc. (1991). In Peter Connor (Ed.) & Peter Connor, Lisa Garbus, Michael Holland, & Simona Sawhney (Trans.), *The inoperative community.* Minneapolis: University of Minnesota Press.

Newbold, Webster. (1999). Teaching on the internet: Transactional writing instruction on the world wide web. *Kairos, 4*(1). Retrieved February 2, 2004, from http://english.ttu.edu/kairos/4.1/features/newbold.

Palloff, Rena M. & Pratt, Keith. (1999). *Building learning communities in cyberspace: Effective strategies for the online classroom.* San Francisco: Jossey-Bass.

Pratt, Mary Louise. (1992). *Imperial eyes: Travel writing and transculturation.* London; New York: Routledge.

Pratt, Mary Louise. (2002). Arts of the contact zone. In David Bartholomae & Anthony Petroksky (Eds.), *Ways of reading* (6th ed., pp. 604–619). New York: Bedford/St. Martin's.

Ratcliffe, Krista. (1999). Rhetorical listening: A trope for interpretative intervention and a "code of cross-cultural conduct." *College Composition and Communication, 51*(2), 195-224.

Roberts-Miller, Trish. (2003). Discursive conflict in communities and classrooms. *College Composition and Communication, 54*(4), 536-557.

Selfe, Cynthia. (1999). *Technology and literacy in the twenty-first century: The importance of paying attention (studies in writing and rhetoric)*. Carbondale: Southern Illinois University Press.

Spigelman, Candace. (2001). Argument and evidence in the case of the personal. *College English, 64*(1), 63–87.

Welch, Kathleen. (1999). *Electric rhetoric: Classical rhetoric, oralism, and the new literacy*. Cambridge, MA: MIT Press.

Van Slyck, Phyllis. (1997). Repositioning ourselves in the contact zone. *College English, 59*(2), 149-170.

Youngs, Gillian. (1999). Virtual voices: Real lives. In Wendy Harcourt (Ed.), *Women@Internet: Creating new cultures in cyberspace* (pp. 55-68). London; New York: Zed Books.

7

CRITICAL AND MULTICULTURAL

PEDAGOGY GOES ONLINE

Lesliee Antonette

The work of constructivist theorists, like James Berlin in the field of Composition and Rhetoric, began a shift away from a current traditional understanding of a classroom as a group of like-minded students who patiently await instruction from an all-knowing professor. This shift allowed for the development of an understanding of Difference as that which may not be necessarily marked by physical characteristics, but may, more accurately, be concerned with relationships between individuals who possess a number of cultural and personal characteristics, habits, and abilities.[1] This shift allowed educators who practice a multicultural pedagogy that has largely depended upon the representation of ethnic or racial difference to begin a shift away from a reliance on those conservative practices to a more critical enunciation of Difference itself (Antonette, 2004).

---

[1] In the 1980s, the recognition of race as a biological myth, which remains a powerful marker of cultural difference, and the realization that students in any given classroom actually display a mind-boggling number of differences, both marked and unmarked, have led to the development of a series of educational theories that address the need for understanding student differences in ways that move us away from a reliance on race. One among them is critical multiculturalism.

Understanding Difference as a social construction has allowed for the development of strategies that decenter the physical class space to empower students to act on their differences, and thereby bring a level of critical engagement, agency, and self-efficacy into the physical class space. A pedagogy that begins with the understanding that Difference is "essentially a politically constructed category which has no guarantees in nature" allows a student to recognize that "we all speak from a particular place out of a particular history" (Hall, 1995, p. 227). This shift is significant because it allows the teacher's voice to become one of many. In a physical class space, this message may be presented pedagogically, but is often undermined by the visual cues of that kind of space. The chairs are organized into rows all pointing toward the one direction from which comes knowledge, the teacher, positioned at the front of the room, usually next to the door, marking who enters and exits. Movement in the physical classroom can be monitored even by the most collaborative and decentered teacher. In the physical class space, one has the option of opening up the space to a critical recognition of Difference and a renegotiation of the relationships in it. However, in the online class space, this is not optional. There are no visual cues, and even trying to perpetuate current traditional teaching and learning habits can become unsatisfying or complicated for both student and instructor, although current technology continues to mimic them.

The online classroom can become a space that can be "constructed . . . with and through difference, which is able to build those forms of solidarity and identification which make common struggle and resistance possible but without suppressing the real heterogeneity of interests and identities" (Hall, 1995, p. 225). This is critical in a space that requires representation. Online class members must present themselves to the class; there is no silent participation. This level of student agency seems to be something that online pedagogy, as represented by the software programs, has not yet learned how to fully employ because this form of collaborative learning cannot simply rely on traditional representation that allows for a certain level of student apathy. Hall (1995) stated that "representation is possible only because enunciation is always produced within codes which have a history, a position within the discursive formations of a particular space and time" (p. 226). Software that attempts to mimic the traditional physical class space seems to be an attempt to enunciate a current traditional representation of the learning experience. This disregard for the Difference between a physical class space and an electronic class space may, in part, explain University of Phoenix's current decision to offer both online and in classroom instruction. The enunciation of traditional class-

Critical and Multicultural: Pedagogy Goes Online   *135*

room representations may not be translating effectively into the electronic class space. It seems to be time to shift pedagogy to fit this new space.

Unlike the conservative or even most liberal multicultural pedagogies found in physical class spaces, a critical multicultural pedagogy assumes that every student in a classroom will exhibit a substantial number of differences that are cultural, social, economic, or, will be displayed in terms of learning abilities and approaches, from his or her classmate.[2] This pedagogical approach is based on the projected need to allow those differences to work to the benefit of not only the student, but also the group of students in a given classroom setting.

In their article, "Multicultural Education and Postmodernism: A Movement Toward Dialogue," Carl A. Grant and Judyth M. Sachs (1995) discussed the fact that, in discussions of multiculturalism, the idea that culture has more to do with race and ethnicity than it has to do with "normative characteristics of behavior, [or] group and individual lifestyles . . . reflects . . . our vested disciplinary interests in characterizing 'exotic otherness'" (p. 98). The reliance on race and ethnicity in discussions held under the auspices of American multiculturalism has led American educators to think in solipsistic ways about differences between and among American students. A critical multicultural pedagogy attempts to remedy this imbalance, and the online class space, a space within which there can be no reliance on physical markers of difference, like Race and ethnicity, or where visual cues cannot undermine attempts at shifting the center of power, can provide a starting place for a shift in pedagogy. This shift allows for the recognition that ethnicity and race are concepts that have historically served processes of marginalization, displacement, and dispossession, and that these are not strategies that will serve the educational systems of a global society (Hall, 1995).

One of the most important relationships inside a class space is the one between student and teacher. In a critical multicultural pedagogy, students learn to interact with the teacher as a voice of experience, yes, but not an

---

[2]The use of the word critical alludes to the work of the Frankfurt school. Some of the members include Max Horkheimer, Teodoro Adorno, Walter Benjamin, and Louis Althusser. These theorists took the economic theories of Karl Marx and translated them into cultural theories of art, literature, and political structures. There are three fundamental premises in the critical theory developed by the Frankfurt School: (a) theory must be translatable into practice, (b) practice must serve the end of producing an egalitarian state, and (c) the theorist must self-reflexively reconsider his or her own practice (Antonette, 1998, p. 40).

omnipotent being. When this shift occurs, students are then able to recognize the value in their own voices. This is a critical step for successful collaborative work. The difference between group work and collaborative work is that collaboration requires the respect and equal participation of all the voices (Antonette, 1998). This cannot happen in a class space that carries the subtextual message that only the teacher really knows the answer.

Some of the software and hardware developed for online instruction attempts to reproduce the illusion that the teacher is omnipresent and in control of the class space. Picturetel seems to replicate the panopticon of traditional teacher power. Cameras are placed in the "location" and set up to continually scan the room. Software such as Webct can provide students with immediate teacher feedback by programming certain canned responses to quiz and test data. This can also be used to simulate the act of looking over a student's shoulder. However, a study done by Mulligan and Geary (1999) suggested that electronic classrooms that depend on teacher-centered, current traditional teaching strategies such as these are, at most, only as effective online as they are in a physical classroom. The hope for the online classroom is that it will allow more students more access to education and that more students will be successful in higher education. This cannot happen if the success rate remains the same in the online class space as it is in the physical class space.

Critical methodologies are needed in the online class space because "online learning is active in nature and is not handed from one individual or source to another intact" (Mulligan & Geary, 1999, p. 2). A pedagogy that is based on the concept of Banking education (Freire, 1987), or the idea that knowledge can be transmitted from one person to another, Mulligan and Geary suggested, is not the most effective model to use in an online class space. A model that can allow students to exchange knowledge with the teachers, and between and among themselves, is a model that can allow for active/collaborative learning.

Susan Hardwicke (2000) wrote:

> Very few studies have been accomplished to date that examine the impact of collaborative teaching and learning on college and university students. Even fewer have examined this approach in a distance-education setting. Despite the plethora of distance learning projects now underway, very little is known, in fact, about the ways in which computer net-worked classes affect interaction among and between students and faculty. (p. 125)

Critical and Multicultural: Pedagogy Goes Online 137

This chapter hopes to contribute to what should be a developing body of work that provides models for shifting collaborative, decentered, critical multicultural teaching strategies into the online class space. My own shift—from being a critical multicultural educator in a traditional class space to teaching online—highlights the need for such work.

As a first-time online teacher, I brought to the electronic classroom my training in critical multicultural theory and teaching strategies that I had designed in a physical class space that encouraged student collaboration and a move toward a "teacher as facilitator" model. Difficulties that may arise from this shift in understanding the social relationships within the class space may be characterized by lack of self-efficacy. Students may have difficulty valuing the voices of other students; they may insist on a more individual relationship with the teacher. This can manifest itself in the use of e-mail to the professor rather than posting responses to a community space. It often comes in repeated statements about how confining the cyber space is for them. These issues, if not addressed, can sabotage the success of an online learning experience, as I learned.

Because there was no distance-education component in the school's Collective Bargaining contract at the time, I could not advertise my graduate course on "Approaches to Teaching Multicultural American Literature" as distance-education, and for this reason I lost three students on the first night. The reasons given were all the same. The students did not have access to the technology at home, and they did not want to learn how to gain access to the technology offered on campus. One man and four women, all of whom presented themselves as highly motivated and interested learners, remained in the course. All but two were classroom teachers at some level of K to12. All except one Hispanic-American female identified themselves as Western Euro-Americans and of middle-class economic status. This does not mean that the differences among them were insubstantial, as we learned. What we all seemed to share in common was that we all approached this new learning experience with a sense of trepidation. We learned, in the end, that only those who could tolerate a shift in the relationships that made up the class would complete the class.

Collaborative work results in a class space where the teacher is a facilitator who becomes one voice among many. Not all students are comfortable with this shift. The one male student in the class, Isaac, wrote,

> Man, this is hard to explain without just talking it (but I am enjoying this process, don't get me wrong). There is so much to say, but I feel like I've written too much already, and we all have plenty to read, so I

138 *Antonette*

> will conclude with, I wish we could meet to discuss the ideas and our
> reactions after reading these chapters. I feel like I'm talking to myself.
> I feel that a lot is lost in communication by online space. It would be
> very nice to be able to experience the whole communication picture
> that is missing i.e.: the spoken word accompanied with vocal intona-
> tion, facial expression, and body language.

Isaac's posting can serve to explain a lot of problems with current traditional teaching and learning practices, but what I would like to focus on is what
seems to be his typical expression of student alienation. He feels confined
by the space and ineffective in his communication. His sense of alienation
seems to stem from the idea that he needs to "see" the other members of
the class.

Much of Isaac's sense of alienation depended on his need for immediate evaluation of his statements. As he explained in a later posting, his own
teaching style heavily depended on modeling. He wrote that the "key to
reaching [students] is in the creativity of the delivery of the message." He
had no model in the chat space. I did not move quickly to offer him one. I
waited a full day to respond to his posting, and while I waited, another student, Consuela, responded to his posting.

Consuela was excited by the syllabus critique exercise, and she was
willing to fully participate in the collaborative class space.[3] She reassured
Isaac that he "[was] not just talking to [him]self on this board." However,
because Isaac saw himself as a teacher—as the transmitter of the message—he likewise believed that, as a student, he was to be the receiver of
the message. He was reluctant to receive Consuela's message because she
was not the teacher. Isaac did not finish the course.

Hardwick (2000) wrote:

> It has been well documented in numerous prior studies that computer
> networks are ideal vehicles for fostering collaborative learning tasks

---

[3] I begin to move away from the traditional teacher role as quickly as possible by
asking students to participate in a revision of the syllabus, which includes negotiating the distribution of grades. Traditionally, the teacher holds complete authority
over the ways in which the work produced in response to the course content is valued. Opening those practices up to student critique allows me to rethink course
material choices (but not necessarily change them) and the ways in which I value
student performance. It also places responsibility for success in the class squarely
on the students' shoulders. They choose it, they in effect design it, and they
become invested in making it work.

Critical and Multicultural: Pedagogy Goes Online 139

> and activities (see for example Davits, 1988; Din, 1991; Owen, 1993; Tinker, 1993). Because of the flexibility and non-linear nature of computer net-worked assignments, collaboration may also be enhanced among students in the same classroom or in students widely dispersed in remote classrooms. (p. 126)

The online class space is a wonderful, nonlinear space within which students can best utilize collaborative techniques. However, this cannot be done until the relationship that privileges the interaction between teacher and student shifts to a relationship that can privilege all of the voices in the class space. Isaac would not or could not do this. As it turns out, this shift was a difficult process for everyone, including the teacher.

My favorite teaching strategy, problem posing, is based on the work of Brazilian philosopher Paolo Freire and developed into classroom practice by Ira Shor (1987). It is not by definition a critical multicultural strategy, but it is a wonderful tool for allowing students to engage in a consideration of differences in relation to a specific topic or problem. In this strategy, the teacher takes a problem posed by a student and makes it the focal point of the class. The entire class works to resolve the problem in a way that is useful to the majority of the students. Isaac, as it turns out, had merely summarized a concern that all of the students had. They felt that they needed to "see" one another. This seems to be related to their need to "see" me. As I discovered, it forced me to consider my own need to "see" them.

After trying to answer a question posed by Consuela, I wrote: "Here we are in this new-fangled mode where my server keeps timing me out and I cannot use the looks on your faces to gauge whether or not you understand what I am saying [writing]." I was feeling just as confined and frustrated as Isaac had felt, and I finally understood what the students were experiencing. As a result, the class took some time off from the syllabus to discuss the problems and potential of online education, and a serious difference between students became apparent in that conversation.

Unlike the students who were feeling emotionally disengaged and alienated, Sabena had a software package that was not compatible with the software at school. As she discovered, the inconsistent provision of services at the school made it quite difficult for her to participate in the chat space discourse. She wrote: "This is becoming very inconvenient. Unfortunately my desktop publishing system at home is not compatible with the college's PC so I cannot transfer data from my disk. So I will type this again quickly." Because of this problem, she came to my office to ask about opting out of the online space discourse. I agreed and responded by writing: "Some of you are still having trouble with e-mail. Do not worry— we can use snail mail or just drop hard copy in my mailbox in the English department." Consuela responded:

> I apologize up front for being a pain in the ass, especially to you Sabena because frustration is a difficult thing to bear. I am asking, however, if it is possible, please continue to post as much as you can. I read everybody's responses and learn a little something from each of them. If only Lesliee gets to read them, then I feel a little cheated. I don't want to make your life hard. I am only asking that if it is not too much trouble for you, please continue to post. You have an audience of more than one.

Sabena responded:

> I agree with Consuela that it shortchanges the other students to not view what we all write. Thank you for the offer to assist me but I think that for the full impact of the course for all students I will continue to post. Bear with me while I work out all of the glitches.

This is collaborative work that engages Difference in ways that can only occur in class spaces that allow for it. Sabena had an out that I had officially given her. However, despite the fact that she was economically strapped, worked a full-time job, and had to work on two different machines all semester, Sabena found a way to stay with the class because her classmates let her know how important she was to the space. For Sabena, this meant extra hours at school, more time in the car, and fewer hours at home. She was getting none of the superficial benefits of online education. Yet the collaborative environment of the class space offered her some kind of a payoff.

Sabena exhibited economic differences from her classmates that, prior to the discussion, had appeared to me to be someone with a bad attitude. She often posted responses laced with sarcasm. I think we both believed that this was because she disagreed with my teaching methods. She wanted me to give her the information to study so she could repeat it on the test and be done with it. This is what she thought distance education was "supposed to do." We found out later that her attitude was, in part, resistance. However; it was also just being tired and stressed out because she did not have the economic stability that allowed her to participate in the course with the same level of comfort that she perceived the other students to have.

Critical and Multicultural: Pedagogy Goes Online   *141*

The negotiation between the two women in class demonstrates what I see as the function of a critical multiculturalism. In class I was working on modeling a means by which the dialogue surrounding a text or set of ideas could be opened up to allow students to take a proactive part in the dialogue and not simply wait for me to tell them what or how to think about the content. This is what the two women in the class did. They negotiated the problem *around* me, which, to my surprise, caused me a little bit of discomfort.

My own assumption was that both students would still have access to me—the traditional model for the student–teacher relationship would still be met. As Consuela points up, this is not enough in the collaborative classroom. I would like to think she learned that from me. However, the transcript shows that I did have some trouble shifting gears. To one of Consuela's postings, I responded:

> You asked a question as part of completing your assignment and I went on WAY TOO LONG giving you THE ANSWER. WHAT-I ASK YOU—Are we supposed to do, or think, or feel about this [teacher/student] relationship. It seems inevitable that we maintain and perpetuate it. OR, is it enough that we make it a topic of our conversation? Will change that values BOTH of our contributions to this conversation equally, result from the conversation itself?

It is amazing how long-long-windedness looks on the screen. I have deleted the majority of the address I presented and provide here just the tail end of my comments. When I go on like that in class, I rarely notice it. However, looking back at the screen and seeing my voice go on and on, I realized that even in this mode of communication I was attempting to become the voice of the space.

For a student to gain self-efficacy in the online class space, he or she must become comfortable as an active learner. This cannot happen in a space that does not allow the student to negotiate his or her relationship with the teacher *and* the other students. As I have written elsewhere, "[d]ecentering the authority in the classroom, *and* privileging multiple voices [allows us to] hear a dialogue in the classroom (Antonette, 1998, pp. 100–101). I had to catch myself taking up all the classroom space with long-winded responses to questions because it is "when the voices in the classroom become parts of a dialogue, [that] the privileged position of knowledge constantly shifts from one voice to another," and this is how students become empowered and active learners (p. 101). They begin to take own-

142   *Antonette*

ership of the space, and "one voice is the authority only until it is challenged by another voice. It is important that the teacher's voice is just one among the many (although this really is not easy to achieve, if it is at all possible, but the attempt is important and poignant)" (p. 101). This is not to say that there are not instances in which a long answer is required. Rather, it is to point out that I actually became aware of the possibility that there are instances in which a long answer really is not necessary.

There is no material way to decenter teacher power. As long as teachers give the final grades, they hold the ultimate power. However, there is a lot of space within which students can exercise power in both the physical and virtual class space if they are given the option. Michel Foucault (1984) said that, "Liberty is a practice" (p. 245). Power that comes from liberty cannot be given; it must be exchanged. Any educational experience that depends on the liberty of a student must allow that student to practice power through pedagogical instances of liberatory learning. Sometimes that means taking a short hiatus from what seems to be directly related to the course content. Sometimes that means allowing a space within which the student can negotiate that which she believes oppresses her. Sometimes that means letting students negotiate their own relationships with one another. At all times that means the teacher must be willing to move away from the center of the learning space.

Students bring differences into the classroom that we cannot see. The way they process information, the way they interact with information, and the way they approach their educations are all different in subtle and important ways. If distance education continues to grow into the future of higher education that it promises, practitioners must begin to self-reflexively design and develop pedagogy that addresses the different needs of all those students. There is no single model that will ever be able to do this. Even within the field of critical multiculturalism, there is a wide range of practices. However, the ability to approach the online classroom as a field of difference is an advantage that a critical multicultural pedagogy provides.

Because I was teaching a graduate course for teachers, about teaching, the detour we took was an invaluable experience, Although I thought I had set up a space in which the students could exercise power and privilege in their interaction with each other, I found that I had harbored the assumption that what was really important was that they had access to me.[4]

---

[4]A critical multicultural approach can work in a content-heavy area such as biology because the pedagogy "focuses its gaze on the classroom, and, within the parameters of that classroom, it focuses its gaze upon the relationships that exist within

Critical and Multicultural: Pedagogy Goes Online 143

Because I was willing to pose and explore this problem, they were able to take control of the discussion by sharing their knowledge of both technology and course content. This allowed them the space to ask for what they needed from one another and me to be successful in the course.

Everyone in this class learned that there are as many different ways to teach and learn as there are teachers and learners. We learned that an effective class space is less a product of uniformity and control and more a result of interaction and responsibility. A critical multicultural pedagogy is a model. Each teacher must necessarily take away from it what he or she is comfortable with and what he or she believes will benefit his or her own experience. However, the teacher must interrogate those pieces of the pedagogy he or she takes away and the ways in which he or she uses them (Antonette, 1999). Not every teacher in this class will use all of the tools my critical multicultural pedagogy offers. Those that use some of them will not use them in the same ways that I did. What matters is that we allow for the shift that online education seems poised to provide us and develop pedagogies using that space to embrace the idea that "we all speak from a particular place, out of a particular history, out of a particular experience, a particular culture"; in this way, the classroom becomes a place where all of those particularities are strengths and not obstacles (Hall, 1995, p. 227).

We ended the semester by reading my own book on critical multiculturalism, "The Rhetoric of Diversity." Chapter 4 is a description of the first class I taught using the critical multicultural pedagogy that I have developed. That course had to be listed with the University of California as an experiment with human subjects. The idea that shifting the exchange of power in a classroom is an experimental topic that requires the protection of its subjects is a statement about the current traditional model of education. The idea that students must be protected from learning how to generate their own thoughts and expressing their own opinions is an important idea to pay attention to because it is embedded in every software program currently offered for distance education. This imbrication suggests that there is a finite set of effective teaching and learning relationships. However, the online classroom seems to be a space wherein that finite set of practices can be extended.

Sabena ended the semester in a surprising way. She had resisted most of what we had read and discussed in terms of opening up class spaces for

---

that classroom" (p. 97). It is more a matter of rethinking the exercises by which students demonstrate comprehension in those content-heavy areas than it is a matter of shifting content.

144   *Antonette*

a more independent learning environment. After reading chapter 4 she wrote:

> The chapter accurately presented the struggle I have been experiencing from day one both from a teacher's and a student's perspective. From both views there is the move from the traditional to the critical that creates discomfort because of the unfamiliarity and the uncertainty change brings. To see the quirks of implementation played out in this chapter helps me to see that the problems are not all insurmountable. Student passivity appears to be a major obstacle. Students have been conditioned to take an inactive role in their education. They have been in the "feed me" mode from the moment they were first able to process information, expected to absorb what is being taught and regurgitate it back on command. This fact is what makes the critical transition so difficult for them. It is much easier to resort back to what is familiar than to keep trying to break the traditional mode of thought.

Sabena had resisted the idea of change. She did not want to change the way in which she interacted with the class. She did not want to change the way in which she taught her own classes, and she could not change her computer. However, she did change. Throughout the semester, she utilized the class space to discuss her alienation and to come to understand her own lack of self-efficacy. This will allow her to become a more effective teacher because she will be able to help her students change ideas, habits, and mindsets that inhibit their abilities to interact effectively with a larger and constantly changing world. This kind of shift is requisite in the online space.

It is an exciting moment in educational history, and our students will be the ones to teach us the limits of its possibilities. As Consuela wrote at the end of the semester:

> You know, the more we do this web page thing, the more I like it. It's like having class and individual instruction all at the same time. Is anybody going to ask us for our feedback on this format? They should. We have valuable experience, don't you know.

Consuela understands the idea that students know something, and that they do not enter the class space as blank slates. They enter as humans with lives that have been lived and will continue to be expressed in a million different ways. No single teacher can accommodate every single difference. However, the promise of distance education is that more students will become comfortable, as Sabena has, being an active, engaged, and collaborative learner in a virtual class space.

REFERENCES

Antonette, Lesliee. (1998). *The rhetoric of diversity and the tradition of American literary study: Critical multiculturalism In English.* Westport, CT: Greenwood.

Foucault, Michel. (1984). Space, knowledge and power. In *The Foucault reader.* New York: Pantheon.

Freire, Paolo. (1987). Letter to North-American teachers. In Ira Shor (Ed.), *Friere for the classroom: A sourcebook for liberatory teaching* (pp. 211-214). Portsmouth, NH: Boynton/Cook.

Grant, Carl A., & Sachs, Judyth M. (1995). Multicultural education and postmodernism: A movement toward dialogue. In Barry Kanpol & Peter McLaren (Eds.), *Critical multiculturalism: Uncommon voices in a common struggle* (pp. 89-105). Westport, CT: Bergin & Garvey.

Hall, Stuart. (1995). New ethnicities. In Bill Ashcroft, Gareth Griffiths & Helen Tiffin (Eds.), *The post-colonial studies reader* (pp. 223–227). New York: Routledge.

Hardwicke, Susan. (2000). Humanising the technology landscape through collaborative pedagogy. *Journal of Geography in Higher Education, 24*(1), 123-129.

Meisel, Steve & Marx, Bob. (1999). Screen to screen versus face to face: Experiencing the differences in management education. *Journal of Management Education, 23*(6), 719-732.

Mulligan, Roark & Geary, Susan. (1999). Requiring writing, ensuring distance-learning outcomes. *International Journal of Instructional Media, 26*(4), 387-396.

Shor, Ira. (1987). *Freire for the classroom: A sourcebook for liberatory teaching.* Portsmouth, NH: Boynton/Cook.

8

FEMINIST CIVIC ENGAGEMENT AND THE ROLE OF THE BUREAUCRAT

GRADUATE EDUCATION, DISTANCE LEARNING, AND COMMUNITY ACTION

Melody Bowdon

The most important benefit I have observed from my online service-learning experience is that it breaks down barriers—not just time and distance barriers, but, most importantly, social barriers. Because I did not have to worry about impression management, the intimate and supportive environment allowed me to risk being more honest than I would have dared in the traditional classroom setting. The online format gave me the freedom to express my joys and fears more honestly than I have ever dared to before—and to my surprise, I was not ostracized for taking the risk—I received more support than I have ever experienced in any other professional or academic setting.

—Denise,[1] Graduate Student

---

[1] All names have been changed to protect students' privacy.

When we move our courses from traditional classrooms to the Internet, we disrupt our students' and our own senses of time and space. The apparently hard-and-fast realities of our teaching and learning experiences become more noticeably unstable. We can make a nothing of this disruption—find emptiness in the lack of familiar markers of person and place and find comfort in the buffer of anonymity and flexibility this shift creates—or we can make a new something of it. In this chapter, I explore some ways in which we can capitalize on this rupture to improve our students' and our own learning experiences and begin to alter the social geography of our communities. I demonstrate how the combination of service-learning and Web-based learning in one graduate program has helped students build a virtual community that understands and values the power of rhetoric for social change. I will explain how an emphasis on distance learning jump started a program, altered its constituency and curriculum, and launched a meaningful pattern of civic engagement. I do these things using the model of action that I call *specific feminism*.

The epigraph at the beginning of this chapter was written by a student enrolled in the Graduate Certificate in Professional Writing program at the University of Central Florida (UCF). Our department of English launched the certificate in 1999, during my first semester at the institution. Late in that academic year, I was asked to take an administrative lead in the new program because of a shift in staffing. As a newly minted PhD, I was suddenly in the role of a low-ranking bureaucrat and charged with the fairly daunting task of helping the certificate to grow.

The program was approved in 1998 by the Florida Board of Regents. The expectation was that it would provide support to our burgeoning local research industry, offering training in writing and document design for middle managers at companies like Siemens, Lucent, AT&T, and the many other multimillion dollar corporations with offices in the research park adjacent to our Orlando, Florida, campus. Research sectors of all of the branches of the armed forces have a presence in this area, as do corporations like Lockheed-Martin that support the defense and space industries. The research park population was a prime target for our certificate, and it seemed logical to put a program designed to serve business employees in one of the fastest growing cities in the nation.

Despite needs assessment studies and logical marketing, however, these business people did not sign up for the program in significant numbers. During that first year of coordinating the certificate, I expended a great deal of energy and postage trying to recruit local business people. I made phone calls and site visits, posted fliers, gave public seminars, went

Feminist Civic Engagement and the Role of the Bureaucrat 149

to Chamber of Commerce luncheons, and joined professional groups. I received little response from this work. I began to wonder if there was a real market for the program at all. Then came the move to the Web.

Just as we were struggling to find a vision for the certificate, university administrators asked our department to consider making the program available entirely online. This plan made sense in light of UCF's strong commitment to using the latest technologies to enhance accessibility and quality of education. Once called Florida Technological University, UCF has built a reputation on our optics lab, our computer science program, and similar science initiatives. This focus colors virtually everything on campus, and related funding supports a solid system for high-tech delivery of instruction, including interactive television, Web-based learning, and other media enhancements. The leaders of our distributed learning program were looking for entire programs that would move smoothly to the Web.

Expanding the certificate via the Web also fit with UCF's goal to increase graduate enrollments in general. The growing university is committed to increasing its research profile by sustaining graduate programs in a wide range of fields. In addition, a Web-based model has important practical benefits for UCF because space on campus is at a premium. UCF's enrollment expanded from approximately 26,000 students in 1994 to approximately 42,000 in 2004, and our president projects enrollment to be at 48,000 in 2010. Because of a population explosion in the state of Florida, many of our schools—from the smallest local elementary campus to the largest university—struggle with these limitations of physical space. It makes sense that a college formed to support the space industry in the 1960s would seek answers to its serious overcrowding problems in cyberspace.

The professional writing certificate was a logical program to move to the Web because our students would, by definition, be working with people from throughout the central Florida region. While I was spending time on the process of getting faculty recruited and trained to teach online, getting new courses approved, and writing proposals to lobby for new lines to support the promising but still small program, students continued to hear about the program and to apply. Yet these students were not coming from corporate America for the most part. They were coming from a wide range of backgrounds and from across the state of Florida and beyond. One student, Catherine, explained her interest in this way: "I chose this program because I wanted to ease back into school after a 20-year hiatus. I wanted to refresh my skills as a professional and technical writer, and to possibly gain a new perspective on writing."

The people who applied to the program as it moved to the Web were writers like Catherine. They were school teachers who wanted to improve their writing skills, a local horse trainer who wanted to learn to write grants, and leaders of nonprofit agencies who wanted to improve their fundraising skills. Our first graduate was a lieutenant in the Orlando Police Department who created documents for our local Big Brothers/Big Sisters organization during his courses in the program. A diverse and committed community was forming in the midst of the transition to the Web, and its focus was shifting to civic responsibility rather than corporate gain. The students brought professional objectives and experiences to the program, but they also brought personal goals and community commitments. They were looking for opportunities to connect, grow, and develop. In introducing herself to her professional writing classmates, Catherine wrote, "I am a technical writer for Howard Corporation by trade. . . . In my spare time I volunteer with various animal rescue groups, mainly German Shepherd Rescue. I'm a member of various conservation groups, and would love to use the skills I gain from this program to pursue a job in the nonprofit arena."

Like most of the students who apply for the Web-based version of our program, Catherine began with the goal of using the skills gained from the course to address concerns beyond the corporate world. Many students previously unable to participate in our traditional program because of life issues were able to explore it due to this shift. The values of these women, whether raising children or working extra hours while seeking supplemental training in an effort to break through glass ceilings for themselves and those who see them as role models, shaped the program significantly. What I saw as a feminist bureaucrat and teacher was a diverse population of applicants with a shared commitment to changing more than their own economic status.

THE SPECIFIC FEMINIST

I call myself a *specific feminist*, drawing on Foucault's (1980) concept of the specific or local intellectual, as presented in *Power/Knowledge*. A specific or local feminist seizes available opportunities to bring about gender equity and to promote the intellectual, social, and economic welfare of women. Taking advantage of the agency my bureaucratic role has offered me, I am able to accomplish this goal. The flexible entrance requirements for the program allow me to accept some students with patchy undergraduate transcripts or with low or no GRE scores when they make a strong argument for their goals for attendance. They demonstrate commitment and potential through professional achievement, through successes in career-oriented training, and through presenting writing portfolios and business plans. This flexibility has led to diversity in our program. We have men and women of a range of ages and ethnicities. We have a growing and changing community that is shaping the world beyond our classrooms.

In *As If Learning Mattered*, Miller (1998) narrated a series of moments in the history of British and American higher education from Matthew Arnold to the Open University through contemporary debates about the role of the public intellectual. Ultimately, Miller suggested that the role of the bureaucrat, although widely considered among the ranks of academics and beyond to be a constraining, distasteful, and anti-intellectual one, can be marshaled for purposes of social reform within the institution and beyond. Miller wrote,

> . . . for those of us weary of feeling utterly powerless—those of us interested in translating into a workable plan of action the dissatisfaction with institutional life that makes itself known everywhere in all of our lives—overcoming the deep revulsion we feel for the bureaucratic conditions that simultaneously constrain and enable our labor in the academy may well be the best chance we have for shaping how the business of intellectual inquiry gets carried out in the future. (p. 216)

This notion that Miller suggested—that as bureaucrats we have an opportunity to influence the shape of intellectual work and institutional structures—then, informed my work with the graduate certificate. I tried to present a model of the specific feminist, one who acts locally, marshaling the power of her capacity for concern and her commitment to justice to make changes in her community. She sees her own self-interests and self-existence as critically tied to the fate of those around her, but also believes that the future of the community relies on her ability to make good decisions for her own life. She neither eschews nor obsesses on her obligations to the people in what Noddings (2003) would call her "chain" of relationships.

GENDER AND THE WEB

Anecdotal evidence suggests that the majority of students in Web-based courses in the United States are women. At UCF, for example, women rep-

152   *Bowdon*

resent more than 55% of all students in Web-based classes, and the percentage is higher on the graduate level, according to our Office of Institutional Research. Indeed 85% of students in the Graduate Certificate in Professional Writing are female, and a majority are working mothers. This makes gender an unavoidable and important issue in the program. The complexity of gender identity in a Web-based environment is significant.

Much has been written about gender differences and the politics of cyberspace. In *Technologies of the Gendered Body*, Balsamo (1996) bemoaned what seems to be a frequently missed opportunity to bring about social improvements through new identity-challenging technologies. She suggested that although virtual communication, for example, has theoretically made it possible for us to move past embodied gender, in fact this technology has reified old models of gender so that females and males online are often reduced to caricatures of their sexes.

Balsamo encouraged feminists to address this problem when she wrote:

> . . . the challenge is how to harness the power of technological knowledge to a feminist agenda while struggling against an increasing industrial imperialism that eagerly assimilates new techno-workers to labor in the interests of private enterprise. The question is how to empower technological agents so that they work on behalf of the right kind of social change. (p. 156)

Haraway (1991) offered useful suggestions for taking up this challenge as she explored the connection between humans and machines and the politics of the cyborg. Haraway advocated a situated knowledge model of inquiry, which invites feminists to draw on their disciplinary knowledge, personal experience, and other individual contexts to take action in their communities. She argued:

> Situated knowledges are particularly powerful tools to produce maps of consciousness for people who have been inscribed within the marked categories of race and sex that have been so exuberantly produced in histories of masculinist, racist, and colonialist dominations. Situated knowledges are always *marked* knowledges; they are re-markings, reorientatings, of the great maps that globalized the heterogeneous body of the world in the history of masculinist capitalism and colonialism. (p. 111)

Feminist Civic Engagement and the Role of the Bureaucrat   153

Students in the certificate who are struggling to integrate academic learning, professional experience, and personal knowledge into projects in and beyond their courses find this model of situated knowledge useful. Applying the situated knowledge methodology in their community-based research and writing helps students capitalize on their strengths to take local action.

Authors like Balsamo and Haraway underscore what my students and my colleagues know to be true—that virtual education can be an isolating enterprise, but that it can also be a dynamic and exciting activity full of opportunities to make changes in the material conditions of our communities. I strongly believe that meaningful engagement in local communities converts a potentially flat experience into a vibrant and meaningful one. This can help students recognize that technology can serve as a tool for marshalling resources to make our communities more just.

Many students come to our program in moments of transition and even crisis as they attempt to find ways to take control of their lives and their futures. They are widowed, divorced, experiencing empty nest syndrome, trying to engineer career changes, or hoping to make themselves more marketable. What they find when they enter this program that so heavily emphasizes civic engagement is a kind of empowerment that only comes through the process of reaching out to others in the community and seeing the impacts of your rhetorical decisions. Through their formation of a vibrant virtual community, these students see beyond the ethic of care that feminine ethicists like Noddings (2003) and Carol Gilligan (1993) advocate and see the power that comes from active social engagement.

MAPPING NEW SPACES

The successful conversion to a program available entirely via the Web has altered this group meaningfully. As we have moved from traditional classrooms to the 24-hour learning centers of the Web, the shared learning space has been redesigned. I was initially quite skeptical about this space. When I started my own training for teaching via WebCT, I lamented that I would be losing out on the joy of connecting with my students face to face and getting to know them. I prepared for that loss, but it has not happened. After explaining the logistical advantages of Web-learning related to parking, child care, and scheduling, one student, Risa, suggests that this changed space can be uniquely comforting. She writes,

> Perhaps the biggest plus for me comes from my hesitance to speak in a classroom setting. I am not a talker. I am the last to make a comment in class—if I make a comment at all, which I normally do not. However, in a Web class, I find that I can voice my opinion. Perhaps that is because I do not have to look at anyone as I do so; whatever the reason, it is a good thing. If I were in a classroom, I would not be giving this opinion no matter how relaxed the class, but I feel comfortable enough to give it here.

In our cyber classroom, my students and I connect more frequently and in a more substantive way than I have ever experienced as a student or teacher in a traditional course. There is a kind of peer accountability that I have not seen before. Students take their responsibility for providing formal and informal feedback to their classmates more seriously than I have seen them do in a traditional course. They engage, make connections, share commitments, and take action. They are not passive or disconnected: They make a new space together and it is mapped in their imaginations. It also is making a difference in our local community.

David Harvey (1997) shed light on the politics of space and social change through his model of historical-geographic materialism. He argued:

> Social relations are, in all respects, mappings of some sort, be they symbolic, figurative, or material. The organization of social relations demands a mapping so that people know their place. Revolutionary activity entails a re-mapping of social relations and agents who no longer acknowledge that place to which they were formerly assigned. From this it follows that the production of spatial relations (and of discourse about space relations) is a production of social relations and to alter one is to alter the other. (p. 112)

Harvey's work serves to augment Marxist ideas about material conditions and their impacts to include the variable of geography, which is overlooked in most of these philosophies. He argued that space always matters when it comes to processes of power and social justice. This intervention is critical from a feminist perspective. Space has always been a crucial force in the shaping of gendered power structures, from the confines of the home to restricted access to pulpits, meeting halls, board rooms, and centers of technology. The power of space plays out clearly in the politics of the map of our program. In changing spaces, in entering the space of the Internet, our program has shifted, and the values and social arrangements in it have changed. Because the cyber classroom helps us think about

Feminist Civic Engagement and the Role of the Bureaucrat   155

learning spaces in a new way, it is a good opportunity to let students think about their communities as a dimension of the changing space of the classroom.

BUILDING A CYBER CITY

Since our program went online, the applications have exploded. We have grown from four in Spring 2000 to 42 in our latest numbers (Spring 2005). Students come to this program for a chance to do graduate work without the necessity of living in the metropolitan area. Many of our students are women with small children who could not get to campus to take courses if they were not offered online. Some have disabilities that limit their access to campus; others face economic constraints that require them to work too many hours to take advantage of traditional courses. Others, like Risa, express fear at the thought of entering a traditional graduate classroom— fear that their voices will not be welcomed or they will not be able to find those voices. In our virtual classroom, many of these students find power. They take control of their own learning, take responsibility for supporting their classmates' efforts, and take pride in the agency they discover when they use their skills to improve their communities.

I do not mean to suggest that the virtual classroom is a utopia. Students who feel alienated in an online class are often less likely to take action to rectify their situations than they might be in a traditional class. Some students simply are not intellectually or temperamentally suited to Web-based learning; some of my students have felt alienated and frustrated by the experience of taking a Web-based course. People can lose their sense of agency in any situation, but clearly the shift in this program has created a new space for many students.

What has emerged in this program over the last two years, then, is an ethnically diverse group of students with strong civic commitments who are serious about making changes in their local communities. They are doing that by working with schools, hospitals, government offices, and nonprofit agencies. Although the original plan for the program emphasized preparing students to move up in the corporate world and improve their own economic lots, what has grown here instead is a group of writers who come in believing that they will be role models for others. By listening to the students' needs and incorporating our own commitment to the model of rhetorical education as training for active citizenship, our faculty has

156   *Bowdon*

been able to support this shift. Denise, the student quoted in the epigraph, explains what this means to her.

> As a minority, a woman in the midst of major life changes, a former immigrant, and now a naturalized citizen, I may be able to offer you a unique perspective. For me the program is less about professional growth than about service. I am reminded of the quote that says, "When you educate a man you educate an individual, and when you educate a woman you educate a family." I would add that you also educate a community.
>
> So, I agree wholeheartedly that the service component of this program does offer a more rhetorically meaningful experience for me personally, but I think it offers an opportunity of equal value to my community in that it demonstrates to others like me that often the most potent barrier we face is the one between our ears.
>
> Many of those I come in contact with from economically and socially disadvantaged backgrounds are intuitively entrepreneurial and financially astute—yet they discount these skills and abilities because they did not acquire them from college, but from surviving life. To the extent that the service-learning component of this program and other university outreach efforts increase the visibility of persons like me in the community, and add our voices to the collective, they validate all kinds of experiences and help people see that anything is possible, instead of the prevailing view that everything is impossible.

In *Justice and the Politics of Difference*, Young (1990) made a point similar to Denise's. Young took on prevailing models of social justice that emphasize equity of distribution as the key to justice. In other words, Young argued that the simple notion that justice comes when everyone has theoretically equal opportunity to access goods and power is bogus. She wrote, "Evaluating social justice according to whether persons have opportunities, therefore, must involve not a distributive outcome but the social structures that enable or constrain the individuals in relevant situations . . . " (p. 26). Young suggested that access to the opportunity for education, for example, is not the same as the opportunity to participate in the practices of power in the community, which result in decisions about education and other public policies. When students like Denise are part of a program that trains students to return to their workplaces and communities prepared to bring about change through their rhetorical practice, it accomplishes something significant. Interestingly, Young's ideal model for addressing issues of social injustice is the city. She stated:

Feminist Civic Engagement and the Role of the Bureaucrat

> I propose to construct a normative ideal of city life as an alternative to both the ideal of community and the liberal individualism it criticizes as antisocial. By "city life" I mean a form of social relations which I define as the being together of strangers. In the city persons and groups interact within spaces and institutions they all experience themselves as belonging to, but without those interactions dissolving into unity or commonness. (p. 237)

Young's model suggests that justice comes from people with diverse histories and experiences participating together in the creation of their community because each individual has an interest in the success of the group. This model is connected well with the work we are trying to do in this program, and doubtless others are attempting as well. UCF is part of a growing group of institutions across the country known as *metropolitan research universities*. These campuses focus on research with an emphasis on problem solving for the metropolitan areas they serve. The kind of learning that is happening in our program, driven largely by the local civic commitments of the students, fits this model perfectly.

Clearly there are residence requirements for the virtual city of our program. First, the students in the certificate are finished or nearly so with bachelor's degrees. To participate in an online class, students must have regular access to computers; because the courses involve peer review of documents, they must have specific word processing software, virus protection, and Internet access. Yet this is a group that wants to bring about social justice through their use of language, and it is a group that welcomes everyone who shows up.

Young argued that distribution is not the key to justice—that making opportunities is not the final goal, and that relationships and having a sense of agency make the difference. She does not want to do away with difference by making a universal kind of community—she believes in the model of the city—a place of diversity and common interest as a model for justice. This connects mightily with the role of the feminist bureaucrat who recognizes that it is not enough to make opportunities available to a wide range of students; one must develop the connections and the community where relationships can grow and change can happen. When we make civic commitment central to our teaching, we move toward that goal. This work can be transformative.

The key to the success of our certificate community is the combination of service learning and distance learning. This combination allows a remapping of social spaces, creating a new way for students and teachers to comprehend their work. This reconfiguration can help disrupt our understanding of the university's role in our communities. Rather than breaking down communities by dispersing students and decentralizing the learning experience, this combination can create a kind of reconceiving that can actually improve our sense of community.

OUR VIRTUAL COMMUNITY

Through incorporating a service-learning and civic engagement emphasis in core courses of the certificate, my faculty colleagues and I created a rudimentary infrastructure for a virtual civic community. Our students, however, have brought it to life through their actions as writers. In courses such as Writing for the Business Professional, Professional Editing, and Proposal Writing, students design and produce a wide range of projects for local community agencies. Several have created curricular tools, assessment reports, and fundraising materials for local public schools and school districts. One pair of students created a volunteer guide for the members of a local hospital board. Students have produced brochures, grant proposals, Web pages, posters, fliers, and other materials for groups including Big Brothers/Big Sisters, the United Way, various humane societies and animal rescue groups, environmental programs, a neighborhood association, AIDS support organizations, campus groups with philanthropic goals, and many others. One student started a newsletter for a children's cancer research program. Another wrote a grant proposal to fund a recycling initiative at a local YMCA. Because the online environment fosters collaboration in a unique way and encourages students to rely on each other's input and support so strongly, *all* of the students have done *all* of these activities. A paralegal in Tampa offers help on a grant proposal to a public school teacher in Jacksonville. A community college teacher in St. Augustine provides feedback on a brochure about mental health to a technical writer in Clearwater. All of this work takes place in the new public space of the virtual classroom, where each member of the class can take pride in the process and the products of the community they build together.

Sometimes students deal with "real" complex ethical dilemmas through this work. Denise, whose words began this chapter, designed a portion of the annual report for her local Boys and Girls Club of America (BGCA). In one section, she was writing feature stories about some of the program's successes—kids who had come out of hard times safely and happily through the support of BGCA. The program's director wanted

Feminist Civic Engagement and the Role of the Bureaucrat   159

Denise to include the story of her own son's experiences with the program. This created a serious dilemma for Denise, who was anxious about writing about her son's problems and concerned about how she might find the emotional and intellectual distance for which the task called. She turned to her online classmates for help and received a great deal of support. She was able to find a way to transcend her personal issues with the project, change her feeling that this personal connection was a liability, and use it to apply the rhetorical training she was gaining in class. She was able to use her voice to make this happen, and she insists that this would not have been possible in a traditional classroom. Her classmate, Hannah, describes the power of the virtual learning space:

> I believe that we, as students, are better able to help one another on our own time with individual needs in an online course. We don't have to spend class time sitting in a windowless room discussing something that some of us may be already familiar with, as we are all from different backgrounds. However, if someone has a personal concern or obstacle to overcome, there are plenty of people to help with advice. And this process helps all of us to keep learning.

In response, Denise writes:

> I can honestly say that this level of intimacy and trust has helped me to be more productive, more creative, and to learn more about myself and my craft than any other learning experience I have had to date. Then there is the enormous feeling of stature that it adds to my sense of self-worth to be able to say that I made a contribution to an organization in my community that no one else was able or willing to do— and to know that the organization has truly benefited from my efforts in equal measure.

THE FEMINIST BUREAUCRAT

As a specific feminist, a teacher, and a program coordinator, I sometimes have conflicting feelings and impulses about how best to engage in my work. As a feminist, I want to promote equality and equity among all my students. I want to help students find ways to empower themselves through what they are learning from the study of rhetoric. I want to make learning accessible for people with family commitments, and for economically challenged and physically disabled students. I want to create a class environment where all students, including women, can speak with confidence and feel that their contributions to important and meaningful conversations are valued. As a professional and technical writing teacher, I want all of our students to know that the work they are doing as writers and rhetors is significant, and that the training they are receiving through participating in this program will be valued beyond the classroom. As a bureaucrat, I need to see application and enrollment numbers rising, and students completing the program and going on to seek new jobs or admission to our MA program for further study. I need to produce evidence that results of this program warrant the resources put into it. For me, the key to this process of serving as a feminist bureaucrat is the combination service- and distance-learning approach. This model invites students to gauge the value of their training through concrete feedback from authentic users of documents. It fosters a community with shared civic values and taps into the experiences of a diverse group of students.

When we get rid of classroom walls by teaching online, we find that the class can expand infinitely to reach all kinds of places where what students are learning matters to communities. Something new happens when we combine distance learning, rhetoric, and service learning—something that I think Miller is advocating when he imagines a new way to understand the role of the bureaucrat. When we enter this new space of the cyber classroom, the physical spaces in which students enact their rhetoric can shift to local communities. This can break down barriers between universities and communities and allow us to understand our worlds differently—particularly the connections between our own work and the communities around us.

REFERENCES

Balsamo, Anne. (1996). *Technologies of the gendered body.* Durham, NC: Duke University Press.
Foucault, Michel. (1980). *Power/knowledge.* New York: Pantheon.
Gilligan, Carol. (1993). *In a different voice: Psychological theory and women's development.* Cambridge MA: Harvard University Press.
Haraway, Donna. (1991). *Simians, cyborgs, and women: The reinvention of nature.* New York: Routledge.
Harvey, David. (1996). *Justice, nature, and the geography of difference.* Malden, MA: Blackwell.

Miller, Richard E. (1998). *As if learning mattered: Reforming higher education.* Ithaca, NY: Cornell University Press.

Noddings, Nel. (2003). *Caring: A feminine approach to ethics and moral education* (2nd ed.). Berkeley: University of California Press.

Young, Iris Marion. (1990). *Justice and the politics of difference.* Princeton, NJ: Princeton University Press.

IV FUTURES

Online Distance Education and the "Buffy Paradigm": Welcome to the Hell Mouth

Cynthia L. Jenéy

Learning at Light Speed in Neal Stephenson's The Diamond Age

Veronica Pantoja

Distant, Present, and Hybrid

Peter Sands

9

ONLINE DISTANCE EDUCATION AND THE "BUFFY PARADIGM"

WELCOME TO THE HELL MOUTH

Cynthia L. Jenéy

Postsecondary institutions used the Internet more than any other mode to deliver distance education. . . . 84 percent of four-year institutions will offer distance-education courses in 2002.

—Cornelia Ashby (United States General Accounting Office Testimony Before the U.S. Senate Committee on Health, Education, Labor, and Pensions, 2002)

Oh, at first it was confusing. Just the idea of computers was like— whoa! I'm eleven hundred years old! I had trouble adjusting to the idea of Lutherans.

—Anya (*Buffy the Vampire Slayer*)[1]

---

[1] Anya, a character from the show *Buffy the Vampire Slayer*, arrives in Buffy's hometown of Sunnydale, California, as the 1124-year-old vengeance demon Anyanka. Later she loses her powers, becoming a mortal woman and an ally of the slayer. Her new-found talents for accounting and finance inspire her to learn how to use computers, and her restored humanity causes her to help friend Tara through her initial college-student technophobia.

165

One of the most responsible approaches that educators and administrators can take in regard to distance-education, especially courses delivered via the Internet and World Wide Web technologies, is to acknowledge that we face an uncertain mix of existing and future conditions. Commercial development, institutional policies, intellectual property legislation, copyright laws, and the technology, in all of its stages—from R&D to retail licensing—will change constantly as far into the future as we can reasonably foresee. The issue is not what we know, but how little we know and how little we can predict.

No one who has looked critically at the responses of higher education to increasing demands for "English online " to date can ignore just how difficult it is to put online distance education into perspective:

- Some college educators and administrators view Internet projects as experiments, watching with varying degrees of interest or detachment, possibly expecting the novelty to wear off, whereas others see the online component as one part of many permanent, growing, and changing technological developments in the delivery of composition and other English courses.

- Some composition programs must deal with online distance-education as a political, state-mandated initiative, whereas others see the development of online teaching technologies as best cultivated by private enterprise and independently funded academic research projects.

- Some educators and critics believe they can characterize various online distance-education design approaches, collect accurate outcomes data, and predict online success both qualitatively and quantitatively; others feel that the state of the technologies and the user population is dominated by uncertainty.

- Some institutions have poured resources into the development of online courses, even offering entire programs or degrees online, almost in a feverish race against time. Others have stepped aside, preferring to watch and learn from the current successes and failures of their counterparts, referring online learners to other institutions' Internet offerings.

- Some online educators believe there are specific "best practices" and preferred technological solutions to the challenges and problems of online teaching; others prefer to improvise and push the newest edges of technological envelopes, expanding and redefining goals and processes as they go.

- Companies that provide proprietary servers and course-delivery products make claims and promises in the face of changing demands, whereas skeptical educators hesitate to commit their design and development time to any one particular system that could be gone tomorrow.
- Online course-delivery systems are often seen as a technological path to substantial economic savings in budget-conscious adminispheres. However, many educators insist on basing online course development on sound pedagogical and theoretical foundations before pressing for large-scale enrollment in computer-mediated classes.
- Although statistical and qualitative data are being gathered on student success, tuition cost-benefits, and student-centered technological design, the stressors and challenges to teachers (many of whom are adjuncts and graduate teaching assistants) are often voiced in propagandistic terms, celebrating their abilities to "adjust" and "innovate"—regardless of the cost in time and activities that might weigh more heavily with hiring committees and with tenure and promotion committees.
- Much thinking about online distance education at the institutional level is still configured in terms of old, established models of curricular organization, whereas students and teachers often see the Internet as a more malleable, borderless entity.
- In the face of security and safety issues, many academics continue to lull themselves into a blissful state of naiveté concerning the threats posed by hackers, code crackers, fraudulent and inadequate service providers, and any number of possible internal and external systems abuses, although systems administrators rank these among their own top concerns.[2]

---

[2]Begun in 1990, The U.S. Campus Computing Project is the largest continuing study of the role of information technology in American higher education. The project's national studies draw on qualitative and quantitative data to help inform faculty, campus administrators, and others interested in the use of information technology

168   *Jenéy*

These are, of course, only a few of the issues that face developers of online distance-education programs in higher education. Woven into these challenges are the unique pedagogical and practical dimensions of teaching English composition and literature in computer-mediated environments, and the task for most educators assigned to online distance courses is often daunting. The new and unpredictable variables are so staggering in number that the discussion almost begs for an escape into chaos theory or postmodern[3] inscrutability.

Yet the time for privileging the inscrutable and multivalent features of online communication is over for teachers and students who are faced with the rapidly changing surrealities of online distance education. A number of superior academic studies of online composition teaching environments appeared in the last decades of the 20th century,[4] many of which have dealt with the pragmatics, pedagogies, and semiotics of computer mediated communication. With the exception of philosophical technocritics (such as Alvin Toffler, Jacques Ellul, Neil Postman, Allucquère Rosanne Stone, and

---

in American colleges and universities. The U.S. Campus Computing Project also provides the foundation for affiliated research projects in other nations, including Brazil (University of Sao Paulo), China (Peking University), Hong Kong (University of Hong Kong), and South Korea (Ewha Woman's University).

Each year more than 600 two- and four-year public and private colleges and universities in the United States participate in the Campus Computing Survey, which focuses on campus planning and policy issues affecting the role of information technology in teaching, learning, and scholarship (Campus Computing Project, *http://www.campuscomputing.net*).

According to the U.S. Campus Computing Project 2003 National Survey of Information Technology in U.S. Higher Education, "Nearly half, or 279, of the colleges and universities surveyed reported increases in money available for security. In some cases, those increases were being spent on making campus networks more secure, Mr. Green said. In other cases, the increased spending was for the salary of a security officer" (Olsen, 2003). (http://chronicle.com)

[3]Rather than imply that *postmodernism* is an umbrella term for inscrutability or pseudonihilistic rejection of paradigms, I suggest here that the postmodern discussion of internetworked computer-mediated communication often centers on features of play and semiotics—it is critical and analytical, to be sure, but for purposes of this discussion it is perhaps a shorthand for all that is distancing, smug, and reactionary (albeit descriptive and often illuminating) in the sphere of online distance education studies, rather than visionary.

[4]Compare such wide-ranging projects as Selfe and Hilligoss' (1994) edited collection *Literacy and Computers: The Complications of Teaching and Learning with*

Online Distance education and the "Buffy Paradigm"

Ellen Ullman) and some thoughtful arguments put forth by Cynthia Selfe's (1999) *Technology and Literacy in the Twenty-First Century: The Importance of Paying Attention*, few studies propose specific political, institutional, or social activism as important avenues for development in the online distance-education projects and challenges we face.[5]

For quite some time, the voices of composition educators involved with computers and writing have seemed more or less content to configure themselves within a mythos of colonization—as the "explorers" and "homesteaders" of the electronic "frontier."[6] The Internet has been widely accepted as a virtual space—a technological environment whose efficaciousness is controlled and altered by means of electronic tools. Popularized in Howard Rheingold's (1993) *The Virtual Community: Homesteading on the Electronic Frontier*, the geographic metaphor serves designers and users well: A classical strategy of memory and thought described by Cicero and by the author of the *Rhetorical Ad Herennium*, using the *topos* of "place," aids us both in memory and the organization of thoughts.

Yet even Rheingold acknowledged that the electronic frontier is not a neutral place. As the 21st century gets underway, educators faced with the spaces and places of teaching in online environments are realizing that the information age is not merely becoming an "info-glut age," but more of a techno-monster age. That is, the technologies now developing are bigger, stronger, faster, and potentially meaner than those from any previous age

---

Technology; Hawisher, LeBlanc, Moran, and Selfe's (1996) *Computers and the Teaching of Writing in American Higher Education 1979-1994: A History*; Palmquist, Kiefer, Hartvigsen and Goodlew's (1998) *Transitions: Teaching Writing in Computer-Supported and Traditional Classrooms*; Ilana Snyder's (1998) edited collection *Page to Screen: Taking Literacy into the Electronic Era*; Haynes and Holmevik's (1998) edited collection *High Wired: On the Design, Use, and Theory of Educational Moos*; Hawisher and Selfe's (1999) edited collection *Passions, Pedagogies, and 21st Century Technologies*; and especially the accomplished and top-notch journal *Computers and Composition* edited by Hawisher and Selfe.

[5]Naturally, we must concede that activism involving issues of diversity, discrimination, tolerance, and equal opportunity is frequently advocated in the field of Computers and Writing, but activism concerning the policies, infrastructures, and design of the technologies *qua* technology in the context of postsecondary online English teaching at various state, private nonprofit, and private for-profit institutions is rarely the focus of discussion.

[6]This frontier metaphor is most famously characterized in Howard Rheingold's (1993) *Virtual Community: Homesteading on the Electronic Frontier*.

170   *Jenéy*

of technological upheaval. Increasingly, we must deal with capricious search engines, spyware,[7] cut-and-paste student culture, murky intellectual property regulations, creeping featurism,[8] administrative demands for "increased output" in online distance-education offerings (often in the form of raised enrollment caps), and any number of unforeseeable and often unprecedented challenges. The "settler on the frontier" mythos is cracking, if it ever was whole.[9]

Still it is useful to have a mythos if for no other reason than to have some model for comparison—some framework within which to plan and develop our online teaching environments. To put it in terms of social psychology:

> [I]ndividuals construct cognitive representations of "possible selves" (i.e., the hopes, fears, and goals that one holds for self) to serve as standards for self-evaluation. . . . Furthermore, perceived matches and mismatches between self and these evaluative standards result in self-directed affect, which in turn motivates efforts toward self-regulation. (Ford et al., 2002, p. 204)

In other words, people feel good or bad, and blame or reward themselves, whether they do or do not live up to an internally constructed "possible self." Each of us has a personal mythos—a configuration against which we measure ourselves. In the case of composition teaching, both in classrooms and online, the actual selves tend in large numbers to be

---

[7]The term "spyware" has come into popular use. According to the online "Webopedia" (2004), an encyclopedia of online terminologies,

> Also called adware, spyware is any software that covertly gathers user information through the user's Internet connection without his or her knowledge, usually for advertising purposes. . . . Once installed, the spyware monitors user activity on the Internet and transmits that information in the background to someone else. Spyware can also gather information about e-mail addresses and even passwords and credit card numbers. (http://www.webopedia.com)

[8]Donald Norman (*The Design of Everyday Things*) described "creeping featurism" as the tendency for designers to add to the number of features that a device can do, often extending the number beyond all reason.

[9]Although not completely rosy, Rheingold's (1993) vision of the Internet as a mixture of small "virtual communities" as well as "larger metropolitan areas of cyber-

Online Distance education and the "Buffy Paradigm"

female, well educated (either possessing or in the process of earning a higher degree), and often underemployed as part-time adjunct faculty, contract lecturers, or graduate teaching assistants. If we configure ourselves as beleaguered settlers, eking out a sparse survival in a hard place, waiting for slow-moving legislation, and lagging adjudication to aid and rescue us as we pick our way through the new electronic learning landscapes, we may begin to *act* like settlers, like little school ma'ams on the electronic prairie, standing in the doorway of the General Store while the high-tech cattle rustlers, sheriff's posses, snake-oil hustlers, gold prospectors, fur trappers, railroad profiteers, Pony Express riders, desperadoes, and Lone Rangers shoot it out in the town square. Our "virtual homesteads," as institutional educators, are often delimited and defined by the resources we have been assigned to as state governments and proprietary developers continue to use college educators as thinly disguised (and sometimes undisguised) free beta-testers for new proprietary technologies.

There can be no question but that there are hundreds of compositionists in higher education who have made astoundingly creative and effective online courses out of the seeming chaos of Internet resources supplied by their institutions, various funding benefactors, and, in some instances, thin air. I would argue that many of these educators are not settlers in the Internet frontier of online education. Most, if not all, of the most successful online educators have begun to design and build Internet environments from a model that does not merely *react* to technological developments. They are innovators, instigators, and when necessary, activists. They have begun (some long ago, some more recently), regardless of ethnicity, economic class, or gender identity, to work within a versatile and effective model that has grown within a small sphere of discussion shared by an unlikely pair of groups: academics who study popular culture and military intelligence planners. The mythopoeic model under discussion at the intersection of these seemingly unrelated circles has come to be known as the "Buffy Paradigm."

---

space" (p. 19) pushed powerfully against 1990's popular rhetoric of the Internet as a kind of "Infobahn" or "Information Superhighway." The initial popular press misapprehensions and glib satirical snapshots of online real-time and asynchronous CMC "chat" and "usenet" environments subsided in the mid-1990s, and soon online commerce and gaming took off, followed by a massive surge in both legal and illegal file sharing of music and video packets, which eventually proved the superhighway metaphor too one-dimensional for most users' conceptual understanding of the Internet and its interfaces and infrastructures.

The Buffy Paradigm is the problem-solving conceptual framework described and named by Anthony H. Cordesman (2001) in a white paper for the Center for Strategic and International Studies (CSIS) entitled "Biological Warfare and the 'Buffy Paradigm.'" The paper is constructed in response to the post-September 11 perceived need among U.S. military and intelligence organizations to shift methodologies away from traditional systems and time-worn strategies of information gathering and warfare. Standard mid-20th-Century methods of defense planning are currently viewed as ineffective in combating terrorist aggression. Seeking a vital and illustrative analogy for the counterterrorist methodologies he advocates, Cordesman reminds us that *Buffy the Vampire Slayer* is a TV series about "a teenage vampire slayer who lives in a world of unpredictable threats where each series of crises only becomes predictable when it is over and is followed by a new and unfamiliar one." The *Buffy* series ran for seven successful seasons (1997–2003) and remains popular in syndication, enjoying extremely high production values as well as cleverly conceived and well-crafted screen writing. Attesting to its quality is a modest, but growing, body of substantive scholarship, including the impressive 2002 collection of academic essays, *Fighting the Forces: What's at Stake in Buffy the Vampire Slayer*, and the peer-reviewed online journal *Slayage*. The "Buffy Paradigm," as Cordesman intriguingly laid it out in his white paper, shows how the structure of the plots, characters, themes, and ideas in the series reflect the situational difficulties met by those who must grapple with new and unknown challenges in the technological age:

- What expertise there is consists largely of bad or uncertain advice and old, flawed, and confusing technical data.
- The importance of any given threat changes constantly, past threat behavior does not predict future behavior, and methods of delivery keep changing.
- Arcane knowledge is always inadequate and fails to predict, detect, and properly characterize the threat.
- The more certain and deterministic an expert is at the start, the more wrong they turn out to be in practice.
- The scenarios are unpredictable and have unclear motivation. Any effort to predict threat motivation and behavior in detail before the event does at least as much harm as it does good.
- Risk taking is not rational or subject to predictable constraints, and the motivation behind escalation is erratic at best.
- It is never clear whether the threat is internal, from an individual, or from an outside organization.

Online Distance education and the "Buffy Paradigm" 173

- The attackers have no firm or predictable alliances, cooperate in nearly random ways, and can suddenly change method of attack and willingness to take risks.
- All efforts at planning a coherent strategy collapse in the face of tactical necessity and the need to deal with unexpected facts on the ground.
- The balance among external defense, homeland defense, and response changes constantly.
- No success, no matter how important at the time, ever eliminates the risk of future problems (Cordesman, 2001).

Although there may be little sustainable usefulness in configuring the challenges of teaching online as "battling evil" (at least in the religious or geopolitical sense), the mythos of *Buffy*—and perhaps, more important, the lessons to be gleaned from the actual "Buffy Paradigm"—are such that online college teachers can adopt and embrace them as useful in meeting and beating the complications of combining distance, technology, and pedagogy.

Even though Cordesman emphasized the battle-worthy dimensions of *Buffy*, it should be clear from his summary of the paradigm that the show is just as much about problem solving in an uncertain environment as it is about fighting the forces of evil. For each different type of vampire, demon, ghost, ghoul, or monster that climbs out of the Hellmouth (a dimensional portal positioned beneath the high school in the fictional town of Sunnydale, California), Buffy Summers and her band of friends must employ research methodologies, tactical planning, feature design, collaboration, networked communications, troubleshooting, reconnaissance, and the exploitation of individual talents and specializations. Although careful not to take itself too seriously, the show also incorporates ironic and sometimes poignant personal struggles that feature core ethical and moral dilemmas. Over time, for example, Buffy becomes a stickler for precise terminology concerning her calling. She is a slayer, and she slays soulless monsters. She pointedly corrects anyone who refers to her as a "killer" or "murderer." Her job is eradicating evil, not assassinating mortals or other worthy entities. Of this she is certain, even when situations create unclear choices about whom to slay, and whom to leave to the jurisdiction of society or perhaps even some otherworldly authority.

The new electronic technologies available to teachers of writing pose many of the same kinds of difficult choices for professionals who not so long ago had little (if anything) to do with the technological infrastructures and management of technology resources at their institutions. Frequently

174   Jenéy

new online distance-education and computer classroom teachers secretly
configure information technology specialists and systems administrators
on their campuses as "forces of evil," and they engage in adversarial dia-
logues that create unnecessary tensions between members of their academic departments and the technology managers hired to assist them. In
the Slayer mythology, this is called "The Yoko Effect"—blaming the wrong
person for a breakdown in workplace communication or cooperation.

> Spike: "The point is, [the Beatles] were once a real powerful group. It's
>   not a stretch to say they ruled the world. When they broke up,
>   everyone blamed Yoko, but the fact is, the group split itself up,
>   she just happened to be there." (Petrie, 2000)

Spike, the evolving part-good, part-evil, nouveau-punk vampire provides here an astute (if cynical) analysis of group-splintering social dynamics, which will sound familiar to members of even the most functional and
amiable academic institutions. These social, hierarchical dynamics powerfully influence individual—and programmatic—self-directed affect. Add
this network of interdependent elements to programmatic, publicly
released "mission statements" that are virtually aglow with politically idealistic (and frequently propagandistic) language describing the aims and
outcomes of distance-education, and the result can be unrealistic expectations and sharp criticism when these expectations are not met. Online distance-education courses, especially lower-division introductory and basic
writing courses, are notorious for high attrition rates, possibly due to low
motivation and other problems related to student populations identified as
at risk. When the heroic "settlers of the virtual frontier" encounter student
resistance, technological design flaws, inadequate support, and other challenges, the "pioneer" mythos has no built-in paradigm for success other
than perseverance, patience, and experience. When servers crash, trunk
lines go down, bandwidth clogs, and software incompatibility issues arise,
there is no "cavalry" waiting over the next rise to rescue us; even if we can
muster a posse, they will not know what to do. In the face of such daunting daily uncertainties, the Buffy Paradigm offers an exciting *mythos*, that
appeals to scholars and educators whose body of criticism and research
reveals layers of cultural *identification*[10] worthy of a new and frequently
unpredictable professional environment.

---

[10]*Identification* is meant here in the sense explained by Kenneth Burke (1966) in
his lecture, "Rhetoric and Poetics":

Myth and folklore play an important role not only in self-directed affect, but in our base assumptions supporting pragmatic systems of problem–solution activities, both internally and in sociocultural settings. Classics scholar G.S. Kirk (1974) explained that anthropologists have constructed five "monolithic theories," whereby discursive analyses have been applied to the structures and purposes of myths. Kirk defined myth in the broadest terms possible as "traditional tales" (p. 23). The first universal theory (proposed by philologist Max Müller, 1848) explaining the human tendency to create and perpetuate mythologies "maintains that all myths are *nature myths*" (i.e., myths that refer to cosmological and meteorological phenomena). The second monolithic theory (championed by Andrew Lang, 1848, and others) is loosely referred to as *aetiological*: myths that explain causes and origins of something in the real world. The third anthropological theory (often associated with Bronislaw Malinowski, 1948) is that "myths should be considered as *charters* for customs, institutions or beliefs" (Kirk, p. 59). The work of Claude Lèvi-Strauss (1963) evolved from this theory and provides us with our strongest reason for maintaining myths in the Scientific Age: They help us work through problems in symbolic and fictionalized form that we are too personally involved in or biased about to engage with openly. The fourth theory about myths arises out of Mircea Eliade's arguments that myths "evoke, or actually re-establish in some sense, the *creative era*" (Kirk, p. 63). Eliade (1963) proposed in vari-

---

The concept of Identification begins in a problem of this sort: Aristotle's Rhetoric centers in the speaker's explicit designs with regard to the confronting of an audience. But there are also ways in which we *spontaneously, intuitively,* even *unconsciously* persuade ourselves. In forming ideas of our personal identity, we spontaneously identify ourselves with family, nation, political or cultural cause, church, and so on. . . . The concept is also relevant because it admonishes us to look for modes of Identification implicit or concealed in doctrines of "Autonomy" that figure prominently in our theories of technological specialization. Simplest instance: If the shepherd is guarding the sheep so that they may be raised for market, though his role (considered in itself as guardian of the sheep) concerns only their good, he is implicitly identified with their slaughter. A total stress upon the autonomy of his pastoral specialization here functions *rhetorically* as a mode of expression whereby we are encouraged to overlook the full implications of his office. Identifications can also be *deliberately* established, as with the baby-kissing politician's ways of kissing women on their babies. [italics original]

176   *Jenéy*

ous works that by telling and retelling ancient tales, a culture is capable of returning to an earlier golden era or the dream time of ages past, connecting with ancestors and predecessors long cherished and revered. The fifth theory (arising from the early 20th century lectures and work of W. Robertson Smith) asserts that myths are closely associated with *rituals*, and myths may actually be derived from rituals, which over the course of time "seem pointless and obscure and therefore give rise to aetiological tales that purport to explain them in some sense."

Kirk (and his predecessors) are of course laying forth theories that categorize and explain the existence of *traditional* tales—stories that arise from the oral tradition and are passed down through generations of storytellers. As any romp through the Aarne–Thompson tale-type indexes will show, there are literally thousands of mythologies and tales from which to draw paradigmatic assistance, so why, of all story groups, choose *Buffy*? One answer lies in the unique gender and power politics of the show:

> Read metaphorically, Buffy stands in for various groups of girls who experience justified feminist anger at having their lives directed by circumstances or individuals beyond their control . . . there is ample reason for diverse girls' frustration and anger at the injustices of living within a culture that objectifies women and encourages passivity and obedience to authority and social norms. Thus, as heroine, Buffy's response to these injustices is instructive. (Helford, 2002, p. 24)

Buffy as metaphor need not stop with teen girls, or even with girls, because the story continues into Buffy's college years, into her 20s, where even at the fictional U.C. Sunnydale she must keep her identity as the slayer secret from all but her chosen inner circle. Unlike older, more well-known pop-culture superheroes with secret identities, Buffy is uniquely suited to the type of "possible selves" composition teachers (I argue) need to construct for themselves when faced with the uncertainties and complexities of the new computer and Internet technologies:

- Buffy is a woman, and a petite one at that; often she is discounted or even overlooked as a resource by conventional "official" authority figures, which frequently is a disadvantage.
- Buffy is a woman, and a petite one at that; often she is discounted or even overlooked as a threat by the forces of evil, which can often work to her advantage, putting them off guard.

- Buffy is an expert with highly specialized skills, yet even those who know about her prowess and service to humanity rarely take the time or effort to acknowledge her.
- Buffy's "day job" as a student and social creature is portrayed with a deeper sense of the real ironies and dangers of growing up in America (and in the American public education system) than any of her precursors (i.e., Super Girl, Wonder Woman, various Marvel Comics freaks of nature).
- Buffy's circle of helpers and friends forms a rational, sophisticated configuration of the "cooperative/collaborative" model: Each member contributes to the problem-solving task from a skill and knowledge base different from the others. Overlaps in knowledge and abilities work as fail-safe systems, rather than frustrating redundancies: Usually each member's knowledge base is checked and balanced by alternative perspectives within the team.

This is only the beginning of a metaphorical comparison between teaching in uncertain environments and the slayer's adventures in Sunnydale, which those familiar with the *Buffy* stories can draw out even further. Yet what can we see as useful in this otherwise banal and vaguely interesting set of comparisons?

There are several answers. The most practical is at the point of conceptual theory. Stuart Blythe (2001) noted in his *Computers and Composition* essay on user-centered design in online distance education that, "It has become commonplace to suggest that distance learning via the internet forces instructors to become designers as well as teachers" (p. 329). Design begins at the conceptual level—a level influenced by society, culture, politics, economics, religion, and education. All of these influences on our inventing processes are to some degree socially constructed. As much as we might deny any religious affiliation, we do know the primary formats of the dominant religious belief systems in our world. As much as we might deny any affinity for fairy stories or folk tales, we do recognize the characters and plots that echo out of our own cultural past. As J.R.R. Tolkien, Max Luthi, and others have argued, our mythical construction of ourselves contributes a great deal to our inner lives and to our ability to move and function in the world around us. The stories we tell and those told by others reveal us, teach us, warn us, amuse us, and comfort us; we in turn, most often subconsciously and unaware of their power and pervasiveness, behave according to the lessons and explanations provided in our traditional mythologies and lore.

178 *Jenéy*

> Willow: Giles says everything's a part of the earth. This bed, the air, us.
>
> Buffy: Explains why my fingernails get dirty even when I don't do anything.
>
> Willow: Plus you stuck your thumbs in a demon. (Espenson, 2002)

If we accept that choosing a metaphor or mythos can be used as a helpful cognitive framework, or at least a set of mental touchstones by which we can roughly or even subliminally measure our own progress against some chosen, "constructed self," then for teachers of online composition courses there is no better ally than the irreverent, tradition-busting *Buffy*. Although she is small and female, she is strong and fast, mighty and smart. No one outside her small circle of friends expects her to show courage and expert skills in the face of trouble. She does not fail in her efforts when ordinary authority figures misrepresent, disparage, or overlook her. Folklorist Karen Rowe (1991), among others, observed that the old, traditional fairy tales—the stories embedded in our cultural identities and lexically interwoven into our mental metaphors—"are not just entertaining fantasies, but powerful transmitters of romantic myths that encourage women to internalize only aspirations deemed appropriate to our real sexual functions within a patriarch" (p. 348). She went on to remind us that, in folk and fairy tales of Western tradition,

> Romantic tales exert an awesome imaginative power over the female psyche—a power intensified by formal structures which we perhaps take too much for granted. The pattern of enchantment and disenchantment, the formulaic closing with nuptial rites, and the plot's comic structure seem so conventional that we do not question the implications. Yet, traditional patterns, no less than fantasy characterizations and actions, contribute to the fairy tale's potency as a purveyor of romantic archetypes and thereby, of cultural precepts for young women. Heroines, for example, habitually spend their adolescence in servitude to an evil stepmother, father, or beast, or in an enchanted sleep, either embalmed in a glass coffin or imprisoned in a castle tower. On one level an "enchantment" serves as a convenient metaphor to characterize the pubertal period during which young women resolve perplexing ambivalences toward both parents, longingly wish and wait for the rescuing prince, and cultivate beauty as well as moral and domestic virtues. (p. 357)

Online Distance education and the "Buffy Paradigm"   *179*

In other words, Rowe insisted, the old model teaches us that "[s]tatus and fortune never result from the female's self-exertion but from passive assimilation into her husband's sphere."

Although there is nothing new about composition teachers and administrators characterizing themselves and their jobs for various rhetorical purposes as mythical figures, the online environment has brought us into a realm so pedagogically new and untried, the mere act of explaining to fellow instructors and other education professionals the scope and nature of the challenges has become an exercise in poetics: We need analogous references to help us explain what it is we are trying to accomplish, especially when the terminologies of Internet technologies become daunting or confusing to all involved. Novels, scholarly works, and the popular press have all adopted the metaphor of place as a way to discuss online environments, and frequently teachers have used it to help their colleagues and administrators visualize the challenges. Yet quickly during the 1990s the idea of virtual space or virtual reality began to fade into the jargon and contextual spheres of computer game production and marketing, or of novelty pastimes. More often than not, we think of it in the context of high-tech exploration and experimental engineering design. Virtual spaces, places, and phenomena discussed with such excitement in the mid-1990s seem to have become online course-delivery systems. As quickly as the excitement about object-oriented teaching environments such as MUDs and MOOs rose to the forefront of discussion, they seem to have almost faded in popularity and emphasis. In their place have arisen proprietary "courseware in a box" services, prepackaged and available for large subscription fees to colleges and universities around the world.[11] Just as the composition teaching homesteaders began to move onto the new electronic frontier, we might say that the Railroad companies arrived to carry students off to a standardized, prefabricated train station. Proprietary courseware comes at a price some might think too dear: Its adoption sometimes "railroads"

---

[11] According to the National Education Association (2002) report "The Promise and the Reality of Distance-education,"

> Distance learning has proven [sic] to be no cheaper than a traditional education, and it is not likely to get any cheaper. Blackboard and WebCT, two major providers of distance-education technology platforms, have recently raised prices of new software options because of a growing complexity and demand for new features. The new WebCT product is especially pricey in the six figures. (p. 3)

teachers who might otherwise have developed exciting course designs and online learning environments. Teachers (especially those with little or no voice in curricular decisions, such as adjuncts and graduate teaching assistants [GTAs]) are then easily pressured into squeezing their Internet classes into the formulaic databases of the adopted courseware. The "online pioneers" quickly become docile workers, shopping at the Company Store.

This pattern of configuring "introjected self-guides" (externally defined expectations or standards of conduct that one does not fully accept as one's own), based on self-defeating cultural tales, usually leads to frustrated abandonment of the paradigm. In the end, no Internet Pedagogy Cavalry is expected (not really, anyway) to rescue and support the efforts of composition teachers who are working to design and teach online courses that make sense, serve student needs, and display a high level of usability and intuitive design. In fact the more likely and ominous outcome is that various unforeseen Big Bad Wolves will take advantage of the (often uncompensated) hard work and ingenious methods employed by online teachers, even to the point of pirating—if not outright stealing—course materials and environmental designs created by individuals for their own online classes. The passive frontier-settler syndrome might explain, to some extent, some of the confounding dead ends, and confusing online dynamics of Internet composition teaching. One unexpected dynamic is described in Laura Brady's (2001) eye-opening article, "Fault Lines in the Terrain of Distance-education." She noted that in online course exit questionnaires, students using drop-down menus evaluated the instructor as "Not Applicable." Brady feels that "the *not applicable* responses suggest that student perceptions of teaching change with a distance-education approach. Without face-to-face interaction, the teacher disappears or becomes not applicable" (p. 351).

It is entertaining to imagine the underlying mythos of those online students—must not they have felt themselves on some level to be acting out the famous Beauty and the Beast story? For an entire semester, these people functioned in an online environment whose furnishings were satisfactory: Their needs were met, their lessons were learned, the experience overall was rated by a positive score, but the host (the Beast!)—the teacher, the designer and builder of the educational electronic space—was to them *invisible*.

On the one hand, recommending a mythological paradigm as a conceptual framework for dealing with technology is a mental exercise, a flight of fancy perhaps. On the other hand, it can be seen as an important starting place for conceptualizing modes of institutional and political movement—of determining and possibly participating in decisions concerning

Online Distance education and the "Buffy Paradigm"   *181*

where online teaching technologies and employment practices are headed. In the world of *Buffy the Vampire Slayer*, vampires, demons, and evil creatures of the night are not "at war" with humans so much as they are simply behaving in their own (super) natural way, which unfortunately is often deadly to mere mortals. They are not exactly *neutral* in nature, and they are sometimes used in allegorical ways to illustrate the harshness and uncertainties of life in our technological world (South, 2001). Still their *behavior* is strange, unpredictable, and often dangerous, albeit the *intent* of various monsters and dark creatures frequently is not personal or vicious at all; they hunt, feed, and wreak havoc as a matter of habit and natural impulses, sometimes even as an unintended by-product of their very existence, not out of any kind of concerted desire to commit specific harm. Computer technologies, especially in educational environments, share many of these specific traits; even when students or educators experience frustration or harm, the technology has no evil intention. In fact it has no intention at all—although its creators cannot be held to that same neutral judgment. In the show, over time as the season arcs progress, it becomes interesting to watch the Slayer's mission evolve: She differentiates among various "baddies" and often shows mercy or even generosity to those creatures who do no harm to people. In other words, the Slayer's world is not black and white: Not every new and surprising monster is bad. Neither is every human ally good.

> Willow: There's a Slayer handbook?
>
> Buffy: Wait. Handbook? What handbook? How come I don't have a handbook?
>
> Willow: Is there a T-shirt, too? 'Cause that would be cool. . . .
>   (Noxon, 1997)

Buffy's task is difficult because she specializes in controlling potentially dangerous forces; because of her special strength and skills, she cannot assimilate into "average" society—in this, she represents the classic embodiment of the hero.

Sunnydale is a place where the mindless and dull-witted cannot survive for long. The same is true of online teaching: internetworked computer technologies are full of bugs, snafus, programming glitches, and other mechanical failures, but they are also a playground for hackers, crackers, embezzlers, identity thieves, cheaters, and other intentional abuses of computer technologies that can catch teachers and students off guard at any moment. Even hybrid and computer-classroom teachers have learned to prepare alternate activities for every planned online exercise and remind students of unsafe information sharing in case of technofailures or online swindle zones. Like the Slayer, online distance educators must think on their feet, learn alternate systems and pedagogies, and develop networks of unusual and innovative resources.

In addition to the "Buffy Paradigm," Cordesman (2001) identified a feature of the show that he calls the "Buffy Syndrome":

> The characters in Buffy constantly try to create unrealistic plans and models, and live in a world where they never really face the level of uncertainty they must deal with. They do not live in a world of total denial, but they do seek predictability and certainty to a degree that never corresponds to the problems they face. (p. 5)

This added dimension of the *Buffy* mythology illustrates in powerful metaphor a syndrome that almost all who work with Internetworked computer technologies must periodically both suffer from and deal with in others. Social psychologists have noted that people tend to believe that computers can do things that they cannot (i.e., "understand" concepts, "read" human language, intuitively interpret incorrectly entered data, etc.), and people do not believe that computers are capable of doing things that they were actually designed to do and can accomplish quite easily (i.e., tracking financial records, cracking security encryptions, spoofing individual identities, logging transactions, communications, personal data, Internet use, etc.). If we as users and manipulators of technology and its communications interfaces are often in denial about the risks and dangers of Internetworked teaching, imagine the varying states of blissful denial and technophobic paranoia our students, colleagues, administrators, and fellow citizens must be feeling. Should we password protect every chatboard, log-in site, and Web page? Possibly. Should we encrypt grade information with e-mail PGP technologies? Perhaps. Should we relax and put it all online and let the pixels go forth, multiply, and influence for the better where they may? Only if we can do so without violating Buckley-amendment policies and other privacy requirements. All of these and thousands more questions lurk just beneath the surface of a slightly uneasy, mildly neurotic band of online distance education teachers of written composition.

I have asked to be humored in my fanciful plan to configure online distance education composition teachers not as passive settlers on a metaphorical "electronic frontier." I have asked that we consider the Buffy Paradigm as a helpful pattern of thinking—not only in clarifying our posi-

Online Distance education and the "Buffy Paradigm"

tion in relation to technologies that are *not* neutral, but are each capable of great good and great evil dependent on our uses and abuses of them. The Internet has long since expanded to a broader dimension than the "superhighway" of the early 1990s, and it has taken on layers of potential still unknown and untapped. It may not be a Hell Mouth into a demonic dimension, but rather a Sunnydale: a bright and cheerful looking place to live and work that nevertheless sits atop an abyss of wonder and horror. If we ask ourselves to become Slayers—to train and study, to prepare and practice our second-guessing and thinking-on-our-feet skills—if we note the hopelessness of our task with irony and humor, but with genuine concern for our students and the subjects we teach, I believe we can become better designers, better online teachers, better Internet *personae* with textual voices and memorable (if pixellated) personalities that students can rely on and trust.

Internet technologies, especially those employed by budget-strapped colleges and universities, are both blessed with astounding communications and workspace capabilities and at the same time plagued with bugs, hacker attacks, system overloads and breakdowns, design flaws, broken connections, and just plain malfunctions. Passively waiting for our Techno-Cavalry to come to the rescue is not the answer. According to testimony by the General Accounting Office to the Senate Committee on Health, Education, Labor, and Pensions:

> Overall, about 1.5 million out of 19 million postsecondary students took at least one distance-education course in the 1999-2000 school year. These 1.5 million distance-education students differ from other postsecondary students in a number of respects. Compared to other students, they tend to be older and are more likely to be employed full-time and attending school part-time. They also have higher incomes and are more likely to be married. Most students take distance-education courses at public institutions, with more taking courses from two-year schools than from four-year schools. The Internet is the most common mode of delivery for providing distance-education. (p. 3)

The job ahead of online distance education teachers is not one of "homesteading," of sitting around on the frontier and waiting for students to join us in bliss and harmony. It just is not going to happen that way. The technologies in place are new, shaky, and untried on any grand scale (consider a bridge that only collapses once a month or a traffic light that only malfunctions every 100th hour). Many of us who have agreed to venture into these online teaching projects have often done so in the style of Buffy without knowing it and will continue to do so. Yet others may follow and stand still, may tolerate poorly made technologies and blame themselves for malfunctions that result from bad design; they may waste numerous hours exploring fruitless catacombs of technohorrors expecting rewards for their students at the end of the endless tunnels. We can pool our resources and skills, listen to each other (resist the Buffy syndrome), learn from each other, demand better design, better technological products and management *without blaming or demonizing* the workers at our institutions who try very hard to provide what we are asking for—if only we take the time to ask in terms they understand (cf. the character of Giles in *Buffy*, who tirelessly conducts research into arcane manuals and guide books that may or may not be of any help).

We have a long road ahead in the development, design, and implementation of strong and effective online courses. Yet the technology is not the only complication as the demand for online education continues to increase. I would propose that a certain amount of activism and political involvement at the curricular and administrative levels is appropriate for the further advancement of good pedagogical online distance education practices. When possible, for instance, faculty and writing program administrators charged with online teaching responsibilities should consider some of the following:

- Faculty should request and receive sufficient "front-loading" time and resources to investigate new and innovative software and Web technologies.
- Institutions should critically analyze proprietary course-delivery systems licensed to them and offer alternatives when possible.
- Students should be surveyed regularly concerning issues of usability and connectivity.
- Educators should make informed and well-reasoned decisions about their own "presence" in online distance education courses—including images, video, and textual personality in electronic classes.
- Courses offered online should be consistent with the practices of the college or university, not just added on for profit or marketing purposes (National Education Association, 2002).
- Online teachers should enlist the aid of systems administrators, instructional technologists, software experts, and, of

Online Distance education and the "Buffy Paradigm" 185

course, each other to learn as much as possible about the available technological options.

- Educators should be willing to act as advisors and consultants to upper level administrators and governing boards when they make major institution-wide online distance education decisions.
- Institutions, governing boards, and legislators should be willing to put money and resources into development efforts made by faculty and writing programs to develop effective and updated online courses.
- Proprietary, for-profit online distance education enterprises should be separate from—and even in competition with—established, traditional institutions of higher education, rather than hired on and wedged into curricula that may or may not be well suited for their use.
- Online distance education writing courses should not be seen as exploitable "cash cows" for departments or colleges looking to load large numbers of students into writing-intensive freshman courses.

We can choose to let software and systems industries configure our place in the sphere of online distance education, or we can rescue good designs and ideas before they are snatched away from our peers. We should learn to become more willing and able to stake the bad ideas through the heart, expel the buggy systems, close down the fragile and unstable online environments, and eliminate poor pedagogical designs *before* they get a chance to harm the mortals in our care.

Like Buffy, we can save the world—
A lot.

REFERENCES

Ashby, Cornelia M. (2002). Growth in distance-education programs and implications for federal education policy (Statement of Director, Education, Workforce, and Income Security Issues: United States General Accounting Office, Testimony Before the U.S. Senate Committee on Health, Education, Labor, and Pensions. GAO-02-1125T).

Blythe, Stuart. (2001). Designing online courses: User-centered practices. *Computers and Composition, 18*(4), 329-346.

Brady, Laura. (2001). Fault lines in the terrain of distance-education. *Computers and Composition, 18,* 347-358.

Burke, Kenneth (1966). Rhetoric and poetics. In *Language as symbolic action* (pp. 295-307). Berkeley: University of California Press.

Cordesman, Anthony H. (2001). Biological warfare and the "Buffy Paradigm." Washington, DC: Center for Strategic and International Studies [online]. Available: http://www.csis.org/burke/hd/reports/Buffy012902.pdf.

Eliade, Mircea. (1963). *Myth and reality* (Willard R. Trask, Trans.). New York: Harper & Row.

Espenson, Jane. (2002, October 8). Same time, same place (James A. Contner, Director). In Joss Whedon (Producer), *Buffy the Vampire Slayer.*

Ford, Thomas E., Stevenson, Peter R., Wiener, Paul L., & Wait, Robert F. (2002). The role of internalization of gender norms in regulating self-evaluations in response to anticipated delinquency. *Social Psychology Quarterly, 65*(2), 202-212.

Hawisher, Gail E., Paul LeBlanc, Charles Moran, & Selfe, Cynthia. (1996). *Computers and the teaching of writing in American higher education, 1979-1994: A history.* Norwood, NJ: Ablex.

Hawisher, Gail E., & Cynthia Selfe (Eds.). (1999). *Passions, pedagogies, and 21st century technologies.* Urbana, IL: National Council of Teachers of English.

Haynes, Cynthia, & Holmevik, Jan Rune. (Eds.). (2001). *High wired: On the design, use and theory of educational MOO* (2nd ed.) Ann Arbor: University of Michigan Press.

Helford, Elyce R. (2002). My emotions give me power: The containment of girls' anger in *Buffy.* In Rhonda V. Wilcox & David Lavery (Eds.), *Fighting the forces: What's at stake in* Buffy the Vampire Slayer (pp. 18-34). Lanham, MD: Rowman & Littlefield.

Kirk, G. S. (1974). *The nature of Greek myths.* New York: Penguin.

Lang, Andrew. (1901, c. 1884). *Custom and myth.* London: Longmans, Green and Co.

Lévi-Strauss, Claude. (1963). *Structural anthropology* (Claire Jacobson & Brooke Grundfest Schoepf, Trans.). New York: Basic Books.

Malinowski, Bronislaw. (1954; c. 1948). *Magic, science and religion, and other essays* (Robert Redfield, ed.). Boston: Beacon Press.

Müller, F. Max. (1881; c. 1848-1859). *Chips from a German workshop* (Vol. II). New York: C. Scribner's Sons.

National Education Association, Office of Higher Education. (2002). The promise and the reality of distance-education. *Research Center Update, 8*(3) [online]. Available: http://www.nea.org/he/heupdate/vol8no3.pdf.

Norman, Donald. (2002; c. 1988). *The design of everyday things*. New York: Basic Books.

Noxon, Marti. (1997, November 24). What's my line, Part 2 (David Semel, Director). In Joss Whedon (Producer), *Buffy the Vampire Slayer*.

Olsen, Florence. (2003). Wireless networking makes strong inroads on campuses, survey shows. *Chronicle of Higher Education*. 20 Oct. 2003: http://chronicle.com/prm/weekly/v50/i10/10a03402.htm.

Palmquist, Mike, Keifer, K., Hartvigsen, J., and Goodlew, B. (1998). *Transitions: Teaching writing in computer-supported and traditional classrooms*. Greenwich, CT: Ablex.

Petrie, Douglas. (2000, May 9). The Yoko factor (David Grossman, Director). In Joss Whedon (Producer), *Buffy the Vampire Slayer*.

Rheingold, Howard. (1993). *Virtual community: Homesteading on the electronic frontier*. New York: HarperCollins.

Rowe, Karen. (1991). Feminism and fairy tales. In Martin Hallett & Barbara Karasek (Eds.), *Folk and fairy tales* (pp. 346-367). Peterborough: Broadview.

Selfe, Cynthia. (1999). *Technology and literacy in the twenty-first century: The importance of paying attention*. Carbondale and Edwardsville, IL: Southern Illinois University Press.

Selfe, Cynthia L., & Hilligoss, Susan. (1994). *Literacy and computers: The complications of teaching and learning with technology*. New York: Modern Language Association of America.

Snyder, Ilana (Ed.). (1998). *Page to screen: Taking literacy into the electronic era*. New York: Routledge.

South, James B. (2001). All torment, trouble, wonder, and amazement inhabits here: The vicissitudes of technology in *Buffy the Vampire Slayer. Journal of American and Comparative Cultures, 24*(1/2), 93-102.

Spyware. (2004). Webopedia. Jupitermedia Corporation [online]. Available: http://www.webopedia.com/TERM/s/spyware.html.

U.S. General Accounting Office. (2004). Growth in distance-education programs and implications for federal education policy. Testimony before the U.S. Senate Committee on Health, Education, Labor, and Pensions, September 26, 2002.

10

LEARNING AT LIGHT SPEED IN NEAL STEPHENSON'S *THE DIAMOND AGE*

Veronica Pantoja

In addition to the many collections of journals, books, Websites, and other sources of critical information about online learning and educational technology, science fiction can be a supplemental approach from which to re-imagine the potential of technology-mediated education and the importance of critical use. Science fiction offers fresh perspectives to seemingly commonplace events by creatively erasing limitations of time, space, technology, and human interactions with an imaginative eye. In his article about the role of science fiction in the 20th century, Hugo Award-winning writer Robert J. Sawyer explained that science fiction is not purely escapist entertainment. Instead he claimed that science fiction is about reality—about looking at the ramifications of science and technology on real people and speculating what can come from the impact. Sawyer (2000) asserted that science fiction asks readers to "look with a skeptical eye at new technologies" (pp. 9, 10), instead of simply using them without considering their possible consequences. He agreed with cyberpunk author William Gibson, who claimed that the job of the science fiction writer is to be "profoundly ambivalent about changes in technology" (as cited in Sawyer, 2000, p. 6). Science fiction, then, can compel readers to consider a "critical imaginative" approach where the normal and expected ways of doing things can be sent on a rocket ship to Mars, examined under an electron microscope, or even studied within an electronic classroom of the future.

Sawyer's assertion about science fiction's role in speculating about the ramifications of technology parallel Gail Hawisher and Cynthia Selfe's (1991) assertion about the critical use of technology in the classroom. As increasing numbers of teachers and students make use of distance-education technologies, their perceptions of online learning and teaching are rapidly changing. To provide for continued quality education, Hawisher and Selfe wrote that teachers are obligated to be mindful of their use of technology and its effects on learning environments. They suggested that teachers can succeed in using technology to improve educational spaces only if they "take a critical perspective and remain sensitive to the social and political dangers that the use of computers may pose" (p. 56). Universities and colleges are increasingly incorporating various models of distance-education curriculum in their efforts to reach more students who may not be able to commute to campuses or who are searching for more convenient ways to attain their education. From more traditional distance-delivery courses, where students attend classes at satellite centers or watch their instructors over cable networks (instructional TV), to courses conducted solely online, where students and instructors may never actually see each other, distance-education models are continually being adapted to meet the needs of institutions and their students. Educators, informed with current research on distance-education models and technologies, are working to meet those perceptions by critically integrating technology into their pedagogy.

Neal Stephenson's (1995) Hugo Award-winning science fiction novel, *The Diamond Age or, A Young Lady's Illustrated Primer*, provides new perspectives for educators interested in constructing a critical pedagogy that integrates technology to establish effective interactive teaching and learning environments. By projecting educational approaches of the past and present into the future, the novel illustrates highly interactive uses of technology and re-imagines what is possible as it tells the story of a young girl, her technologically advanced computerized primer, and how it impacts her life and education. In addition to illustrating innovative twists to current educational practices, the novel also encourages educators to look at what is possible now and in the future with a science fiction-based critical imaginative.

FUTURISTIC VISIONS OF DISTANCE LEARNING

Stephenson's novel provides a model of teaching and learning that illustrates the principles of a critical engagement of technology through the fictional depiction of a young girl's education through a highly developed form of distance education, made possible with some fantastical scientific and computerized advances. The novel is set in the relatively near future, the "Diamond Age," so named because the fuel of choice for all advanced technology is diamond-based. In this future world, society is divided into various *phyles*, or social strata, where the New Victorians are the wealthy elite, and *thetes* comprise the lower working class. Members of the New Victorian phyle make up the intelligent engineering workforce behind the nanotechnology based machines on which everyone relies. These molecular machines saturate everything: Air-scrubbing atomic-sized tools keep the atmosphere clean, miniature grids of spinning molecules filter water, and twitching nanosites can be implanted on muscles to build bulk without having to exercise. Nanotechnology also spawns *ractives*—an extrapolated form of today's Web-based interactive entertainment. A ractive, shortened from "interactive," is a narrative-based, real-time shared experience in which participants take part by using nanosite implants and other technologies. For example, I could choose to participate in a ractive of *Taming of the Shrew* and choose to play Kate. Other people would choose other roles, and we would all meet in the virtual ractive space to perform the play. Some participants could be professional *ractors* who have spent considerable amounts of money and time to implant themselves with specially constructed nanosites to more fully develop and perform an array of characters. For example, a ractor may choose to implant vocal nanosites down her throat to act with different voices and textures during her performances.

One of the central characters in the novel is John Percival Hackworth, an affluent New Victorian computer engineer who builds computer codes (despite his ironic surname) for molecular machines. One day his superior, Lord Alexander Chung-Sik Finkle-McGraw, commissions him to design something special with which to educate his young granddaughter. Finkle-McGraw feels she needs a new kind of education to instill in her a subversiveness that he feels is missing in her current education. He explains to Hackworth: "In order to raise a generation of children who can reach their full potential, we must find a way to make their lives interesting. And the question I have for you, Mr. Hackworth, is this: Do you think our schools accomplish that?" (Stephenson, 1995, p. 24). Her more traditional schooling is too didactic, Finkle-McGraw complains, and he takes it on himself to find a way to teach her "refreshingly nihilist" and subversive thinking that he feels is missing in his granddaughter's education and necessary for her to break out of their phyle's complacency.

After he builds the Primer, which looks like an antique book (except with highly sophisticated mediatronic pages), Hackworth secretly makes a copy for his own daughter. However, he is mugged on his way home by a boy named Harv, who senses the value of the Primer and gives it to his younger sister, Nell. She opens the Primer, and, as it is designed, it bonds with her, responding only to her commands and questions. Therefore, Nell becomes the unintended recipient of all the Primer is intended to teach despite her lower class status. Although highly imaginative, Nell does not go to school and is often ignored and left alone by her drunken mother, Tequila, in their lower income housing unit. Yet, Nell is intelligent, sensitive, and hungry for the education that the Primer can provide. For Nell, the Primer becomes a handbook, teacher, mentor, caregiver, and mother figure.

The Primer's method of teaching is exceedingly individualized, and Nell's first experience with it is soothing and refreshing, as she has not received much caring attention before and is not sure what to do with it. The first time the Primer addresses Nell, she shuts it immediately, flinging it under her bed. The next time Nell opens the Primer, she is busily putting her stuffed animal "friends" to bed; the Primer reacts to her activities:

> "Nell was putting her children to bed and decided to read them some stories," said the book's voice. Nell looked at the book which had flopped itself open again, this time to an illustration showing a girl who looked much like Nell, except that she was wearing a beautiful flowing dress and had ribbons in her hair. (Stephenson, 1995, p. 95)

The Primer continues to relate a story to Nell, using her as the main character, Princess Nell, in an educational ractive:

> Once upon a time there was a little Princess named Nell who was imprisoned in a tall dark castle on an island in the middle of a great sea, with a little boy named Harv, who was her friend and protector. . . . Princess Nell and Harv could not leave the Dark Castle, but from time to time a raven would come to visit them. (Stephenson, 1995, pp. 95–96)

Learning at Light Speed in Neal Stephenson's The Diamond Age   *193*

When Nell asks the Primer what a raven is, it responds with more than just a simple answer. Instead Nell's Primer helps her internalize her language learning by interacting with her and providing answers to her questions. It shows Nell an illustration of an island seen from above. Then,

> The island rotated downward and out of the picture, becoming a view toward the ocean horizon. In the middle was a black dot. The picture zoomed in on the black dot, and it turned out to be a bird. Big letters appeared beneath. "R A V E N," the book said. "Raven. Now, say it with me."
> "Raven."
> "Very good! Nell, you are a clever girl, and you have much talent with words. Can you spell *raven?*"
> Nell hesitated. She was still blushing from the praise. After a few seconds, the first of the letters began to blink. Nell prodded it.
> The letter grew until it had pushed all the other letters and pictures off the edge of the page. . . . "R is for Run," the book said. The picture kept on changing until it was a picture of Nell. The something fuzzy and red appeared beneath her feet. "Nell Runs on the Red Rug," the book said. (Stephenson, 1995, p. 96)

Nell is unaware of the inner workings of her new teacher. The Primer is an elaborate ractive, facilitated by a ractor named Miranda Redpath. As a ractor, Miranda is able to choose her assignments, but as she participates more and more with Nell through the Primer, she chooses the assignment permanently. She assumes that Nell is alone most of the time because of the long amount of time she spends with the Primer; Miranda also knows that Nell's life is a dangerous struggle because of the stories she presents to Nell through the Primer.

The Primer does not remain merely a tool for learning for Nell—it becomes a strong force both in Nell's life and in the actions that affect all the characters in the novel and the revolution that Nell eventually leads. As the novel progresses and Nell becomes a young woman, the lessons from the Primer become much more complicated, and the stories of Princess Nell develop intricate patterns to correspond to the real events in Nell's life. With the Primer's guidance, Nell develops skills previously unavailable to her; she learns martial arts and self-defense, and, perhaps more important, she learns to trust her instincts. Her success from the Primer's lessons comes from the Primer's mirroring the real-world events in Nell's life and having Nell work through them in the Primer's virtual ractive space. However, the true success comes when she attains the confidence to apply her Primer lessons to events and obstacles.

THE PRIMER: THEN, NOW, TOMORROW

Nell's Primer is certainly no ordinary primer and is unlike the primers used as educational tools in the past to teach children their ABCs, good manners, and prayers. Although it appears to be an old book, it is instead a multimedia-rich, highly interactive computer that alters itself in response to its owner, whomever that little girl may be, imprinting her face, voice, and experiences into its memory. As Hackworth explains to Finkle-McGraw, "[the Primer] will see all events and persons in relation to that girl, using her as a datum from which to chart a psychological terrain, as it were. Maintenance of that terrain is one of the book's primary processes. Whenever the child uses the book, then, it will perform a sort of dynamic mapping from the database onto her particular terrain" (Stephenson, 1995, p. 106). In other words, the Primer is specifically designed to teach its student by interpreting her life into lessons that will be useful, applicable, and interesting for her.

The Diamond Age Primer also evokes American primers of the 17th and 18th centuries that were used to teach children moral values and basic literacy skills; many of these primers were written with singsong verses to more easily teach the dictates of virtue and piety. Unlike its traditional prototypes, the education Stephenson's Primer demonstrates is not the standard, "virtuous" education for the typical New Victorian young lady. *The New-England Primer*, for example, used simple religious teachings to indoctrinate young children into their society and culture. Stephenson's Primer uses its staggering databases of knowledge to encourage its students to think outside their prescribed roles in New Victorian society and culture. David Watters (1985) claimed that primers like *The New-England Primer*, first published in 1727, are recognized for their immense influence on early American literature, but they are seldom the subjects of literary criticism due "to the distaste in modern times for its view of infant corruption" (p. 193). Primers defined for children their place in relation to their communities and parental, civil, and religious authority figures, and they were a jumble of texts and lessons: alphabet books, advice, proverbs, guides to behavior, prayers, catechisms, poetry, and cautionary tales in simple language that was easy for children to memorize (Watters, 1985, p. 193). The Primer constructed by Hackworth and Finkle-McGraw is similar to the "distasteful" primers of the past in its mission to shape (or corrupt) a child's behavior. However, it differs in that it can truly interact with its student to provide an education that is, in Finkle-McGraw's term, "subver-

Learning at Light Speed in Neal Stephenson's The Diamond Age   *195*

sive."[1] Peter Brigg (1999), in his analysis of Stephenson's use of such an antiquated teaching tool in *The Diamond Age*, wrote that,

> the Neo-Victorian world [of Stephenson's novel] focuses on order and morality, while the Primer is focused on going beyond those bounds to a fuller realization of human potential. . . . The Primer's function is to permit the young women who possess it to see beyond the highly artificial bounds of the Neo-Victorian upbringing by developing them emotionally and educationally so they are both free and powerful. (p. 122)

Instead of passively teaching only necessary information in no particular order, the Primer is nearly alive, capable of talking and interacting with its student, asking provocative questions, providing useful information at the right times, and constructing a safe environment that reflects and includes its student's real-life experiences within its ractive space. It is the subversive element of nontraditional learning and teaching that enables Nell to lead the society of *The Diamond Age* into a new age (which is what forms the other major storyline in the novel). It is from a character whom Nell meets that we get a sense of Stephenson's idea of education and knowledge:

> The difference between ignorant and educated people is that the latter know more facts. But that has nothing to do with whether they are stupid or intelligent. The difference between stupid and intelligent people—and this is true whether or not they are well-educated—is that intelligent people can handle subtlety. They are not baffled by ambiguous or even contradictory situations—in fact, they expect them and are apt to become suspicious when things seem overly straightforward. In your Primer you have a resource that will make you highly educated, but it will never make you intelligent. That comes from life. (Stephenson, 1995, p. 283)

Because Nell is able to transfer the knowledge she gains from her Primer into her experiences in her real physical world, she attains a critical aware-

---

[1]Finkle-McGraw's ideas of subversive teaching echoes Neil Postman and Charles Weingartner's (1969) *Teaching as a Subversive Activity*, in which they advocate a nontraditional approach to education that is "capable of generating enough energy to lead its own revitalization" (p. xv).

196 *Pantoja*

ness of the situations in which she finds herself. When the Primer's methods of teaching resonate with Nell's needs at the time, it is much more effective, and its instruction is retained because of its usefulness.

LEARNING GOES THE DISTANCE: ADJUSTING FOR CHANGE

As institutions continue to accommodate the demands of distance teaching where arenas of interaction are altered in multiple ways, students and teachers alike must also adjust their ways of thinking about the learning and teaching process and consider the possibilities beyond (and within) the face-to-face conventional classroom. Technologies are more than just tools; if integrated critically, they can transform pedagogy as they shift interactions among students, teachers, and course content. As Hawisher and Selfe (1991) reported, many writing teachers extol the virtues of online communication in their courses because online interactions allowed for more one-on-one time with individual students and more opportunities for sharing. However, as Hawisher and Selfe (1991) soon discovered in their classroom observations, writing teachers were not making use of the technology in innovative ways and were at times simply giving presentations or electronic lectures with little interaction from the students. They stressed that computers themselves "do not automatically create ideal learning situations" (p. 60).

One common concern about distance education and online teaching is that technology cannot facilitate the relationships and interactions that develop in face-to-face classrooms. Although technologies can provide seemingly endless possibilities for teaching and learning, "they also frequently clash with some . . . basic beliefs about the nature of classroom instruction, in all its communal richness and face-to-face complexity" (Anson, 1999, p. 263). For example, in a face-to-face class, students and instructors can rely on nonverbal communication strategies, such as facial expressions, to express themselves and enhance interaction. These strategies are lost in an electronic environment (except for the use of emoticons used in e-mail and online communication). However, I argue that using computers and other technologies will almost always clash with traditional notions of teaching, learning, and interaction as the usual roles of teacher, student, and content are subverted to meet student needs. As Miranda

Learning at Light Speed in Neal Stephenson's The Diamond Age

Redpath's character illustrates in the most complete way, technology can be a way to connect with a student, no matter the distance. Jan Berrien Berends (1997), in his review of the novel, noted, "the Primer would not function were it not for the fact that several people devote themselves entirely, or at least extensively, to Nell" (p. 16). The situation in the novel is indeed based in fiction, but it illustrates the importance of a real person on the other end of the education provided.

Mark Canada (2000) explained that one main difference between a face-to-face course and an online course is that students must "shift their focus in a fundamental way—from viewing the teacher as a source to viewing themselves as seekers" (p. 35). This shift alters the learning process. If students can see themselves as seekers and if teachers work to facilitate the process, students and teachers can construct an educational experience together to promote critical thinking. Joan Tornow (1997) argued that students may already see themselves as "seekers"; because many of them have grown up using the computer network medium, they think of it as their own. It is a "space where they can bring their own language and concerns. . . . On computer networks, whether local or wide, students pursue learning on their own terms" (p. 220). Seeing students as "seekers" in online or technology-assisted learning can remedy another concern about distance learning—that students may become passive learners. David Squires (1999) wrote that educational software should automatically build into its programming a "volatile design" for "subversive use . . . responding to the changing and idiosyncratic needs of learners" (p. 48). The goal of constructivist education software, where students are in control of their own learning, is to create authentic learning where the following situations and conditions apply:

1. Opportunities are provided for the learner to explore the behavior of systems, environments, or artifacts;
2. The learner is able to express personal ideas and opinions, with the environment providing a mechanism for the articulation of these ideas;
3. Learners should be able to experiment with ideas and try out different solutions to problems;
4. A sense of ownership should be a prominent feature of learning;
5. Learners should be presented with complex environments that are representative of interesting and motivating tasks; and

198   *Pantoja*

6. Learners may need help in coping with complexity. (Squires, 1999, p. 49)

The Primer in Stephenson's novel definitely incorporates volatile design because it was built to be subversive. Instead of replicating the educational pattern that the characters in the novel found too conventional, they instead allowed the technology, the student, and the teacher to build their own routes through a terrain of information, echoing the conditions that Squires explains is integral to authentic learning.

LESSONS FROM THE PRIMER

The Primer's capabilities are, no doubt, beyond what current computers can do today, and the support staff for the Primer is extraordinary. Stephenson's novel may not be applicable to all situations and institutions because its setting operates in futuristic contexts and within different societal considerations. Like current forms of distance education, however, the Primer encompasses a wide variety of technology-enhanced methods of teaching, such as interactive TV, online courseware, CD-ROM-based instruction, computer communication, or any combination in between. Although a miracle of technological advances not yet realized presently, the Primer does contain elements that are currently being explored and used in different ways. For instance, Nell's experience with the Primer is similar to MOO spaces that many instructors utilize today. MOOs are shared virtual spaces in which multiple participants interface with each other using text or visual representations in real time for entertainment, education, and socializing, much like the ractives in Stephenson's novel. As in a MOO, Nell is in control of her Primer space (for the most part) because the events that occur in the Primer's story of Princess Nell and her interactions with characters in the Primer space depend on her learning the Primer's lessons or applying lessons she learns (or does not learn) in the real world. In this way, Nell learns best by doing, not by being told or simply memorizing some content. Although Nell controls the Primer's narrative, it does not allow her to skip ahead; she must successfully complete each task along the journey before setting on to the next adventure. This kind of learner-centered teaching promotes active learning and is similar to the volatile design that Squires advocated: It provides opportunities for Nell to see the

Learning at Light Speed in Neal Stephenson's The Diamond Age **199**

effects of her actions on systems within the ractive environment. Additionally, the interactive MOO-like space also encourages Nell to experiment with different solutions to the various problems she has presented—problems that are important to her life as Princess Nell.

As with Primers of the past, Nell's most important initial lessons deal with literacy and language and Nell's essential place within both. The Primer does not allow Nell to be a passive learner. Instead it draws her into the language lesson—she is immediately a part of the Primer's virtual world as Princess Nell, the protagonist of the Primer's narrative, and so is highly invested in what her character does and learns in the virtual world. As Nell matures and moves through the lessons of the Primer, the lessons become subtler, and her ideas of literacy and language expand, as was intended by the creators of the Primer. Although Nell was fundamentally a blank slate on which the Primer could begin its teaching, she advances to complicated levels of literacy, successfully solving elaborate language puzzles in Princess Nell's quests. Literacy lessons like Nell's can be seen with today's listservs, discussion boards, blogs, online tutoring, and instant messaging that so many teachers and students alike utilize for virtual office hours, virtual tours, and other activities.

Stephenson's choice to place an archaic element such as a primer into his novel's futuristic setting is a "complex 'hall of mirrors' situation, in which the future can be used to comment on the present by means of the elements of the past that are selected for projection into it and the attitudes towards those elements" (Brigg, 1999, p. 117). Attitudes and perceptions of primers of the past and about teaching and learning are cast against a new backdrop to reveal some potential lessons today's teachers can apply to their current pedagogy. For instance, the Primer clearly demonstrates what can occur when educational spaces (such as MOOs or courseware packages like Blackboard and WebCT) and the relationships among subject, teacher, and content are subverted to allow students to take control of their own learning. Perhaps one of the most important lessons the novel teaches is the significance of the meaningful relationship that develops between Miranda Redpath and Nell. Although teachers of current distance-based education cannot be as available as the Primer is for Nell, Miranda's role in Nell's education cannot be overlooked. Without Miranda, the Primer's supercomputer intelligence and complicated machinery would not have accomplished much for Nell. *The Diamond Age*, in its futuristic exploration of teaching and learning, allows for and encourages current teachers to examine more critically their methods, students, and implications of teaching with technology, but it also emphasizes the importance of individual attention and personalized instruction.

REFERENCES

Anson, Chris M. (1999). Distant voices: Teaching and writing in a culture of technology. *College English, 61*(3), 261-280.

Berends, Jan Berrien. (1997). The politics of Neal Stephenson's *The Diamond Age*. *The New York Review of Science Fiction, 9*(104), 15-18.

Brigg, Peter. (1999). The future as past viewed from the present: Neal Stephenson's *The Diamond Age*. *Extrapolation, 40*(2), 116-124.

Canada, Mark. (2000). Students as seekers in online courses. In R. Weiss, D. Knowlton, & b. Speck (Eds.), *Principles of effective teaching in the online classroom*, (pp. 35-40). San Francisco: Jossey-Bass.

Hawisher, Gail. & Selfe, Cynthia. (1991). The rhetoric of technology and the electronic writing class. *College Composition and Communication, 42*(1), 55-65.

Postman, Neil, & Weingartner, Charles. (1969). *Teaching as a subversive activity*. New York: Dell.

Sawyer, Robert J. (2000). The profession of science fiction, 54: The future is here already. *Foundation, 80*, 5-18.

Squires, David. (1999). Educational software for constructivist learning environments: Subversive use and volatile design. *Educational Technology, 39*(3), 48-53.

Stephenson, Neal. (1995). *The diamond age or, a young lady's illustrated primer*. New York: Bantam Books.

Tornow, Joan. (1997). *Link/Age: Composing in the online classroom*. Logan: Utah State University Press.

Watters, David. (1985). "I spake as a child": Authority, metaphor and *The New England Primer*. *Early American Literature, 20*(3), 193-213.

11

DISTANT, PRESENT, AND HYBRID

Peter Sands

To say that teaching and learning is performance raises a host of connotative and denotative meanings. We speak of "performance" on tests, and we speak of "improving performance," and we even engage in sequential activities intended to rehearse performance of skills and applications of knowledge. Teachers and students adopt roles, play to different audiences, depend on their responses, and rescript their performances. In workshop-based writing courses, for example, students take on the roles of writers working with peers, editors working with writers, and audiences responding to writers. Teachers, too, take on different roles in different classes: Sage-on-the-Stage, Guide-on-the-Side, and all positions in between. Other metaphors such as facilitating or coaching identify as well roles teachers can play. Traditional physical-presence classrooms, online distance, and emerging hybrid models of teaching and learning can be mapped onto three rhetorical positions, roughly corresponding with those reported in the literature as prevalent in each environment: a hierarchical relationship with the other, isolation of each self from others, and, finally, an invitation to participation that approximates the invitational rhetoric that grows out of feminist rhetorical theory. In this chapter, I argue that the hybrid or blended course is ultimately a richer ground for role-playing in the service of

201

applicable learning than either "pure" course, whether distance or traditional, but that ultimately the three models must co-exist in the 21st-century university.

The model just presented is immediately recognizable as a caricature of the wide variety of teaching and learning situations that occur, ranging from discussion-heavy large lecture classes to teacher-dominated online classes. As such, it is of limited utility other than to bring front and center the tendencies and controlling metaphors inherent in each environment, rather than the individual efforts to overcome those tendencies that regularly occur. Although such a model does not directly reflect empirical reality, it is a good scheme for organizing thought and action with respect to the choices available to educators and students. Certainly, in writing and other workshop courses in particular, the top–down lecture model rarely appears, yet it is still firmly entrenched in the bulk of higher education pedagogy (Brinkley et al., 1999). Likewise, the literature on distance-education contains ample reports of student isolation and content-rich, but interaction-poor, course designs in addition to reports at the other end of the spectrum.

KINDS OF EDUCATION

Traditional education refers to the discussion- or lecture-based, bricks-and-mortar model of the classroom, in which students and teacher meet in a designated physical space at prearranged times each week for a set period of time, and in which the transmission of knowledge from teacher to student is presumed to be the chief purpose of the meeting even if the method of transfer varies widely from highly directive lecture to loosely structured discussions. Online distance-education, then, is that form of education in which teacher and students do not meet at all face to face, but instead complete the coursework through computer-mediated interactions such as content-rich Websites, streamed video and audio lectures, and student postings to a discussion board or synchronous discussions in a virtual space.[1] Hybrid courses replace some of the seat time of the traditional course with

---

[1] Although my focus here is on Internet-based online distance education, the literature extends backward into correspondence courses, noting, for example, their capacity to extend educational opportunities to otherwise isolated individuals. See Keegan (1994). Otto Peters (cited in Keegan, 1994) noted that teachers of corre-

some of the online interaction of the distance course; students complete self-directed tasks, such as writing to a class bulletin board, but also meet with the teacher in an actual, physical classroom. The hybrid course reconfigures the learning experience in time and space: from the unit of the class meeting to the unit of the week or month, and from the constant physical space of the classroom to the distributed physical spaces of the classroom, the home or other location, and the virtual spaces of the Internet.[2] Hybrid courses create good role-playing situations because they bring an element of realism to the course, resist student expectations based on tradition or long experience, reconfigure the physical and temporal experience of the classroom, and remove the teacher from the position of sole authority. These changes put students and teachers into new roles as facilitators, self-starters, and generators of feedback as a matter of course. As Richard Lanham (2002) wrote, "Everyone who has taught online seems to agree that role of the instructor changes, too, from Socratic wise person to magister ludi. The burden of instruction, though not of arrangement, seems to move back onto the student" (p. 161).

While distributing responsibility for performance and improvisation to teacher-students and student-teachers, hybrid courses simulate most accurately the real conditions under which knowledge and skills are applied (rather than just displayed) in the working world (broadly defined to include both careers and other activities outside school) by those who possess them. In that sense, although not entirely escaping the seduction of what Joseph Petraglia (1995) called "pseudotransactional" writing, the simulation of the hybrid course at least moves thinking and discussion toward the conditions of application, rather than focusing on the conditions of performance and display of knowledge. What is more, by creating a variety of situations—some dependent on synchronous physical presence and some dependent on asynchronous virtual presence—the hybrid course reflects

---

spondence courses in 1965 claimed that they were able to give greater personal attention to students and developed as a result of closer personal relationships with their pupils.

[2]This is not a feature that only arose with the advent of the Internet. For example, before WAN and then the Internet, teachers without access to a Local Area Network and appropriate software such as the Daedalus Integrated Writing Environment would sometimes turn their classes into something recognizable today as a hybrid model by using the reserved area of the library to store a computer disk on which students could deposit or check out assignments, read and comment on the work of others, and so on. For examples of this and other applications, see Hickey and Reiss (1977).

lived experience more directly than the artificial designs of all presence or all distance. For example, publication of student writing as an incentive and teaching tool has a long history in the traditional classroom, either as a classroom "book" or, now, as a website or other digital compilation. In a hybrid course that presents students with both in-class editorial meetings and writing time, as well as independent, outside-class writing, editing, and meeting time, the conditions of actual publishing in mass media or advertising are more accurately simulated. Hence, the simulation of the hybrid course brings students into contact with the real-world conditions of work that writers labor under, encouraging a real performance, rather than a scripted one (Sands, 2002).

THREE SCENARIOS

In these conditions, the teacher's role in the hybrid course (or any other) can change in multiple ways: into a completely decentered facilitator with little or no display of traditional authority (although that is a complex fiction); into a strictly hierarchical role devoted to controlling network traffic and interaction in the classroom; or into a mediated, third role that both accepts and appropriately uses teacherly authority, but also distributes much of the power and responsibility that normally inheres in the teacher out into the class.[3]

Each of these scenarios has some constants: (a) use of a course-management system such as Blackboard or WebCT; (b) access to a class listserv; (c) access to a physical classroom at one point or another; and (d) a course that meets partly online and partly face to face. Although much of what I have to say here can be applied to "pure" distance-education, let me stress that the thought experiment which follows is directed at so-called hybrid or mixed-delivery courses that meld the elements of bricks-and-mortar education with distance learning.

In the first scenario, a teacher can set up the course management system (CMS), establish an unmoderated listserv, and distribute a syllabus outlining the various administrative regulations and basic elements of the

---

[3]This is a common enough issue that variants on it appear regularly in the literature (see e.g., Briggs, 2003; Finkel, 2000). The focus in manuals for new teachers on transitioning to a student-centered viewpoint is a clue to its elusiveness in college teaching (see e.g., McKeachie 1999).

course to the students. Following those basic tasks, the teacher can cede power and authority entirely to the students, becoming a peer among peers for the writing workshop, even submitting her writing for workshopping and evaluation during the term. The highly artificial nature of the exercise, and the requirement that all participants in the room ignore the teacher's real and persistent power, tend to breed resentment and an awareness of the artificiality of the setup.[4] This is the kind of course that many in the computers-and-writing community built in the early years of LAN- and WAN-based teaching. Using Daedalus Integrated Writing Environment in my own early classes, and later Norton Connect, personal websites, and listservs, I also used a pedagogy intended to reduce my own authority and empower students. Results ranged from disastrous to middling, not least because the only truly empowered person in the classroom—me—had made all the decisions, but also set the students loose in an environment familiar to me, but alien to them.

In the second scenario, a teacher can set up the CMS, establish a moderated listserv, and distribute a syllabus outlining the course to the students. At this point, this second teacher situates herself at the opposite end of the spectrum: Messages to the class listserv are filtered through her before posting; materials on the CMS are generated and posted by her, and students are clearly in a subordinate position to her, expected to take learning from her; but not return much, if any, in the other direction. This is the metaphor of teacherly authority that sometimes appeared behind early forms of software produced specifically for writing instruction, as Darin Payne (2000) observed,

> On their surface, the programs often do promote collaboration and self-publication in the promising ways described above. But beneath their surface, at levels too rarely scrutinized, they can undermine and even directly counter such promotion, constraining students' self-representations, determining who is allowed to voice their perspectives (or not), and reaffirming traditional social hierarchies.

---

[4]Such course designs seemed fairly common in the early days of ENFI and later, Internet-enabled computer-mediated communication, predicated on the assumption that online anonymity erased markers of power such as gender and teacherly authority. The work of Susan Herring (1993, 1995, 1996), among others, raised critical questions about such assumptions. For additional approaches, see Faigley (1992), especially the chapter, "The Achieved Utopia of the Networked Classroom"; Ray and Barton (1991); Sirc (1989); and Taylor (1998).

206 *Sands*

This position reflects discomfort with the degree of autonomy and distribution of power/control inherent in computer-enhanced writing environments—what Jerome Bump (1999) identified as its association with "the right side of the brain and thus with feeling." What is more, variants of this position often appear unintentionally in practice.[5] Gail Hawisher and Cynthia Selfe (2000) reported that,

> . . . we began to see that the language teachers used when they wrote about using computers sometimes provided incomplete stories that omitted other possible interpretations. . . . The use of computers in these classes seemed to come between teachers and students, preempting valuable exchanges among members of the class, teachers and students alike. (p. 134)

In the third scenario, the teacher sets up the CMS, establishes an unmoderated listserv, and distributes the syllabus. Yet rather than hewing to either extreme, this teacher embraces her position and uses it for its difference from the positions of the students: she is there as a resource, she is teaching the course because she has specialized knowledge and experience that have been translated into institutional authority, and she is expected to transmit, teach, model, and evaluate student performance in the course. This is perhaps the essence of Freirean liberatory pedagogy, as Freire said in a 1992 JAC interview with Gary Olson:

> Repeatedly, [Freire] contends that teachers must "respect the subjectivity of the students," that they must strive to increase curiosity at every turn. What truly makes someone critical, able to "read reality," is "insertion in the struggles in order to intervene in reality. It is praxis."

Nevertheless, this emphasis on students' participation, students' action, and "respect for students and their contexts" does not mean that teachers should surrender authority to some abstract ideal of classroom

---

[5]Hawisher and Selfe (2000) wrote:

> Another kind of computer-supported class we observed reflected traditional practices of writing instruction in American classrooms. The instructor projected a student paper on an overhead projection system, and students critiqued various aspects of the paper. In each instance, classmates seem to be searching for answers to the instructor's preset

democracy. In fact Freire is quite adamant that his liberatory pedagogy does not translate to the teacher's relinquishing of authority. Quite the contrary: "The teacher has the duty to teach," to use his or her authority to good advantage. Despite attempts to read Freire as advocating the dissolution of the teacher's authority as a means to achieve a truly participatory, dialogic teaching environment, Freire argued that the teacher's authority "has to exist." The important point is that it should never "have such power that it crushes freedom."

WRITING TECHNOLOGIES AND HYBRIDITY

The history of writing technologies—especially with respect to their place in the curriculum—is fraught, but also well enough explored to provide some reassurance about the long-term prospects of teaching and learning online. Dennis Baron (1999) noted that "each new literacy technology begins with a restricted communication function and is available only to a small number of initiates" (p. 16), but that that restriction is ultimately overcome as a technology spreads through society. Alternatively, new technologies of writing produce trepidation in the elites who have already mastered what is current: "the virtual university, a Mars in his cradle though it be, questions the main operating assumptions of its parent. Maybe that is why such a baby dose of it has evoked so much strong feeling" (Lanham, 2002, p. 160). The pressures on universities to produce efficient and profitable online courses is frequently remarked and has led to private-sector competition unlike any previously faced in the history of the American university. Nelly Stromquist (2002) found that "much of the investment by private firms in education is geared to the provision of distance-education or telecommuting. Consortia on distance-education are multiplying rapidly" (p. 51), and that this is leading to a globalized, homogenized form of online education. Neff and Comfort (2002) wrote that,

> questions. And only three or four students were participating in these rather contrived discussions. . . . The use of technology in these classes, far from creating a new forum for learning, simply magnified the power differential between students and the instructor. Ostensibly computers were being used to "share" writing, but the effect of such sharing was to make the class more teacher-centered and teacher-controlled. (pp. 134-135)

the implementation of distance-education often conflicts with values traditionally associated with English studies. Going from a [face-to-face] class to a distance class is not a simple transition or adaptation of what we currently do for a different delivery system. In distance-delivery systems, many individuals in addition to the instructor have authority over curriculum and pedagogy. (p. 191)

As Lanham (2002) said, "The whole tone and spirit of online writing frees students from trying to imitate their professors. Written for the class and not for the instructor, it is sometimes incorrect and often inelegant, but it has the breath of life" (p. 161). Recall, too, Lanham's observation of the changing role of the instructor online.

It is a commonplace idea that the pace of digitally enhanced change appears to be accelerating in a kind of educational Moore's Law.[6] Responses to the rapid changes in computer-enhanced teaching and learning (see Maeroff, 2003) that threaten established order can lead to top-down imposition of particular course designs, particularly those that are presentation, rather than interaction heavy (Neff & Comfort, 2002). As Palloff and Pratt (1999) put it,

> Clearly, the role of the instructor, either in a traditional face-to-face or online setting, is to ensure that some type of educational process occurs among the learners involved. As we have discussed, in the face-to-face classroom that role is generally of the expert imparting knowledge to willing learners. (p. 74)

---

[6]*Chronicle of Higher Education* (June, 13 2003):

> When online education began garnering widespread attention in the 1990s, some pundits predicted that it would be short lived and never compete successfully with traditional face-to-face education. Others said students of the future would take all their courses online, interacting with their professors and classmates through home computers and watching Webcast lectures in their underwear.
>
> In the years since, however, rising enrollments have made distance education a viable industry for colleges and companies as administrators and faculty members have learned what works online and what doesn't, both in marketing and in teaching. At many institutions that paid attention to those lessons, distance enrollments have remained strong even after the dot-com implosion of 2000 and 2001 — and after several high profile experiments in distance education

Distant, Present, and Hybrid 209

In their ideal formulation, "the role of the instructor becomes that of an educational facilitator" online, but that has not always been the experience of online teachers. As Neff and Comfort (2002) noted, "tension arises when composition faculty bring a social constructionist pedagogy and a facilitative ethos into a system that promotes portable, self-contained units of instruction and independent rather than interdependent learning" (p. 186). As they said,

> It is not easy to enact a facilitator role in distance settings in which technology constructs the teacher as a dispenser of information and invites students to "time their own learning." . . . No doubt, a presentational mode of delivery serves the pedagogical goals of many disciplines, but it works against contemporary composition and rhetoric theory and pedagogy. (p. 186)

Neff and Comfort's discomfort, however, is specifically directed at a system in place where they taught as untenured new members of the faculty, and is not universally held among distance educators, including those who teach writing. However, as Soomyung Cho and Zane Berge (2002) documented, such "barriers to distance-education" are common. Cho and Berge, in "Overcoming Barriers to Distance Training and Education," identified 10 barriers to effective distance-education: technical expertise, administrative structure, evaluation of effectiveness, organizational change, social interaction, support for students, feelings of being threatened by technology, access to technology, compensation, and legal issues.

---

crashed and burned. Columbia University's Fathom and New York University's NYUonline, to name two, were multimillion-dollar experiments with course offerings that seem, in retrospect, to have been too eclectic and, in the case of Fathom, not career-oriented enough.

Now both traditional colleges and new virtual institutions are enjoying success with distance-education programs. Virginia Tech enrolled 1,054 students in for-credit online courses in the fall of 1998, for example, but that number grew to 2,557 in 2002. Monroe Community College, in Rochester, N.Y., enrolled 277 students in distance education in 1998, and in 2002 it had 1,723. Capella University, a privately held company, has had three consecutive quarters of profitability and has seen its enrollment in its online-only degree programs nearly doubled, from 3,730 in 2001 to 6,578 in 2002. (Carnevale & Olsen, 2003)

In keeping with Neff and Comfort's implicit criteria, the more explicit criteria of Rena Palloff and Keith Pratt (1999)—a well-constructed, interactive, community of online learners—puts in place a situation that acknowledges that "key to the learning process are the interactions among students themselves, the interactions between faculty and students, and the collaboration in learning that results from these interactions" (p. 5). As Frank H. T. Rhodes (2001) put it in his recent *Creation of the Future*, "education is not a spectator sport; it is a transforming encounter. It demands active engagement, not passive submission; personal participation, not listless attendance" (2001, p. 65). Palloff and Pratt (1999) concur with Neff and Comfort in noting that,

> one of the basic requirements for education in the twenty-first century will be to prepare students for participation in a knowledge-based economy; knowledge will be the most critical resource for social and economic development. . . . The traditional educational model, based primarily on the concept of the school and the teacher in a classroom as islands, standing alone and not interconnected with society or other educational institutions, will not generate competence in a knowledge society. (p. 166)

Yet they differ in that they believe that such a community can be created and nurtured online

Neff and Comfort (2002) are not alone in noting that,

> when instructors teach face-to-face (f2f) classes in mediated rooms or computer labs, they can rely on the more adept students to work with the novices at their workstations, and classmates are usually happy to help out. This kind of collaboration supports a social constructionist pedagogy and lists some of the pressure to "know it all" from the instructor's shoulders. But because distance-education students are usually physically isolated, it is much more difficult for them to provide each other with hands-on help. (p. 187)

In a sense, this observation points toward either traditional or hybrid models as potentially more successful. Yet theirs is not the only view or experience. Indeed commentators more and more acknowledge the futility of seeking a single solution for all varieties of higher education. Diane Harley, an anthropologist who looks at distance-education in the culture of the university, said in an interview (Foster, 2002) that,

Distant, Present, and Hybrid   211

no one person can come up—I think—with one theory. Over the course of the year-plus that we've been working on this project, it's pretty clear that to understand it, you have to disaggregate institutions. Different institutions are going to respond differently.

In a counterexample to the assumption that hybridity or tradition are to be favored, Michael Marx, for example, more than a decade ago reported that connecting students in two different classes at a distance provides advantages such as a willingness to give and attend to honest criticism that might have been masked by social niceties in the face-to-face classroom. Such candor and attention to language have long been documented advantages of computer-enhanced teaching of writing and literature, even after long years of experience have tempered early enthusiasm.

Increasingly, commentators are presenting blended or hybrid classrooms as the inevitable or necessary outgrowth of computer-mediated teaching—a return to some forms of face-to-face learning following awareness of the limitations of purely online learning (Dreyfus, 2001; Ess, 2003). Institutions such as my own—the University of Wisconsin–Milwaukee— and University of Central Florida in Orlando have begun classroom-based research and faculty development projects aimed at gathering empirical data necessary to justify, understand, and improve hybrid and distance-education. They are building on the finding of "no significant difference" between online and face-to-face instructional modes, as well as on the findings that certain student populations, such as those with stronger intrinsic motivation and maturity, both desire and benefit from online or hybrid courses (see "The 'No Significant Difference Phenomenon' " at http://teleeducation.nb.ca/nosignificantdifference/). The RITE research shows that most distance-learning students at their campus are also taking traditional courses; there is no local difference in ethnic distribution among any of the available course-delivery methods, although true distance-education courses attract more women students; fully online course tend to attract older students than other kinds of classes do. About half of the UCF students taking fully online courses work full time as well. Finally, UCF (2001) found that nearly all of the distance- and hybrid-course enrollees have computers at home. The Research Initiative for Teaching Effectiveness at UCF (http://pegasus.cc.ucf.edu/ ~ rite/), the Hybrid Course Development Project (http://www.uwm.edu/Dept/LTC/hybrid.html), and the statewide Dot.Edu hosting and development project (http://www.uwm.edu/Dept/dotedu/index.html) at UWM represent positive institutional responses to both student demand and faculty concerns for quality instruction.

212   *Sands*

Such projects engage the claim that hybridity enjoys advantages but is not a panacea for educational problems, working in the range of commentators such as Ess and Dreyfus, who presented the idea that there is a point at which being online is demonstrably functional and even superior to being present in the body. Beyond that point, however, embodied experience proves more valuable than being online. This converges with developing practices in other spaces as well. For example, offices that had moved to telecommuting have now moved back to a mixed method, in which people can be in the physical office as needed and in the virtual company space the rest of the time. It is a commonplace notion among office workers that it is often easier, more efficient, and more gratifying to stroll down the hall to another workstation than it is to send an e-mail to the person working there. Where once there was a prediction of a paperless office and a virtual business space, there now is an acceptance that some middle ground, with the human body at its center, will be achieved.

These examples point toward an integrative tendency that, in 20/20 hindsight, is easy to identify and observe. Any significant advance in technology may bring calls for a dramatic shift—a sense that an entirely new way of being and doing has come on us. Yet the history of technology, like the history of teaching and learning, suggests that the embodied human will incorporate those changes into that world, rather than take flight into a new and disembodied world. This strikes me now as eminently sensible, even as my earlier, younger self was excited by the prospect of virtuality and cyberspace.

CONCLUSION

The three positions outlined here correspond roughly to typical pedagogical stances adopted—either by intent or, as is often the case in distance-learning programs, because of administrative requirements and a loss of teacher autonomy (Neff & Comfort 2002)—which is not to say that they have any absolute reference point in the real world. Such an expectation is both unreasonable and indefensible; as the paradox states, "absolute statements are always false." Some people really do learn best through rote repetition. Some material is best learned that way. Others and other material are best learned in experiential settings, in clinical settings, or in discussion with others. As Gene Maeroff (2003) argued in his latest book, distance learning has certain advantages and enables reconsideration of entrenched

Distant, Present, and Hybrid   *213*

teaching and learning methods. Yet, as Palloff and Pratt (1999) wrote, with understatement, "the traditional face-to-face classroom is not likely to disappear. It continues to serve the needs of many students and will do so in the future" (p. 167). Maeroff (2003) began his recent assessment of online learning with a short summary of developments, concluding in a section worth quoting in full that online education is here to stay:

> Developments in online learning in just a little more than ten years force one to conclude that this is a sea change, not a fad. By the end of the twenty-first century's first decade, e-learning will be an embedded feature of education, widely available and no longer an object of controversy. Whether it will be a source of financial gain, as some for-profit providers hope, remains to be seen. Nonetheless, online courses will proliferate at traditional not-for-profit institutions, and students will have far more opportunities to choose between studying in a classroom with other students or in a virtual classroom in which they work alone. Almost certainly, most courses—including the vast majority in classrooms—at most institutions of higher education and to a lesser extent in secondary schools will have online components as essential features. Instructors who in coming years ignore the potential of web-based embellishments will be as remiss as their peers of past years who did not expect students to enrich their learning by consulting sources beyond their books. (pp. 2–3)

Maeroff acknowledged "technology's potential for strengthening instruction in the traditional classroom remains enormous" (p. 2), but also noted that "a growing number of classroom-based courses (by 2001) included online portions that personalized education in new ways." Such changes, such as those reported by Peter Saunders in 1998, in which he discussed successful transition from a paper-based case project to a computer-based simulation of the communications problem the case illustrated for MBA students, point the way toward a continually evolving and effective hybridity. Saunders (1998) pointed to the increased realism of the process as a desirable outcome to be assessed:

> by having students work cases in different courses which refer to a single company, and by integrating communication and writing training into the fabric of the learning platform, it is hoped that the relatedness of what we teach will become apparent and the MBAs we graduate will have a greater sense of how to apply what they learn and how to meet the communication challenges that they will face (p. 98)

In a Leibnitzian perfect world, we would not have to consider these questions. Yet neither do we have to cede critical awareness and practice, like Voltaire's Pangloss, and interpret all aspects of the world as perfect because they exist. Like Candide, teachers and learners in the 21st century have to cultivate their gardens. For specific groups, that garden will flourish online—and it should. For others, that garden will flourish in the physical classroom—and it should. The middle way of integration strikes me as the middle way of balance: between the strengths of online role-playing, writing, self-direction, and communication and the strengths of physical interaction, discussion, listening, role-playing, communicating.

REFERENCES

Baron, Dennis. (1999). From pencils to pixels: The stages of literacy technologies. In Gail Hawisher & Cindy Selfe (Eds.), *Passions, pedagogies, and 21st century technologies* (pp. 15-33). Logan: Utah State University Press.

Briggs, John Channing. (1995). Edifying violence: Peter Elbow and the pedagogical paradox. *JAC, 15*(1). Retrieved 5 August 2003, from http://jac.gsu.edu/jac/15.1/Articles/5.htm.

Brinkley, Alan, Dessants, Betty, Flamm, Michel, Fleming, Cynthia, Forcey, Charles, & Rothschild. Eric (Eds.). (1999). *The Chicago handbook for teachers: A practical guide to the college classroom.* Chicago: University of Chicago Press.

Bump, Jerome. (1999, Fall). Hypermedia and the new puritanism. *Currents in Electronic Literacy* (2). Retrieved 5 August 2003, from http://www.cwrl.utexas.edu/currents/fall99/bump.html.

Bump, Jerome. (1999, November 8). The impact of hypermedia on emotions. Retrieved 5 August 2003, from International Online Conference on Teaching Online in Higher Education: http://as1.ipfw.edu/99tohe/presentations/bump.htm.

Carnevale, Dan, & Olsen, Florence. (2003, June 13). How to succeed in distance-education: By going after the right audience, online programs build a viable industry. *Chronicle of Higher Education, 49*(40), A31. Retrieved 5 August 2003, from http://chronicle.com/weekly/v49/i40/40a03101.htm.

Cho, Soomyung Kim & Berge, Zane L. (2002, January). Overcoming barriers to distance training and education. *USDLA Journal, 16*(1), Featured Articles. Retrieved 13 March 2002, from http://www.usdla.org/html/journal/JAN02_Issue/article01.html.

Dreyfus, Hubert L. (2001). *On the internet.* New York: Routledge.

Ess, Charles. (2003). Liberal arts and distance-education: Can Socrative virtue (arete) and Confusius' exemplary person (junzi) be taught online? *Arts and Humanities in Higher Education, 2*(2), 117-137.

Distant, Present, and Hybrid   *215*

Faigley, Lester. (1992). The Achieved Utopia of the networked classroom. In *Fragments of Rationality* (pp. 163-200). Pittsburgh: University of Pittsburgh Press.

Finkel, Donald L. (2000). *Teaching with your mouth shut.* Portsmouth, NH: Boynton /Cook.

Foster, Andrea L. (2002, March 12). Logging in with . . . Diane Harley: An anthropologist studies universities' approaches to distance education. *Chronicle of Higher Education.* Retrieved 12 March 2002, from http://chronicle. com/free/2002/03/2002031201u.htm.

Hawisher, Gail E., & Selfe, Cynthia L. (2000). The rhetoric of technology and the electronic writing class. In N. M. Edward, P.J. Corbett, & Gary Tate (Eds.), *The writing teacher's sourcebook* (4th ed., pp. 129-138). New York: Oxford.

Herring, Susan. (1993). Gender and democracy in computer-mediated communication. *Electronic Journal of communication* [Online] 3(2). Available: < http://www.cios.org/www/ejc/v3n293.htm > .

Herring, Susan. (1995, 8 Nov). Gender differences in computer-mediated communication: Bringing familiar baggage to the new frontier [Http://www.cpsr.org/cpsr/gender/herring.txt].

Herring, Susan. (1996). Gender and democracy in computer-mediated communication. In R. Kling (Ed.), *Computerization and controversy* (pp. 476-489). New York: Academic Press.

Hickey, Dona, & Reiss, Donna. (1997, August 26). Cybersimulations: Low-tech variations of high-tech applications for learning communities. Retrieved 30 July 2003, from http:// online learning.tc.cc.va.us/faculty/tcreisd/resource/cybrsims.htm.

Keegan, Desmond. (Ed.). (1994). *Otto Peters on distance-education: The industrialization of teaching and learning.* New York: Routledge.

Lanham, Richard A. (2002). The audit of virtuality: Universities in the attention economy. In Steven Brint (Ed.), *The future of the City of Intellect: The changing American university* (pp. 159-180). Stanford: Stanford University Press.

Maeroff, Gene I. (2003). *A classroom of one: How online learning is changing our schools and colleges.* New York: Palgrave Macmillan.

Marx, Michael S. (1990, November). Distant writers, distant critics, and close readings: Linking composition classes through a peer-critiquing network. *Computers and Composition,* 8(1), 23-39. Retrieved 5 August 2003, from http://corax.cwrl.utexas.edu/cac/archives/v8/8_1_html/8_1_2_Marx.html.

McKeachie, Wilbert J. (1999). *McKeachie's teaching tips: Strategies, research, and theory for college and university teachers* (5). Boston: Houghton Mifflin.

Neff, Joyce Magnotto, & Comfort, Juanita Rodgers. (2002). Technological imbalances: The English curriculum and distance-education. In C. M. H. David, B. Downing, & Paula Mathieu (Eds.), *Beyond English Inc.* (pp. 181-193). Portsmouth, NH: Boynton/Cook.

Olson, Gary A. (1992). History, praxis, and change: Paulo Freire and the politics of literacy. *JAC, 12*(1). Retrieved 5 August 2003, from http://jac.gsu.edu/jac/12.1/Articles/1.htm.

Palloff, Rene M., & Pratt, Keith. (1999). *Building learning communities in cyberspace: Effective strategies for the online classroom.* San Francisco: Jossey-Bass.

Payne, Darin. (2000, September). Collaborative learning and cultural reproduction: Publishing students in electronic environments. *Journal of Electronic Publishing, 6*(1). Retrieved 5 August 2003, from http://www.press.umich.edu/jep/06-01/payne.html.

Petraglia, Joseph. (1995). Spinning like a kite: A closer look at the pseudotransactional function of writing. *JAC, 15*(1). Retrieved 25 November 2001, from http://jac.gsu.edu/jac/15.1/Articles/2.htm.

Ray, Ruth, & Barton, Ellen. (1991). Technology and authority. In Gail E. Hawisher & Cynthia L. Selfe (Eds.), *Evolving perspectives on computers and composition studies: Questions for the 1990s* (pp. 279-299). Urbana, IL: NCTE.

Rhodes, Frank H. T. (2001). *The creation of the future: The role of the American university.* Ithaca, NY: Cornell University Press.

RITE. (2001). Distributed learning impact evaluation. Retrieved 3 February 2004, from http://pegasus.cc.ucf.edu/~rite/ImpactEvaluation.html.

RITE. (2001). RITE—Research initiative for teaching effectiveness. Retrieved 13 March 2002, from http://pegasus.cc.ucf.edu/%7Erite/.

RITE. (2001, March). Who takes online courses. Retrieved 13 March 2002, from http://pegasus.cc.ucf.edu/%7Erite/Presentations/site%20presentation.ppt.

Russell, Thomas L. (1999). The "no significant difference phenomenon." Retrieved 3 February 2004, from http://teleeducation.nb.ca/nosignificantdifference.

Sands, Peter. (2002, Spring). World wide words: A rationale and preliminary report on a publishing project for an advanced writing workshop. *Academic Writing.* Retrieved 30 July 2003, from http://wac.colostate.edu/aw/articles/sands_2002.pdf.

Saunders, Peter M. (1998). From case to virtual case: A journey in experiential learning. In D. S. Donna Reiss & Art Young (Eds.), *Electronic communication across the curriculum* (pp. 86-101). Urbana, IL: NCTE.

Sirc, Geoffrey. (1989). Response in the electronic medium. In Chris M. Anson (Ed.), *Writing and response: Theory, practice, and research* (pp. 187-205). Urbana, IL: NCTE.

Stromquist, Nellie P. (2002). *Education in a globalized world: The connectivity of economic power, technology, and knowledge.* Lanham, MD: Rowman & Littlefield.

Taylor, Todd. (1998). The persistence of authority: Coercing the student body. In Todd Taylor & Irene Ward (Eds.), *Literacy theory in the age of the Internet* (pp. 109-121). New York: Columbia University Press.

ABOUT THE EDITORS

Jonathan Alexander is Associate Professor of English and Comparative Literature at the University of Cincinnati, where he also serves as Director of the English Composition Program. He is the author of several articles on computers and writing pedagogy and sexuality studies. With Karen Yescavage, he edited *Bisexuality and Transgenderism: InterSEXions of the Others* (Harrington Park Press, 2004), and his book, *Digital Youth: Emerging Literacies on the World Wide Web* (2006), was just published by Hampton Press. With Margaret Barber, he co-authored the textbook *Argument Now* (Longman, 2005). He is twice the recipient of the Ellen Nold Award for the best article in Computers and Composition Studies. For more information, see his Website at http://oz.uc.edu/ ~ alexanj/.

Marcia Dickson is an Associate Professor of English at The Ohio State University, Marion, where she teaches both composition and literature. She has been involved in teaching with technology both in face-to-face classrooms and online for nearly fifteen years. The author of *It's Not Like That Here: Teaching Reading and Writing to Novice Writers*, as well as co-editor of *Portfolios: Process and Product* and *Writing with Elbow*, she also has published a number of articles on writing pedagogy. For more information, see her Website at http://mrspock.marion.ohio-state.edu/dickson2002/.

ABOUT THE CONTRIBUTORS

Lori E. Amy is Director of the Women's and Gender Studies Program at Georgia Southern University and Assistant Professor in the Department of Writing and Linguistics. She holds a BA in English from the University of Hawaii at Manoa, a MA in English from the University of California at San Diego, and a PhD in English with a certificate in Women's Studies from the University of Florida. Her research into narrative, memory, and trauma draws on feminist psychoanalytic theory, cultural studies, and post-colonial /transnational feminist studies. Recent publications include: "The War Story: Cultural Amnesia and the Avenging Angel Fantasy" (*Journal of Politics and Culture*); "Teaching for Peace in a Digital Age" (with Laura A. Milner, *Women's Studies Quarterly*); "Violent Matters, Classroom Practices: Teaching Etel Adnan's *Sitt Marie Rose*" (*Concerns: Journal of the Women's Caucus of the Modern Language Association*); and "Contemporary Travel Narratives and Old Style Politics: American Women Reporting After the Gulf War" (*Women's Studies International Forum*). She is currently working on her first book, *The Wars We Inherit*, which uses critical autobiography to critique the relation between public and private violence.

Currently teaching at East Stroudsburg University of Pennsylvania in both the traditional and the online classroom, **Lesliee Antonette** is the author of *The Rhetoric of Diversity and the Traditions of Literary Study: Critical Multiculturalism in English*, part of the Series on Critical Theory and Education, edited by Henry A. Giroux, and a number of articles on multicultural history, education and literature.

220 *About the Contributors*

Melody Bowdon is Assistant Professor of English at the University of Central Florida, where she coordinates the Graduate Certificate in Professional Writing and teaches face-to-face and web-based writing courses from the undergraduate to PhD levels. She is co-author with Blake Scott of *Service-Learning in Technical and Professional Communication*, part of the Allyn and Bacon series on technical communication, and her work has been published in journals such as *College English* and *Technical Communication Quarterly*. She is currently working on a new book project called *Professional Writing in the Nonprofit Sector*. Her email address is mbowdon@mail.ucf.edu.

Stuart Blersch is Professor of English at the University of Cincinnati, where he has taught basic writing for 29 years. He also teaches courses in Lesbian and Gay Literature and Censorship in Literature and the Arts. His other research interests include Victorian studies and the novels of Daisy Ashford. **Carolyn Stoll** is a Field Service Assistant Professor at the University of Cincinnati, where she has taught for the last 9 years. Prior to teaching at the college level, she taught middle school English and worked briefly in the private sector as a technical editor. She graduated from Miami University of Ohio in 1985 with a Bachelor of Science degree in Education and then received her Master of Arts degree in English from Miami in 1992. She resides in Hamilton, Ohio with her husband and two sons.

John Bryan has taught professional writing at the University of Cincinnati since 1989. Before that, he worked as a writer and marketing manager for engineering firms in Colorado and Missouri for ten year. From 1995 to 2003, he served as associate dean of the College of Arts & Sciences and then as dean of University College at UC. In that latter role, he led the creation of UC's largest and most successful distance-learning degree program. Since 1992, he has been the regular ethics columnist for the Society for Technical Communication's *Intercom* magazine.

Debbie Danowski, PhD, is an assistant professor of English and Media Studies at Sacred Heart University where she teaches journalism and writing. Her areas of research include journal writing and popular women's magazines. The co-author of three popular books, *Why Can't I Stop Eating?* (Hazelden, 2000), *Locked Up For Eating Too Much* (Hazelden, 2002), and *The Overeater's Journal* (Hazelden, 2004), Dr. Danowski has written more than 100 articles for national and local publications, including *First For Women, Woman's Day*, and *Seventeen Magazine*. She has also worked in the journalism and public relations fields serving as a reporter for a local news-

About the Contributors 221

paper, a marketing consultant for a national psychiatric hospital, and Manager of Media Relations for a national nonprofit organization.

Christy Desmet is Associate Professor of English and Director of the First-Year Composition Program at the University of Georgia. **Robert Cummings** is a PhD candidate in the English Department at the University of Georgia, specializing in Rhetoric and Composition, Humanities Computing, and Southern Literature. **Alexis Hart** completed her PhD with an emphasis in Rhetoric and Composition in August 2003 at the University of Georgia. She currently serves as a Robert E. Park Post-doctoral Teaching Fellow and Assistant Director of First-year Composition at the University of Georgia. **William Finlay** is Professor and Head of the Department of Sociology at the University of Georgia. Most of his research is on the workplace, and one of his specific interests is in how technology affects the way in which people work. His most recent major publication is a book on corporate head-hunters (Cornell University Press, 2002), and he is currently working on a project that looks at the training and work of surgical residents.

Ellen Hendrix is an Assistant Professor in the Department of Writing and Linguistics at Georgia Southern University. For the past eight years, she has taught distance learning first-year writing courses, and she acts as the technical liaison for the Georgia Southern Writing Project.

Cynthia Jeney is an assistant professor of English and Technical Communications at Missouri Western State College in Saint Joseph, Missouri, where she has taught both online distance and computer lab courses since 2000. She is an active member of the Alliance for Computers and Writing and a task-force member of the CCCC Assembly on Computers in English. She earned a PhD in Rhetoric and Composition from Arizona State University in 2000, with her dissertation "Extending the Burkean System Online: A Study of Motive and Internetworked Symbolic Action."

Veronica Pantoja is currently teaching writing at Chandler-Gilbert Community College in Arizona. Her research interests include teaching writing with technology and writing center theory and administration. She is also a doctoral student in English (Rhetoric/Composition and Linguistics) at Arizona State University.

Peter Sands is assistant professor of English at the University of Wisconsin-Milwaukee, where he teaches graduate and undergraduate courses in computers and composition, rhetoric, American literature, sf/utopia, and writ-

222 *About the Contributors*

ing. He is co-editor of *Electronic Collaboration in the Humanities* (Erlbaum, 2003), and his articles have appeared in *Academic.Writing, ACE Journal, Kairos, Utopian Studies, Works and Days*, and elsewhere. He is founding editor of H-Utopia, part of the Humanities and Social Sciences Online network, and is currently working on a book-length study of rhetoric, utopia, and pedagogy.

AUTHOR INDEX

A

Adam, A., 122(n6), *130*
Agarenzo, T., 103, *108*
Angelou, M., 81, 82, 83, 84, *94*
Angier, N., 84, *94*
Annas, P., 25, *42*
Anson, C., 21, *42*, 66-67, 76, 102, 103, *107*, 196, *200*
Antonette, L., 133, 135(n2), 136, 141, 142, 143, *145*
Arbuthnot, L., 103, *107*
Arizpe, L., 122(n6), *130*
Ashby, C.M., 165, *186*

A

Balsamo, A., 152, 153, *160*
Baron, D., 207, *214*
Bartholomae, D., 81, *94*
Barton, E., 205(n4), *216*
Beach, R., 102, 103, *107*
Berends, J.B., 197, *200*
Berge, Z., 209, *214*
Berlin, J.A., 102, *107*

Berzsenyi, C.A., 28, *42*
Bizzell, P., 123, *130*
Blythe, S., 177, *186*
Bordia, P., 34, 35, 38, *42*
Bourdieu, P., 115, *130*
Brady, L., 7, *14*, 22, 25, *42*, 180, *186*
Brigg, P., 195, 199, *200*
Briggs, J.C., 204(n3), *214*
Brinkley, A., 202, *214*
Britton, J., 70, 73, 74, 76
Brubakeret, C., 103, *108*
Bruffee, K.A., 63, 68, 74, 76, 76
Brunner, K.A., 26, *43*
Bryan, J.C., 53, 55, *60*
Bump, J., 206, *214*
Burke, J., 34, *42*
Burke, K., 174(n10), *186*
Butler, J., 25, 26, 27, 35, *42*

C

Cabray, R.W., 24, *44*
Canada, M., 197, *200*
Carnevale, D., 208(n6), *214*
Carstarphen, M.G., 119, 119(n5), *130*

223

224 Author Index

Casanave, C.P., 4, *14*
Chickering, A.W., 24(*n*2), *42*
Cho, S.K., 209, *214*
Christensen, L.J., 24, *42-43*
Clark, G., 41, *43*
Clayton, M., 54, *60*
Comfort, J.R., 207-208, 209, 210, 212, *215*
Cooper, M., 39, *43*, 120, 121, 125, *130*
Cordesman,A.H., 172, 173, 182, *186*
Craig, T., 118, 119, *130*

D

Dessants, N., 202, *204*
Dickson, M., 81, *94*
Dreyfus, H.L., 211, 212, *214*

E

Eisenberg, D., 101, *107*
Eliade, M., 175-176, *186*
Emig, J., 38, *44*, 102, *107*
Espenson, J., 178, *186*
Ess, C., 211, 212, *215*

F

Faigley, L., 39, 40, *43*, 113, 118, 119, *131*, 205(*n*4), *215*
Ferrara, K., 26, *43*
Feyton, C.M., 3-4, *14*
Finkel, D.L., 204, *215*
Fitts, K., 112, *131*
Flamm, M., 202, *214*
Fleming, C., 202, *204*
Forcey, C., 202, *204*
Ford, T.E., 170, *186*
Foster, A.L., 210, *215*
Foucault, M., 142, *145*, 150, *160*
France, A.W., 112, *131*
Freire, P., 67, *76*
Frymier, A.B., 24, *43*
Fuller, D., 79, *95*
Fulwiler, T., 102, 104, *107*

G

Gabriel, M., 107, *107*
Gallop, J., 7, *14*

Galusha, J., 87, 88-89, *95*
Gamson, Z.F., 24(*n*2), *42*
Gardner, H., 67, 71, *76*
Geary, S., 136, *145*
George, D., 125, *131*
Gere, A.R., 64, 67-68, 70, 71, *76*
Gilligan, G., 153, *160*
Goffman, E., 26, 27, 29, 35, 38, *43*
Golish, T.D., 24, *43*
Goodlew, B., 169, *187*
Gorham, J., 24, *43*
Graff, G., 112, *131*
Grant, C.A., 135, *145*
Grant-Davie, K., 22, *43*
Green, E., 122(*n*6), *130*
Guri-Rosenblit, S., 7-8, *14*

H

Hailey, D.E., 22, *43*
Hall, S., 134, 135, 143, *145*
Hansen, D.T., 24, *43*
Hanssen, B., 116, 117, 119, 120, 121, *131*
Hanson, D., 99, 100, 101, *108*
Haraway, D., 152, 153, *160*
Hardwicke, S., 136, 138-139, *145*
Harris, L., 118, 119, *130*
Harvey, D., 154, *160*
Hartvigsen, J., 169, *187*
Hawisher, G.E., 168(*n*4), *186*, 190, 196, 200, 206, 206(*n*5), *215*
Haynes, C., 168(*n*4), *186*
Helford, E.R., 176, *186*
Herring, S., 205(*n*4), *215*
Hess, J.A., 24, *43*
Hickey, D., 203(*n*2), *215*
Hilligoss, S., 168(*n*4), *187*
Hiltz, S.R., 30, 35, *43*, 101-102, *107*
Holmevik, J.R., 168(*n*4), *186*
Holstrom, L., 53, *60*
Horner, W.B., 76, *77*
Horowitz, E., 54, *60*
Houser, M.L., 24, *43*
Howard, T., 31, 34, *43*
Howe, F., 25, *43*
Hult, C.A., 22, *43*

Author Index

I

Irvin, L.L., 68, 69, 70, 71, *76*

J

Jay, G., 112(*n*1), *131*
Johnson, K., 30, 35, *43*
Joyce, M., 34-35, *43*

K

Kaplan, N., 8, *14*
Katula, R.A., 106-107, *107*
Kearney, P., 24, *44*
Keegan, D., 202(*n*1), *215*
Kiefer, K., 169, *187*
Kiesler, S., 30, *44*
Kirk, G.S., 175, *186*
Kirsch, G.E., 25, 41, *44*
Knox, R.L., 24, *44*
Kolko, B., 39, *44*

L

Laine, C., 82, *95*
Laine, M., 82, *95*
Lambiase, J.J., 116, 119, 119(*n*5), 120, *131*
Lang, A., 175, *186*
Lanham. R.A., 203, 207, 208, *215*
LeBlanc, P., 168(*n*4), *186*
Lepper, M.R., 24, *44*
Lèvi-Strauss, C., 175, *186*
Lu, M-Z., 25, *44*, 127, *131*
Lynch, D.A., 125, *131*

M

Maeroff, G.I., 208, 212, *215*
Malinowski, B., 175, *186*
Markel, M., 98, *107*
Marx, M.S., 211, *215*
Matheson, K., 38, *44*
McGuire, T.W., 30, *44*
McKeachie, W.J., 204(*n*3), *215*
Menzel, K.E., 24, *42-43*
Mewborn, D., 23(*n*1), *44*
Miller, R.E., 151, 160, *161*
Miller, S.K., 41, *44*
Moore, M.G., 7, *14*

Moran, C., 168(*n*4), *186*
Mouffe, C., 119(*n*4), *131*
Müller, F.M., 175, *187*
Mulligan, R., 136, *145*
Mutnick, D., 129, *131*
Myers, S.A., 24, *44*

N

Nancy, J-L., 111, 129, *131*
National Education Association, 179(*n*11), 184, *187*
Neff, J.M., 207-208, 209, 210, 212, *215*
Newbold, W., 26-27, 40, *44*, 116, 117, *131*
Noble, D., 21-22, *44*
Noddings, N., 151, 153, *161*
Norman, D., 170(*n*8), *187*
Noxon, M., 181, *187*
Nutta, J.W., 3-4, *14*

O

O'Keefe, D., 25, 30, *44*
Olsen, F., 167(*n*2), *187*, 208(*n*6), *214*
Olson, G.A., 206, *215*
Olson, L.N., 24, *43*
Ong, W., 39, 40, *44*
Oran, S.M., 8, *14*
Owston, R.D., 102, *108*
Palloff, R.M., 66, 67, 70, 77, 120, *131*, 208, 210, 213, *216*
Palmquist, M., 168(*n*4), *187*
Patton, J.G., 103, *108*
Payne, D., 205, *216*
Peterson, P.W., 7, 8, *14*
Petraglia, J., 203, *216*
Petrie, D., 174, *187*
Petrosky, A., 81, *94*
Pinker, S., 71, *77*
Piorkowski, J., 82, *95*
Plax, T.G., 24, *44*
Postman, N., 195(*n*1), *200*
Pratt, K., 66, 67, 70, 77, 120, *131*, 208, 210, 213, *216*
Pratt, M.L., 112, 114, 118, 119, 124, 128-129, *131*

Author Index

R

Ragan, T.J., 28, *44*
Ratcliffe, K., 127-128, *131*
Ray, J., 36, 37, *44*
Ray, R., 205(*n*4), *216*
Reiss, D., 203(*n*2), *215*
Rheingold, H., 169, 169(*n*6), 170(*n*9), *187*
Rhodes, F.H.T., 210, *216*
Ritchie, J.S., 25, 41, *44*
RITE, 211, *216*
Roberts-Miller, T., 41, *44*, 118, *132*
Rodriguez, J.I., 24, *44*
Rose, M., 72, *77*
Rothschild, E., 202, *204*
Rowe, K., 178, 179, *187*

S

Sachs, J.M., 135, *145*
Sands, P., 51, *60*, 204, *216*
Saunders, P.M., 213, *216*
Sawyer, R.J., 189, 190, *200*
Schechner, R., 26, *45*
Scheurer, E., 82, *95*
Schlosser, C., 99, 100, 101, *108*
Schutte, J.G., 98, 99, *108*
Selfe, C.L., 64-65, 66, 77, 112(*n*2), 113, *132*, 168(*n*4), 169, *186, 187*, 190, 196, *200*, 206, 206(*n*5), *215*
Sheehy, G., 81, 83, 85, *95*
Shor, I., 139, *145*
Siegel, J., 30, *44*
Simonson, M., 99, 100, 101, *108*
Sirc, G., 205(*n*4), *216*
Smagorinsky, P., 103, *108*
Smith, R., 118, 119, *130*
Snyder, I., 168(*n*4), *187*
South, J.B., 181, *187*
Spigelman, C., 127, *132*
Spyware, 170, *187*

Squires, D., 197, 198, *200*
Stephenson, N., 190, 191, 192, 193, *200*
Stevenson, P.R., 170, *186*
Stromquist, N.P., 207, *216*
Sujo de Montes, L.E., 8, *14*

T

Tannen, D., 83, 89, *95*
Taylor, T., 205(*n*4), *216*
Threnhauser, E., 106-107, *107*
Tornow, J., 197, *200*
Turkle, S., 26, *45*
Turoff, M., 30, 35, *43*

U

U.S. Department of Health and Human Services, 79, *95*
U.S. General Accounting Office, 183, *187*

V

Van Slyke, P., 112(*n*1), *132*

W

Wait, R.F., 170, *186*
Watters, D., 194, *200*
Weingartner, C., 195(*n*1), *200*
Welch, K., 121, 124, 129, *132*
White, P.R., 28, *44*
Whitemore, g., 26, *43*
Wiener, P.L., 170, *186*
Wilkins, H., 28, 30, 32, *45*
Willis, E.M., 8, *14*
Woods, S.J., 103, *108*

Y

Young, I.M., 156-157, *161*
Youngs, G., 122(*n*6), *132*

Z

Zacharias, M.E., 103, *108*
Zanna, M.P., 38, *44*

SUBJECT INDEX

A

adjunct faculty, 1
administrators and distance education,
47-60

B

basic writers, 79-94
Bill Clinton, 2
Blackboard, 204

C

chat, 69
"contact zone", 112, 114, 119-120, 128
CUSeeMe, 3

D

Daedalus Integrated Writing
Environment (DIWE), 50, 205

E

e-journals, 97-107
Early Childhood Learning Community
(ECLC), 2, 5, 79-94

F

feminism, 25
feminist theory, 147-160
Ferris Bueller's Day Off, 97
flaming, 37, 116-118

G

gender, 26, 151-153

H

Head Start, 2, 53, 79-94
hybrid classrooms, 201-214

I

I Know Why the Cage Bird Sings, 82, 84

L

labor issues, 22
language and power, 99-120
listservs, 69

M

MOO, 34-36, 69, 113, 122, 189-199
MUD, 52
multiculturalism, 8, 133-145

228   *Subject Index*

O

online relationships, 28-34

P

postmodernism, 168

S

science fiction, 189-199

T

television talk shows, 6
The Diamond Age, 189-199

V

virtual community, 158-159

W

Web CT, 70, 72, 153, 199, 204

Y

You Just Don't Understand, 83

Printed in the United States
76074LV00003B/70